THE **Waste Not, Want Not** COOKBOOK

THE Waste Not, Want Not COOK BOOK

SAVE FOOD, SAVE MONEY, AND SAVE THE PLANET Cinda Chavich

PHOTOGRAPHY BY DL Acken

TouchWood
Editions

CONTENTS

This book is dedicated to my parents, who taught me that fresh, homegrown food is a precious gift, and one that should never be wasted.

INTRODUCTION: a TERRIBLE WASTE

Imagine going to the grocery store and leaving with three bags of food, then dropping one in the parking lot and driving away. We all do the equivalent of that every week of our lives.

The amount of food wasted in North America is phenomenal—more than 40 percent of all food produced never gets to anyone's plate, according to the US Department of Agriculture (USDA). The production and disposal of all of that wasted food also wastes water and other precious resources, while emitting CO_2 and methane gases, which add to the rapidly escalating problem of global warming. If food waste were a country, it would be the third largest greenhouse gas emitter on the planet, after China and the United States, a staggering statistic.

On California farms, where so many of our favorite fruits and vegetables are produced, tons of produce simply goes unpicked and unsold—oddly shaped and over- or undersized specimens are left to drop from the trees and are piled into the compost because large multinational supermarkets won't buy them. And in some cases, perfectly edible (and cosmetically perfect) food is plowed back into the fields to artificially reduce supply and prop up prices.

At the same time, in major cities across the country, there are "food deserts," areas where 500 or more people live more than a mile from a grocery store. People living in these deserts have trouble both accessing and paying for fresh local food, which makes our systemic waste of healthy produce even more inexcusable.

The impact of food waste, as it contributes to global warming and worldwide food production, is already being felt at the supermarket. Whether it's California droughts and tropical storms or the acidification of our oceans, environmental pressures on agriculture have caused food prices to rise, as the Intergovernmental Panel on Climate Change (IPCC) warned they would.

And so for purely economic reasons, we all face a new reality, where overconsumption and wasting precious food are no longer options.

Now is the time to educate yourself on the issue, to learn about what is being done around the world and in your community to reduce waste, and to find new strategies to reduce your "foodprint" (food-based carbon footprint) at home.

You can be part of the solution to this terrible waste, one meal at time.

Resolve to reuse and recycle what's in your refrigerator or pantry before sending food to the compost pile (or horrors, the landfill!). Find new ways to use up that box of fresh strawberries you scooped up at the market or the bounty of kale bristling in the back garden. Learn why "best-before" dates on packaged foods are only there to protect producers and retailers from liability, or help them restock shelves.

Support fruit recovery programs in your city—those that will pick the apples in your backyard and share them with charities—and initiatives to use commercial produce that's been rejected by wholesale buyers and grocery chains.

Food waste is a massive global problem but one we can all help solve, starting at home. Check out the Think.Eat.Save website (thinkeatsave.org) for tips on everything from cooking and storing food to growing food from the bits you'd usually cut off and throw away. Or head to LoveFoodHateWaste.com, a UK-based nonprofit website dedicated to fighting food waste, a program that Metro Vancouver will launch for Canadians this year.

This book is designed to help you get the most out of the food you buy while it's still perfectly good to eat. You can reuse and recycle so many things—stale bread into sweet and savory puddings, roasts into soups and sandwich wraps, a bounty of fresh fruit or veggies into crisps, smoothies, and freezable soups or sauces—you'll find it's easy to cut down food waste in your household.

My "Weekly Feast" chapter helps you recycle Sunday dinner into creative weekday meals. I encourage you to take the "White Box Challenge" (open the fridge, grab five ingredients, and devise a recipe). And I offer tips on how to freeze fresh food for long-term storage.

This book is brimming with ideas to get dinner on the table fast, while keeping healthy food out of the dumpster.

It's good for you, your budget, and your planet—the first step toward reducing your family's foodprint.

FOOD WASTE FACTS

I was inspired to write this book after a single encounter with Dana Gunders, project scientist for the Natural Resources Defense Council (NRDC) in San Francisco. She was in Portland, Oregon, to speak at a food conference about the incredible impact food waste has on our environment. I now follow her regular posts on the NRDC website (switchboard .nrdc.org). It's a great place to learn more about food waste and what we can do to combat the problem.

The numbers Dana reveals are shocking—only 60 percent of the food Americans produce is consumed, which means a full 40 percent is wasted, even while kids across the country go to school hungry. The resources used to grow this wasted food, including fresh water, soil nutrients, and fertilizers, are wasted, too, while farm machinery and transportation pump excess carbon dioxide and other greenhouse gases into the atmosphere, warming the planet and impacting our oceans and our weather. Dana's NRDC report tells the entire story.[1]

Perfectly healthy produce often doesn't even make it to the market because it is rejected for size or color by supermarkets, while millions of fish are discarded because they are considered bycatch, scooped up in commercial nets by boats licensed to fish for other species, and thus illegal to sell. Conservation group Oceana's 2014 report *Wasted Catch* says global bycatch amounts to 40 percent of the world's catch, or 63 billion pounds (29 billion kg) of fish, per year. That, scientists say, will lead to the total collapse of global fisheries within the next 30 years.

Every year producers, manufacturers, retailers, and consumers around the world toss and waste

1.3 billion metric tons of food that is fit for human consumption, enough food to feed 3 billion people, while more than 900 million are starving.[2] This includes food that is spilled, spoiled, or otherwise lost in the food supply chain as well as food that gets to the consumer but is discarded—globally, one-third of the food produced is lost in the food chain, from farm to plate, with that number rising to nearly 50 percent in industrialized countries.

The UN estimates that North American and European consumers each waste from 210 to 243 pounds (95 to 115 kg) of food per year, while those in sub-Saharan Africa and Southeast Asia waste much less, only 13 to 24 pounds (6 to 11 kg) per person.

Our production and consumption habits are simply unsustainable. Which is why we have the prime responsibility to reduce food waste.

As people tune into the issue, there are more success stories, but there is also still much to be done. Dana Gunders's work at the NRDC focuses on food and agriculture, and she makes the point that cutting down on food waste is a no-brainer, whether you think about it as a moral obligation or as an opportunity to save money. (Some $1 trillion is squandered worldwide each year on wasted food. That's more than $180 billion worth of wasted food in the US alone; plus an estimated $31 billion in Canada,[3] or as much as $100 billion when you factor in the associated costs of wasted energy, fresh water, land, transportation, etc.)

The United Nations Environment Programme (UNEP) and the Food and Agriculture Organization of the United Nations (FAO) have launched a program called Think.Eat.Save to help people around the world reduce their foodprints. The FAO has also published a comprehensive online "toolkit" detailing food waste issues and potential solutions that can be applied around the world.

The US Food Marketing Institute recently formed the Food Waste Reduction Alliance to engage major grocers, food marketers, and restaurant chains (think Safeway, Walmart, Kellogg's, Unilever, ConAgra, McDonald's) in the issue of food waste. Some retailers are now promoting a "ripe-and-ready" bargain section in their supermarkets, and there are non-profits recovering food from restaurants and hotels to feed the hungry.

There are also some creative entrepreneurs rising to the anti-waste challenge in different parts of the world. For example, the Whole Foods Market in Portland, Oregon, created My Street Grocery, a roving trolley that sells fresh, local food in low-income and underserved neighborhoods. And in France, the huge Intermarché grocery chain recently launched its Inglorious Fruits and Vegetables campaign to bring attention to food waste. They buy produce that has been rejected by wholesalers for cosmetic reasons, and sell it, both fresh and in products like juices and soups, at a 30 percent discount.

Sadly, Canada lags behind the US, UK, and EU in addressing the issue of food waste, even though Statistics Canada numbers indicate Canadian food waste amounts to about 269 pounds (122 kg) per person annually, with 51 percent of the total wasted at home.

In 2014, the Value Chain Management Centre (VCMC), a Canadian agri-foods business management group, joined the Provision Coalition, which works to make Canadian food and beverage manufacturers more sustainable, in a project to "map" food waste across the country, concluding that consumers "need to be engaged to tackle the food waste challenge,"[4] while businesses and government regulators need to switch their focus from waste diversion (recycling) to reduction.

Meanwhile, Metro Vancouver is the first Canadian municipality to address the issue of food waste with practical consumer measures. After hosting a Zero Waste Conference in 2014, the city inked a deal to bring the UK's Love Food Hate Waste campaign (and website) to Canada this year (2015).

Metro Vancouver is also spearheading the National Zero Waste Council's Food Working Group and encouraging food retailers to take on new supply chain initiatives to reduce waste, including the donation of edible food. The city's new $750 million waste treatment plant promises to be one of the first to recycle food waste into biofuel and fertilizer.

While much of the food we waste is fit for human consumption, the food we don't eat could also feed the animals we do. According to the US Environmental Protection Agency (EPA), recovering discarded food for animal feed is not new—hog farms, in particular, often accept food scraps for livestock.

Rutgers University in New Jersey sends more than a ton of food scraps a day from its dining halls to feed hogs and cattle at local Pinter Farms. And in Las Vegas, RC Farms feeds 3,000 pigs with food scraps recovered from MGM Resorts International.

During the First and Second World Wars, food shortages and rationing meant every household took steps to make sure that food was not wasted. It's possible to develop this kind of food-saving savvy among consumers today, too, though it may require economic pressure to get the average shopper on board.

While most of us still live in a world of cheap and abundant food, the UN says that doing nothing about current levels of food waste will lead to severe food shortages, and food price increases of up to 50 percent in the future.

We all have the individual power to reduce food waste. We can change our personal shopping and eating habits. We can commit to using the food in our pantries before buying more and to up-cycling our leftovers, in the process saving both money and resources.

It's time to start that war on food waste again!

1. You can find it here: nrdc.org/food/files/wasted-food-ip.pdf.
2. This comes from the Food and Agriculture Organization of the United Nations.
3. This figure comes from a Value Chain Management Centre report on Canada's annual food waste. The recently updated report can be found here: vcm-international.com/wp-content/uploads/2014/12/Food-Waste-in-Canada-27-Billion-Revisited-Dec-10-2014.pdf.
4. A summary of the report can be found here: aofp.ca/pub/docs/Provision-News-Release-Food-Waste-Report%20(2).pdf. The full report is available here: provisioncoalition.com/assets/website/pdfs/Provision-Addressing-Food-Waste-In-Canada-EN.pdf.

the MYTH of COMPOSTING

While composting is one way to manage food waste, reduction is far more important.

Organic waste, which includes food waste, paper, and garden debris, is the kind of trash heading to our landfill sites in the largest amounts—it accounts for about two-thirds of the solid waste stream. The EPA says food waste is the second-largest category of municipal solid waste (after paper), but less than 3 percent of that organic waste is diverted into composting programs.

And though composting is preferable to sending organic waste to the local landfill, cutting down food waste is an even better solution, because with the amount of food we now waste, composting food scraps has become an issue in itself.

Even as consumers learn to divide their trash at home and separate out the organic material, municipalities struggle to deal with it, as there is no easy way to cope with the large volume of food scraps.

There are promising solutions beginning to surface, though, with organizations like sports facilities and universities, and even cities, investing in new high-tech systems to turn food waste into biofuel. For example, FirstEnergy Stadium, home of the Cleveland Browns, is working with InSinkErator to convert the food waste from feeding 73,000 fans into slurry that can be transformed into fuel and fertilizer. InSinkErator's Grind2Energy recycling technology—essentially a large version of a home garburator—collects the ground food waste in a tank that's then transported to a wastewater treatment plant for anaerobic digestion. The Grind2Energy system is also being used at Ohio State University in Columbus.

While it's a promising idea, one that could process food waste for facilities like hospitals, schools, restaurants, and grocery stores, it doesn't address the issues of overproduction, overconsumption, and global warming. And in some cases, where there are conflicts with residents about composting odors or other issues, organic waste ends up back at the landfill. Once buried in landfills, organic waste produces methane, a greenhouse gas that's far more dangerous than CO_2, plus other toxins that can leach into groundwater.

But, in fact, landfilling organic waste may soon be outlawed. The US Composting Council reports that there are now more than 23 states that ban the disposal of organics in landfills, even though few have the facilities for processing these materials for the animal feed, renewable energy, or compost they could become.

Reduction is the key.

IS IT STILL SAFE to EAT?

This is the big question we all ask as we check the sell-by or best-before dates on everything from milk and yogurt to vacuum-packed Chinese noodles.

According to the NRDC, these dates are largely unregulated and rather arbitrary, and confuse most consumers. They may indicate optimum quality for any given product, but not food safety. "Best before" does not necessarily equate to "dangerous after."

Companies use best-before dates to indicate when their product is at "peak quality," which might mean brightest color or optimum crunch.

And food producers are actually becoming more conservative when it comes to best-before dates, mainly in response to food safety scares and liability issues. Most food is perfectly safe after the date, but 90 percent of consumers pitch foods after the best-before dates.

In fact, if unopened and properly stored, many foods, including eggs, milk, and yogurt, are still perfectly fine to consume a few days after their best-before dates, while canned and packaged foods like cookies are safe to eat long after best-before dates. Dried foods like beans, lentils, and pasta last indefinitely, and chocolate is still fine to eat even if it has a white film, which is simply an indication that it has been exposed to air.

In the US, only infant formula is required by law to have an "expired-by" date. Foods with that kind of label should not be consumed after the date has passed. Other dates, including "use by" or "best before," are not legally required; they are included at the discretion of the manufacturer. In Canada, only products that are shelf stable for less than 90 days must be dated. Fresh meat and poultry must have a "packaged-on" date and should be eaten within a few days of packaging. Foods with a "sell-by" date should be cooked or frozen before that date passes, but are perfectly safe when properly handled. In an effort to stem the tide of food waste caused by expiration dates, the EU has proposed that "best-before" dates actually be removed from foods with a long shelf life (coffee, rice, pasta, jams) and that dates used for store-stocking purposes be invisible to consumers.

It's best to use your nose, and some common sense, when deciding when to pitch packaged foods. If snack foods, cookies, and crackers smell stale or rancid, throw them out. When milk products are sour, moldy, or curdled, down the drain. Ditto with food showing signs of spoilage—when in doubt, throw it out.

Rotate canned and packaged foods in your pantry to bring older foods to the front. Discard any cans that are leaking or bulging. Store food in a cool, dark cupboard for longer shelf life.

Some things, like eggs, are tricky—raw eggs last a month in the fridge but only a week if they're hard-cooked. Soft cheeses (including cottage cheese and yogurt) are not safe to eat if they become moldy, but if there's mold on your hard cheeses (Parmesan, Swiss, or cheddar), you can safely cut away the moldy bits and eat the rest.

A great online resource to check before you pitch that food in the fridge is stilltasty.com.

Here are some basic storage guidelines:
- Milk: 7 days after best-before date, opened or unopened
- Yogurt: 7 to 10 days after best-before date, opened or unopened
- Cheese, hard: 3 to 4 weeks opened, 6 months unopened
- Butter: 4 weeks after best-before date, opened or unopened
- Eggs, in shell: 4 weeks
- Eggs, hard-cooked: 1 week
- Fresh meat: 2 to 4 days
- Fresh ground meat: 1 to 2 days
- Deli meats: 3 to 4 days
- Fresh chicken or turkey, whole or pieces: 2 to 3 days
- Fresh ground poultry: 1 to 2 days
- Cooked chicken: 3 to 4 days
- Fresh fish: 2 to 3 days
- Fresh shellfish: 12 to 24 hours
- Leftover soups, stews, casseroles: 3 to 4 days
- Jams and jellies: 3 to 4 months, opened
- Mayonnaise: 2 to 3 months, opened
- Mustard: 1 year, opened
- Ketchup: 6 months, opened
- Salad dressing or vinaigrette, bottled: 6 to 9 months, opened
- Salsa, bottled: 4 weeks, opened

TIPS to STAY on TRACK

Make a List, Check It Twice

Plan meals, check the cupboards for ingredients before you leave home, and only buy what you need. Yes, it takes a little more time, but you won't end up with a pantry full of stale food.

Clean Out the Fridge

Before you shop or call for takeout, make an effort to get creative and eat what's in your fridge today. Then make sure the appliance is shiny and clean and ready to receive the fresh food you buy—with no science experiments lurking in the bottom of the crisper. A clean fridge (or pantry) is easier to manage and more inspiring than one that's overflowing.

Use Your Freezer

When there are leftovers that make a meal, package them like individual TV dinners, then label, date, and freeze. These meals are a treat on those nights when you're alone or just can't face the stove. You can also freeze peeled and chopped ripe pineapple, mangoes, and bananas for future smoothies or fruit pops, as well as bread before it gets moldy (slices thaw quickly in the toaster for breakfast).

Cook Like a Chef

Think about the soup of the day at your favorite restaurant. Soups have long been a clever chef's way of recycling yesterday's leftovers into today's dinner. Today, there is even more pressure on chefs to use all of the precious organic produce and local meats that come into their kitchens—hence the growth of nose-to-tail and root-to-shoot items on the best menus, from house-made sausage and terrines to beet and radish leaves in the salad.

Peasant Cuisine

Wondering what to cook? Imagine some of your favorite foods from a Spanish frittata to a French cassoulet or Italian minestrone, all cobbled together by peasant cooks with limited ingredients. The world of comforting peasant food is vast. Whether you end up with a lentil stew, fried rice, or ratatouille, accessible, inexpensive ingredients are combined to create dishes that are more than the sum of their humble parts.

Save Money and Food

Look for best-before bargains. There are more and more entrepreneurs out there offering deep discounts on food that's near or past it's arbitrary best-before date or too large or small for conventional grocers. For example, look for Amelia's Grocery Outlet in Pennsylvania (with 16 stores), the online shop approvedfood.co.uk in Britain, or Outlet Stam in Holland.

Buy a Small Refrigerator

If you have a small refrigerator, you will shop more often, you will buy less, and you will be more likely to cook what you have before buying more food.

the WHITE BOX CHALLENGE

The best way to avoid food waste is to use up what you have on hand.

So before you head to the supermarket, call for a pizza, or even thaw out something new to cook, take the White Box Challenge.

Like the chefs we see on reality TV food shows, you should be able to open that big white (or stainless steel) box in your kitchen, pull out three or four ingredients, and with some staples from the pantry, cook dinner.

While chefs learn how to creatively combine seemingly random ingredients in the "black box" challenges they face in professional food competitions, most people don't practice this skill. But if you have a few "mother" recipes in your repertoire—whether for soup, stir-fry, risotto, panini, frittata, or omelet—you can come up with some great ideas to recycle or up-cycle what's behind that big Door Number One in your kitchen.

Think of your leftovers as the base for a brand new dish. With pita bread in the freezer, you can always use those leftovers to make a quick personal pizza.

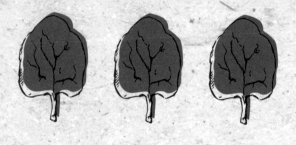

A curry or stew can become a hearty soup with some chicken or beef broth from the pantry. Or you might wrap it up in a flour tortilla (along with the leftover rice or mashed potatoes you cooked with it and some chopped lettuce or tomato) for a fast, portable meal.

Take that steamed broccoli, spinach, or asparagus and fold it into an omelet with some grated cheese. Toss it with pasta and Parmesan. Add it to risotto. Or combine it with some sautéed onions, stock, and cream, and whirl it up into an elegant cream soup.

And before you shop, make an effort to get creative and eat what's already in your fridge. Cauliflower, potatoes, eggs, mushrooms, and cucumbers? Make a frittata with a spicy cucumber salad on the side.

Boiled potatoes, black olives, and green beans? Open a can of salmon, slice some tomatoes, shake up a simple vinaigrette, and create an elegant composed Niçoise salad.

Make sure you refrigerate leftovers right away. Food should never be left at room temperature for more than 4 hours—ideally leftovers should be stored within 2 hours of cooking. But leftover cooked foods will last for 4 to 5 days in the refrigerator when stored in an airtight container.

So make extra rice so you have enough for fried rice—fast-fry it in the wok with chopped vegetables like green onions and peppers, frozen peas and carrots, leftover meats from your refrigerator, a little ginger, and a splash of soy sauce. Or bind the rice with a little cheese sauce, roll, and fry for instant arancini appetizers. To make homey rice pudding, heat leftover rice with milk, sugar, and beaten egg yolks until thick.

Use up what's getting too ripe or on the verge of going off first. Peel and freeze fruits for smoothies. Toss the last of the potatoes, beets, carrots, parsnips, and onions with some olive oil and roast them for a tasty side dish—or add them to a pot of home-style vegetable soup. Freeze whole tomatoes for soups and sauces down the road.

The challenge is to use up as much as you can from that "white box" in your kitchen before you head out to the supermarket to buy more food.

Think of yourself as a chef and start flexing your "blue plate special" and "soup of the day" skills. You will be amazed at what you can do with the ingredients you already have on hand, and how easy your shopping can be when your fridge is well managed.

The Love Food Hate Waste website has more ideas and recipes.

BRING HOME the BOUNTY

Cooking that windfall harvest of seasonal produce from the local farm or the back garden is never easy, but if you embrace what's seasonal (and thus accessible and affordable), you will exponentially expand your repertoire of recipes while dramatically reducing your foodprint.

There's nothing as tasty as freshly harvested fruits and vegetables, the kind that are allowed to ripen on the vine for farm-gate or farmers' market sales. It's night and day compared with food that's picked green and bounced along conveyor belts to be shipped halfway around the world, arriving weeks beyond its prime.

The best chefs know this and are embracing farm-to-table cooking, working directly with local growers and in some cases even producing their own ingredients in their own kitchen gardens.

It doesn't take much to discover the difference—just try that imported supermarket carrot next to the one from a local grower or your own backyard, and you won't go back to big-box shopping.

Some might argue that buying local is more costly, but big issues like climate change and water scarcity are evidence that saving a few cents a pound is a false economy. The hidden costs of industrial-style food production are too high, and too scary; it's simply not sustainable. And as food costs rise, in reaction to climate-related disasters, the price of sustainable, locally produced food may no longer seem prohibitive.

It's also good to remember that processed foods often cost far more than whole foods, especially when you factor in nutrition. A recent USDA report concluded that it all comes down to where you allocate your food dollars. Spend more of your food budget on fruits and vegetables (40 percent), eat ideal portions, and spend a little more time on food prep, and you can actually reduce your grocery bill.

Local and organic fresh produce is far tastier, even when simply cooked, and when you've spent more for better-quality produce, you will be inspired to use it up, not throw it in the trash.

Join forces with a local farm in a Community Supported Agriculture program and get fresh food delivered direct from field to plate, and you will gain a new appreciation for the work of growing fresh food. You'll likely have a windfall of fresh food—inspiration to learn more about cooking it, and storing and freezing it for leaner times.

Finding a source of cheap, even free, local fruits or vegetables is possible in the summer season, too. Look for a food rescue or gleaning project in your area. A big bag of fresh apples or oranges may be as easy as helping a neighbor pick the fruit ripening in their backyard.

Resolve to shop—and eat—in season and you can find the best prices, whether you're buying strawberries or tomatoes. More local shoppers mean more local farms and better supplies—all good for the local economy and stretching your food dollars.

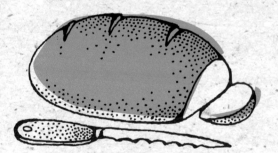

SMART FOOD STRATEGIES

- You can extend the shelf life of staples like sugar, flour, baking supplies, and spices by storing them in glass jars, in a cool dark cupboard.
- Only buy as much fresh food—fruits and vegetables, bread, milk—as you can eat in a week or less.
- Focus a week's worth of menus around a big piece of protein that you can roast on a weekend—go from roast chicken to chicken quesadillas.

- A big pot of tomato sauce or eggplant caponata can be part of your weekly preparations, too, and can do double duty for pasta, pizza, lasagna, eggplant Parmesan, or even crostini topping.
- Shop locally and buy meat, poultry, and vegetables from local farms to reduce your carbon "foodprint."
- Buy in bulk and then plan a "bee" with friends or family to make a favorite dish that you can freeze and pull out for "fast food" dinners later. Think perogies, cabbage rolls, tortellini, lasagna, or Chinese dumplings.
- Get a freezer (or a refrigerator with a large freezer compartment) and a home vacuum sealer for packaging meats, poultry, and fish for freezing. This will extend the storage time by many months and prevent freezer burn. The freezer temperature should be 0°F to 2°F (-18°C to -17°C).
- Learn all about home canning of pickles, preserves, jams, and jellies with a good canning resource book or a cooking class in your community.
- Host a jamming night or pickling party with friends on the weekend to pool resources and labor—and end up with lots of healthy, local products in the pantry. Get inspired by canningacrossamerica.com.
- Clearly label and date anything you put up, whether it's preserves or frozen food, and use it up the same year it's made or frozen.
- Designate a shelf or bin in your fridge as your Use It Up spot and encourage everyone in the family to eat these items first.
- Wrap salad greens in a paper towel and then seal them into a plastic bag and they'll last much longer in the refrigerator. Herbs like parsley or cilantro benefit by standing in a jar of water—make sure to untie them to allow air to circulate.
- Don't store your apples, bananas, citrus, or tomatoes with other produce. The ethylene gas they emit makes other fruits and vegetables spoil faster.
- Have apples with soft spots or tomatoes that are past their prime for eating raw? Before you toss them out, think about cooking them into a sauce, soup, crisp, or cobbler.

- Use technology for culinary inspiration. Stashed merguez sausages in the freezer? Google it and you'll find ideas from Couscous with Merguez and Chickpea Tagine to Spicy Merguez with Spinach and White Beans.
- Take stock of how much waste your household generates in a week and aim for zero waste by tracking your progress. Look online at sites like makedirtnotwaste.org and download their Wasted Food Tracking Sheet, or simply weigh the fruits and vegetables you buy and those you discard.
- Aim to buy sustainable foods when you shop. Ask retailers and talk to farmers at markets about how their operations are sustainable—defined by FAO as "a food system that has a positive effect on health, [and] is economically viable and environmentally and socially acceptable."

HOW to USE THESE RECIPES

The easiest way to reduce food waste in your own kitchen is simply to use up what you have in the refrigerator and pantry before shopping for additional food. So I've divided the book into three sections, based on the kinds of fresh produce, staples, and proteins we usually buy.

Are there avocados you need to eat before they're overripe? Just flip to the first section and look under A. There you'll find information about buying, storing, and serving avocados, lots of ideas for quick fixes (simple how-to's for salsas and salad combos), and some delicious recipes that feature this nutritious treat.

It's the same format in the Staples and Weekly Feast sections, the former including tips for using up things like bread and cheese, and the latter offering "mother" recipes for cooking a large piece of protein when you have the time (think roast beef or chicken), plus several secondary recipes to help you use up the leftovers in creative new ways, without ever serving the same dish twice.

Fresh Fruit and Vegetables

This is an A to Z section of recipes and ideas, from Apples to Zucchini. You'll find out how to choose fruits and vegetables and how to best store your perishable produce. You'll also find quick tips for the best ways to dry, freeze, or can a windfall of garden goodies. There are recipes galore, whether you just need some inspiration (I've done the internet searches for you) or a solid recipe that will impress your guests.

Staples

We all get caught up in a good sale at the supermarket or a big-box store bargain, but a deal is only a deal when you can use it up. An extra-large tub of yogurt, a mega supply of shelled pecans, or a giant block of Parmesan cheese can seem like a good idea, but without a plan, you may find yourself with too much of a good thing.

Hence, this section, where you'll find information on how to buy, store, and serve everything from bacon and bread to cheese, eggs, nuts, and chocolate, along with Don't Waste It tips for quick solutions and several recipes that make each of these staple ingredients shine.

Let's face it—not all foods are produced locally, so you will have to buy some imports. You can definitely save money by purchasing shelf-stable foods in quantity, but be careful about perishable ingredients.

Flats of canned tomatoes, chicken broth, olive oil, and rice are all sensible buys for the pantry, but produce, breads, meat, and dairy products will spoil, so learn how to use them in a timely fashion with this section.

The Weekly Feast

Often, food is wasted simply because we get tired of eating the same thing day after day. But my Weekly Feast section shows you how to cook once and use that leftover protein in new ways, so you can be eating Mexican on Tuesday and Chinese on Thursday, with no need to call for take-out.

On your day off work, plan to cook something you can recycle into meals all week long, whether it's a roasted chicken or an Italian milk-braised pork shoulder. A big piece of protein can feed a family for a week with leftovers for sandwiches, wraps, stir-fries, and pasta dishes.

This section offers mother recipes for cooking a roast beef or whole salmon, followed by tips and recipes to recycle them into dishes like thai beef and cucumber salad or salmon pot pie. It will also show you how to use up those bones and carcasses, whether from a leg of lamb or a roasting chicken, by making stocks for hearty soups.

It's also the place to turn when you need to know how to buy, store, and cook a roast for Sunday dinner, or when you just need some inspiration to use up that bit of leftover ham in the fridge.

FRESH FRUIT and VEGETABLES

APPLES

Buy

There are hundreds of varieties of apples. Buy eating and cooking apples in the late summer and fall. Look for sweet apples for eating fresh (Gala, Fuji, Delicious, Empire); apples that hold their shape when cooked in pies and baked (Jonagold, Winesap); and those that disintegrate when cooked for sauces (Cortland, Ida Red). McIntosh, or Macs, are tart/sweet classics that are juicy and good to eat raw and break down when cooked.

Store

Keep apples in the refrigerator for 2 weeks or in a colder place for longer storage. Apples continue to ripen and get sweeter in storage and keep best at around 34°F (1°C). Consume any bruised fruit first.

Serve

An apple is the perfect portable fruit for lunches or snacks. Eat them raw or sliced into salads (dipped in a bath of water and lemon juice to prevent oxidation and browning). Buy tart apples to bake into crisps and pies with cinnamon and sugar or to cook into chicken curries and savory sauces for meats.

Don't Waste It!

- Combine chopped apples, celery, and walnuts with mayonnaise or yogurt dressing for a speedy Waldorf salad.

- For healthy apple chips, core and thinly slice apples (use a mandoline or the slicing blade on a food processor), brush with a mixture of lemon juice and honey, then dry on a parchment-lined baking tray in an oven heated to 200°F (or in your dehydrator) for 2 hours, turning once, until crisp.

- Caramelize sliced apples with brown sugar and butter to serve over gingerbread or ice cream.

- Make open-faced sandwiches of sliced fresh apples, prosciutto, arugula, and honey-mustard mayo on rye.

- Slice apples and dip in water that's been acidified with a little lemon juice (to prevent browning), then skewer apple slices with slices of sharp cheese (aged gouda or blue cheese) for easy appetizers.

- Sauté onions in olive oil until they begin to caramelize, then add chopped apple and thyme and cook until softened. Serve on toasted baguette with sliced Brie as an appetizer.

- Roast peeled, cored, and quartered apples on buttered baking sheets at 375°F for 3 hours, then purée with a splash of apple cider for pure apple butter. Otherwise, use your slow cooker to cook apples down with some apple cider, sugar, cinnamon, ginger, nutmeg, and apple brandy (an overnight endeavor), then reduce to thicken and purée. Apple butter can be refrigerated for a month, or frozen for longer storage. Include onions, jalapeno, cumin, apple cider vinegar, and salt and it's apple chutney.

APPLE MUESLI

A Swiss standard. The addition of prunes gives this healthy breakfast extra flavor and nutrition. Keep it in the fridge and top with any fresh or dried fruit you have on hand. SERVES 6–8.

In a large bowl, combine the oats, water, shredded apple, prunes, honey, lemon juice, and cinnamon. Stir well and refrigerate, covered, overnight.

In the morning, stir in the yogurt.

To serve, spoon the muesli into serving bowls and top each serving with fruit and nuts. This keeps in the fridge for several days.

1½ cups large-flake rolled oats or rolled barley (not instant)

1½ cups water

2 cups shredded unpeeled apple, about 2 apples

1½ cups chopped pitted prunes

2 Tbsp honey

2 Tbsp fresh lemon juice

½ tsp ground cinnamon

2 cups plain yogurt

Garnishes:

Chopped fresh fruit (blueberries, banana slices, melon slices, pineapple chunks, grapes, etc.)

Dried fruit (raisins, cranberries, apricots, etc.)

Nuts and/or seeds (pecans, walnuts, slivered almonds, sunflower seeds, sesame seeds, etc.)

✎ FOOD FOR THOUGHT
Waste reduction in the US, China, and India alone could provide food for 400 million people.

CHICKEN BREASTS with APPLE and ROSEMARY

An easy way to include apples in a main dish. This recipe works perfectly with boneless pork chops or pork tenderloin medallions, too. Add a rustic mash of yellow-fleshed potatoes on the side. **SERVES 4.**

Season the chicken breasts with the salt and pepper and then dredge in the flour, shaking off any excess.

In a nonstick sauté pan, heat the oil and butter over medium-high. When sizzling, add the chicken. Cook for about 5 minutes per side, until the chicken is nicely browned. Remove from the pan and set aside.

Add the onions to the pan, stirring up any browned bits. Cook until the onions are soft and starting to brown. Add the apples and rosemary to the pan, tossing to combine.

Add the cider and bring to a boil. Simmer for 5 minutes, until the liquid is reduced by half. Return the chicken to the pan and cook together for about 5 minutes, until the chicken is cooked through and the apples are saucy. Season with additional salt and pepper to taste.

Serve the chicken topped with the sauce.

4 boneless, skinless chicken breasts

Salt and freshly ground black pepper

2 Tbsp all-purpose flour

2 Tbsp olive oil

2 Tbsp butter

2 onions, thinly sliced

2 Granny Smith apples, peeled, cored, and sliced

1 Tbsp minced fresh rosemary

2 cups apple cider

APPLE CRISP

Apple crisp, brown Betty—whatever you call it, this is a simple, classic dessert. And it's even tastier if you have a handful of berries to toss in. In the spring, substitute chopped strawberries and rhubarb for the berries, and in the winter, use cranberries. Use tart apples, like Granny Smiths, for the best flavor. **SERVES 6-8.**

In a large bowl, combine the sugar, honey, cinnamon, nutmeg, and brandy, and then add the sliced apples and the blueberries. Toss to coat the fruit with the spices and set aside to marinate for 1 hour, until the fruit releases its juices.

Preheat the oven to 350°F. Butter a shallow baking dish.

Stir the flour into the fruit and spice mixture, and then pour the mixture into the prepared baking dish.

To make the topping: In another bowl, combine the butter, flour, and brown sugar, mixing to form coarse crumbs. Stir in the rolled oats, and add the cinnamon and salt.

Spread the oat mixture evenly over the fruit in the baking dish.

Set the baking dish on a baking sheet (this will save your oven if any juice runs over), and bake for about 45 to 55 minutes, until bubbling and golden brown. Serve the crisp warm with vanilla ice cream or lemon yogurt.

¾ cup granulated sugar

2 Tbsp honey

½ tsp ground cinnamon

¼ tsp ground nutmeg

3 Tbsp brandy, Calvados, or Grand Marnier

5 large Granny Smith apples, peeled, cored, and sliced

2 cups blueberries

3 Tbsp all-purpose flour

Topping:

3 Tbsp butter, softened

¼ cup whole-wheat flour

½ cup packed brown sugar

½ cup rolled oats

1 tsp ground cinnamon

Pinch salt

ASPARAGUS

Buy

Look for fresh shoots in spring with tightly closed purple tips. Spears should be shiny, not shriveled, and should snap at the base when bent.

Store

Break off the tough ends and store spears standing upright in an inch of water in a jar in the refrigerator for 3 days. Before cooking, soak in warm water to remove any grit lodged in the tips, then chill quickly in cold water. Blanch whole spears or tips and then vacuum-seal and freeze. Cooked and puréed asparagus freezes perfectly, too, to use later in soups or flans.

Serve

Serve steamed or roasted asparagus spears whole, piled on a platter. Don't worry, it's considered polite to eat asparagus with your fingers, and it's delicious dipped in hollandaise with your Easter ham. Another classic way to serve asparagus is alongside spring salmon, or steamed and tossed with pasta, wild morel mushrooms, and Parmesan.

Don't Waste It!

- Brush asparagus with olive oil and grill over high heat until just browned and starting to char, then sprinkle with sea salt or good balsamic.

- Wrap a thin slice of prosciutto around a lightly steamed asparagus spear, starting at the bottom and wrapping at an angle to enclose the spear. Serve cold for a summer appetizer (stand spears upright in a glass), or grill just long enough to crisp the meat and heat the asparagus.

- Use a blender to make a fast hollandaise with 3 egg yolks, 2 tablespoons lemon juice, a pinch each salt and cayenne, and ½ cup melted butter, then serve as a dipping sauce with steamed asparagus.

- Roll spears in beaten egg and then in a mixture of grated Parmesan and seasoned bread crumbs. Panfry in olive oil until crisp and serve as an appetizer with lemony or garlicky mayo.

- Cut leftover steamed or grilled spears into chunks and fold into scrambled eggs with cheese for lunch.

- Toss spears with olive oil and roast in a 400°F oven for 10 minutes. Pile on a platter and top with thin shards of Parmesan cheese (peeled off the block with your vegetable peeler).

- Roll steamed asparagus with baby shrimp and wasabi mayo into the center of a sushi rice roll, enclosed in a sheet of nori, then cut into ½-inch rounds for appetizers.

- Trim spears to fit into 2-cup canning jars. Pack tightly into jars, tips up. Add a clove of garlic, a teaspoon of dill seed, some mustard seed, and a pinch of dried chiles to each jar. Make a brine of 8 cups water, 2 cups vinegar, 3 tablespoons pickling salt, and ½ cup sugar. Fill jars with boiling brine, covering tips, then seal and process in a water bath for 6 minutes. Pickled asparagus spears are great with cheese or instead of celery in Bloody Marys and Caesars.

- Slice into rounds and toss into spring potato salad with slivered radishes for crunchy fresh flavor and lovely color.

- Stir-fry 1-inch chunks of asparagus with minced ginger and slices of carrot and onion, until tender crisp, then toss with oyster sauce, rice wine, and sesame oil.

ASPARAGUS RISOTTO

This version of classic risotto uses asparagus for flavoring and color, but you could also add sautéed wild mushrooms, roasted peppers, leftover peas, or seafood (or all of the above). Learn to make risotto, and you have a platform for using up lots of things in your fridge. **SERVES 2 HEARTILY AS A MAIN DISH, OR 4 WITH OTHER COURSES.**

1 lb asparagus

4 cups (about) canned low-salt chicken stock

Pinch saffron threads

2 Tbsp butter

2 Tbsp extra-virgin olive oil

1 medium onion, minced

1½ cups Arborio rice or medium-grain white rice

½ cup dry white wine

1 tsp minced fresh herbs (optional)

1½ cups grated Parmigiano-Reggiano

Salt and freshly ground black pepper

Snap off the tough ends of the asparagus, and discard. Cut off tips and reserve. Slice stalks on the diagonal into ¼-inch to ½-inch chunks. Set aside.

In a small saucepan, heat the chicken stock to boiling. Keep warm. Crumble the saffron threads and add to the stock.

In a large sauté pan, heat the butter and olive oil. Add the onion and sauté over medium heat until tender, about 8 minutes. Stir in the rice and cook together for a minute.

Add the wine and stir until absorbed, then ladle in a little hot stock (about ½ cup) and simmer until the liquid is absorbed, stirring often. Continue adding stock, ½ cup at a time, until it's absorbed, and cook, stirring often, for about 10 minutes. Add the asparagus stalks and the herbs, if using. Add stock, stirring, until the rice is al dente (still slightly firm), about 10 to 15 minutes longer. The risotto should be loose but not soupy.

Add the asparagus tips and continue cooking until the rice is just tender, adding stock as needed to keep the mixture creamy.

Stir in 1 cup of the Parmigiano-Reggiano. Season to taste with salt and pepper.

Serve immediately (risotto waits for no one!) in rimmed soup bowls. Pass the remaining cheese.

> **TIP**
> For a brilliant green risotto, lightly steam half of the asparagus stalks and purée in the food processor or blender with 2 tablespoons of butter. When the rice is almost tender, add the asparagus purée. You can also try this technique with fresh or frozen green peas and fresh mint, or baby spinach leaves.

SPRING PASTA with ASPARAGUS and PRAWNS

This light, creamy sauce dotted with fresh spring asparagus is delicious served over tender ribbons of fresh pasta. **SERVES 2.**

Break the bottoms off the asparagus spears (they will snap where the tough bits end) and discard. Cut the spears into 1-inch pieces, on a diagonal. Bring a pot of salted water to a rolling boil and add the asparagus. Bring back to a boil, drain, and shock in a bowl of ice water, then cool, drain, and set aside.

Using a mandoline (or a vegetable peeler), take thin, lengthwise slices from the zucchini, making 6 ribbons. Set aside.

In a large sauté pan, heat the butter over medium-high. When the pan is hot, add the prawns and cook quickly for 1 minute, until pink. Season with the salt and pepper, and stir in the garlic and tomatoes.

Add the wine to deglaze and cook for 1 minute, until half of the liquid has evaporated, then stir in the cream.

Bring to a simmer and add the reserved asparagus, the pasta, and the reserved zucchini ribbons, tossing together until the zucchini is tender and the pasta is heated through, about 3 to 4 minutes. Add the arugula and toss to combine.

Divide the mixture between 2 large pasta bowls. Top each serving with shavings of fresh Parmigiano-Reggiano.

8 asparagus spears

1 small zucchini

2 Tbsp butter

12 large prawns, peeled and deveined

Salt and freshly ground black pepper, to taste

1 tsp garlic purée

12 cherry tomatoes

½ cup white wine

¼ cup heavy cream

½ lb fresh pappardelle pasta or dried wide, flat noodles, cooked barely al dente (1–2 minutes for fresh pasta)

Handful baby arugula

2 oz Parmigiano-Reggiano, shaved into thin shards

AVOCADOS

Buy

A true superfood, avocados are grown in Mexico and California and are available year round. Choose firm specimens that yield only slightly, not soft fruits. You can usually get a bargain on a bag at the big-box store, but you'll need to use them up.

Store

Keep avocados at room temperature until they begin to soften (just start to yield to pressure), then refrigerate for longer storage.

Serve

A mashed ripe avocado with a splash of lime and chili sauce makes almost instant guacamole, but this rich and healthy fruit is also perfect to slice for sandwiches or wrap up in tortillas with beans or fried fish.

Don't Waste It!

- For classic guacamole, peel and roughly mash 2 ripe avocados with a tablespoon of lime juice and some salt, then mix in chopped fresh tomatoes, chopped green onion, and minced jalapeno chiles. Some recipes include minced garlic, chopped cilantro, chopped radish, minced white onion, or cumin, too.

- For a creamy salad dressing or dip, combine an avocado with a little mayonnaise, plain yogurt, or sour cream as well as some lime juice, cilantro, and garlic, and purée.

- Add sliced avocado to toasted BLT sandwiches (or use to replace the bacon for a vegetarian version).

- Cubed avocado is a nice addition to a classic tomato, onion, and cilantro salsa.

- Stuff avocado halves with baby shrimp salad for a lovely luncheon dish.

- Purée avocado with spinach, apples, and lime for a rich and healthy green drink.

- Combine chopped avocado with chunks of canned white tuna (drained), cherry tomatoes, lemon juice, and a little olive oil, then pile on toasted crusty rolls or sliced baguettes, top with grated cheese, and broil until bubbly for open-faced tuna melts.

- For crispy avocado fries, dip avocado pieces in seasoned flour, then beaten egg and panko bread crumbs, then bake on a rack at 425°F.

- For a cold soup, whirl 2 ripe avocados, 2 chopped tomatillos, and ¾ cup each buttermilk and chicken stock in a blender until smooth, season with salt and pepper, minced garlic, and lemon juice to taste, then garnish each bowl with 2 ounces cold crabmeat.

EGG and AVOCADO SALAD

A scoop of this rich and tasty salad on a bed of salad greens makes a healthy lunch. **SERVES 2**.

In a bowl, mash the eggs and stir in the green onion, mayonnaise, salt, pepper, and cayenne. Halve the avocado, remove the pit, and score the flesh into cubes. Scoop the cubes out of the skin and place them in a bowl. Toss with the lime juice.

Fold the avocado into the egg mixture and top with the cilantro. Serve on a bed of greens.

3 hard-cooked eggs, peeled

1 green onion, minced

2 Tbsp low-fat mayonnaise

¼ tsp salt

A few grindings black pepper

Pinch cayenne

1 ripe avocado

1 Tbsp fresh lime juice

1 Tbsp chopped fresh cilantro

Mixed salad greens

GRILLED CHICKEN and AVOCADO SALSA WRAPS

This is a quick way to serve chicken, especially on busy nights when everyone is on the run. **SERVES 4.**

Combine the oil, lemon or lime juice, garlic, cumin, paprika, oregano, chili powder, and cayenne (if using) in a small bowl. Slather the rub over the chicken on all sides and set aside in the refrigerator for 10 minutes.

For the salsa, combine the tomatoes, avocado, lime juice, cilantro, jalapeno, salt, and cumin in a bowl. Set aside to marinate at room temperature while you cook the chicken.

Grill the chicken over medium heat until browned and cooked through, about 7 minutes per side. Or place the chicken in a single layer on a baking sheet lined with parchment and bake at 375°F for about 30 minutes, just until juices run clear when the chicken is pierced.

Slice the chicken and roll it up into the flour tortillas with the salsa and rice.

1 Tbsp olive oil

2 Tbsp fresh lime juice or lemon juice

1 clove garlic, minced

1 tsp ground cumin

1 tsp paprika

1 tsp dried oregano

1 tsp chili powder

¼ tsp cayenne (optional)

4 boneless, skinless chicken breasts (or about 1 lb boneless thighs)

Salsa:

3 ripe Roma tomatoes, seeded and diced, about 1 cup

1 ripe avocado, chopped

Juice of half a lime

¼ cup chopped fresh cilantro

1 Tbsp minced fresh jalapeno chile

Pinch salt

Pinch ground cumin

4 large (or 8 small) whole-wheat tortillas

2 cups hot cooked brown rice

> **TIP**
> To quickly cube an avocado, slice in half around the pit and twist apart. Whack the pit with the blade of your chef's knife, then twist to remove. Cut through the flesh in both directions, down to, but not through, the skin. Scoop the cubes out with a spoon or turn the skin inside out and pop the cubes free.

BANANAS

Buy

Regular sweet bananas can be purchased green to ripen at home, but if they look gray, avoid them—they've been chilled and won't ripen. Baby or finger bananas and red bananas are the sweetest, while plantains are big, starchy, and hard, meant for cooking in Caribbean stews or making fried tostones.

Store

Store bananas at room temperature (refrigerating will ruin them) and speed ripening by putting an apple in a paper bag with your bananas. Once ripe, you can refrigerate the bananas for 3 days. Peel ripe bananas and freeze whole or halved in plastic bags for smoothies, or mash and freeze in measured portions for baking.

Serve

The banana is the perfect package—portable, easy to peel, and a starchy and satiating fruit, which is why it's carried in lunch bags around the world.

Don't Waste It!

- Always add a banana to your fruit smoothie for sweet flavor and smooth texture.
- Whirl a frozen banana, a couple of tablespoons of peanut butter and cocoa powder, plus a splash of almond milk together in the blender for a killer shake.
- Layer sliced bananas with caramel or vanilla pudding and crumbled ginger cookies in small jars or glasses, then chill and top with a bit of whipped cream for an easy dessert.
- Split bananas lengthwise (in the skin), and fill with chocolate chips. Wrap loosely in foil and grill for a campfire treat.
- Slice bananas and sauté in butter with brown sugar and rum to pour over ice cream.
- Mash or slice bananas and spread inside peanut butter sandwiches.
- Cut ripe bananas into chunks and freeze, then whirl (frozen) in the food processor to create a banana "ice cream." Top with chocolate sauce.
- Chop or mash ripe bananas and stir into your morning oatmeal with a little vanilla, cinnamon, and almond milk.
- Make peanut butter and banana sandwiches, then soak in a mixture of beaten egg, milk, vanilla, and cinnamon, and fry, French toast–style, in butter until brown.
- Combine a mashed banana with a cup of rolled oats, some chopped dates and nuts, and a dash of cinnamon and vanilla, then roll in chopped nuts or coconut for vegan energy balls.

BANANA BREAD

Banana bread has long been the solution to overripe bananas. This recipe uses ground flaxseed and organic canola oil, along with whole-grain flour, to make it an even healthier solution. **MAKES 1 LOAF.**

Preheat the oven to 350°F.

Butter and flour an 8- × 4-inch loaf pan (grease the pan and then tap 2 teaspoons of flour around inside of it; this will prevent sticking).

In a large bowl, combine the brown sugar, buttermilk, egg, and canola oil, and whisk until smooth.

In another bowl, combine the all-purpose flour, whole-wheat flour, flaxseed, baking powder, and baking soda. Add to the wet ingredients and stir just to mix. Add the banana and blend well.

Pour the batter into the prepared pan.

Bake for 40 to 50 minutes. Turn out onto a rack to cool.

½ cup packed brown sugar

½ cup buttermilk

1 large egg

3 Tbsp organic canola oil

¾ cup all-purpose flour

½ cup whole-wheat or rye flour

¾ cup ground flaxseed

1 tsp baking powder

1 tsp baking soda

1 cup puréed banana (or substitute pumpkin or applesauce)

TIP

Craving banana bread with a big bunch of bananas, but none are overripe? Try this trick: bake bananas, unpeeled, on a parchment-lined sheet at 300°F for 30 to 40 minutes until blackened and soft, then cool and proceed with the recipe!

BANANA FLAPJACKS

You can keep this batter covered overnight in the fridge so you're ready to flip flapjacks at a moment's notice. MAKES 12.

In a large bowl, combine the whole-wheat flour, all-purpose flour, baking powder, baking soda, cinnamon, nutmeg, brown sugar, and salt.

In another bowl, whisk together the buttermilk, butter, egg, and mashed bananas.

Make a well in the center of the dry ingredients and pour the banana mixture into it. Stir with a fork until everything is barely moistened.

Heat a nonstick frying pan over medium-high and brush it with a little oil or melted butter. Reduce heat to medium and spoon batter onto the pan, forming 3- to 4-inch pancakes. When you see bubbles rising and breaking all over the top of the pancakes, they're ready to flip. Cook the second side until nicely browned. Keep the pancakes warm in an oven heated to 200°F while you finish cooking.

Serve them topped with sliced bananas and maple syrup.

½ cup whole-wheat flour

½ cup all-purpose flour

1½ tsp baking powder

½ tsp baking soda

¼ tsp ground cinnamon

¼ tsp ground nutmeg

2 Tbsp brown sugar

Pinch salt

1 cup buttermilk
or plain yogurt

2 Tbsp melted butter or
oil, plus more for the pan

1 egg

3 medium overripe
bananas, mashed
(about 1 cup to 1¼ cups)

Extra sliced bananas
and maple syrup

CHOCOLATE BANANA CREAM PIE

This is a dense, nutty chocolate pie, filled with fresh bananas and topped with Amaretto cream. **SERVES 6–8.**

For the crust, pulse the flour, sugar, and butter in a food processor until finely blended. Add the egg, egg yolk, lemon juice, and vanilla, and pulse just until a ball forms. Divide the dough in 2 balls and flatten into disks. Wrap the disks in plastic and chill for 30 minutes. (This makes enough for two 10-inch tarts—the extra dough can be frozen.)

Preheat the oven to 350°F.

For the cream filling, in a small saucepan, bring the cream to a boil over medium-high heat. Remove from the heat, and stir in the chocolate, whisking until smooth. Cool to room temperature.

Using the food processor, combine the butter, salt, ¼ cup of sugar, ground almonds, cornstarch, and Amaretto, and purée until smooth. Pour in the chocolate mixture, and process until creamy. Add the eggs, one at a time, and pulse to combine well.

Press one of the disks of dough into a 10-inch tart pan with a removable bottom. Pierce the shell with a fork in several places, and pour the chocolate filling into the shell.

Arrange the banana slices over the filling and sprinkle with the remaining 3 tablespoons of sugar. Bake for 40 to 45 minutes.

For the topping, in a medium-sized metal bowl, whip the cream with the sugar until stiff. Add the Amaretto and mix well. Chill.

Remove the pie from the oven and set on a rack to cool. Cover with plastic wrap and refrigerate for several hours. When chilled and set, cut into wedges and serve, topping each slice with a dollop of Amaretto cream.

Crust:

2¼ cups all-purpose flour

½ cup granulated sugar

1 cup less 2 Tbsp butter

1 egg

1 egg yolk

Squeeze lemon juice

Splash vanilla extract

Filling:

⅓ cup heavy cream

¼ lb good-quality bittersweet chocolate, chopped

⅓ cup unsalted butter, softened

Pinch salt

¼ cup plus 3 Tbsp granulated sugar, divided

1½ cups finely ground almonds

2 Tbsp cornstarch

1 Tbsp Amaretto or nut-flavored liqueur

2 large eggs

3 bananas, sliced

Topping:

1 cup heavy cream

2 Tbsp granulated sugar

1 Tbsp Amaretto or nut-flavored liqueur

BEANS

Buy

Fresh-picked green and yellow beans are crisp and velvety. They should be slim and smooth (the seeds inside should not be visible), with tips intact. Thin haricots verts are usually more tender than yellow beans.

Store

Store fresh green or yellow beans in a perforated plastic bag or container in the refrigerator for up to 5 days (don't wash first). Or blanch in boiling water for 2 minutes, submerge in ice water to stop the cooking, drain well, and dry, then use a vacuum sealer to package the beans and freeze them (frozen beans will keep for a year this way).

Serve

Simply steamed with a little butter and dill, fresh beans are best when cooked until tender but still crisp. Chopped raw beans add crunch and color to potato or green salads, and slim green beans may be served raw as crudités. Beans are also great in stir-fries. Remove the tops (stem end) before cooking.

Don't Waste It!

- To "smother" green beans, sauté them with chopped bacon, onions, garlic, and chopped tomatoes.
- Dip beans in an egg wash and seasoned bread crumbs to coat and deep-fry until crispy, then serve with chili mayo for dipping.
- Stir-fry green beans with garlic and ginger in a little canola oil, and finish with a spoonful of black bean sauce.
- Combine leftover steamed beans with a little Italian dressing and some chopped red onion and tomato for a simple salad.
- Sauté mushrooms, onions, garlic, and green beans in butter until tender, then finish with a bit of heavy or sour cream and a dash of nutmeg for an update on the classic green bean casserole.
- Combine cold cooked green beans with chopped white mushrooms, minced shallots, diced Swiss cheese, and fresh herbs (dill, parsley, chives), and toss in a Dijon vinaigrette.
- Steam your green beans, then sauté some sliced blanched almonds or pine nuts in butter, just until the butter begins to brown, and pour over the beans.
- Blanch beans and then toss with olive oil and roast at 400°F until crisp. Seasoned with salt these make a tasty, easy snack.
- Boil green beans until just tender crisp—about 4 minutes—then chill in ice water to set the color. Drain and, when ready to serve, quickly sauté with garlic and butter.
- Pack fresh beans upright in jars with a clove of garlic, some dill, and a dried chile. Make a brine of equal parts water and vinegar, with a little salt and sugar, pour it over the beans, seal, and process in a boiling water bath for 10 minutes. Pickles—voila!

TOSSED SALAD NIÇOISE

This is a potato salad with gourmet cachet—a tossed version of that classic composed salad of potatoes, green beans, fish, and garlicky mayonnaise. Serve it in a big shallow salad bowl lined with butter lettuce leaves to make it look extra appetizing on the potluck table. **SERVES 6.**

In a large bowl, whisk together the mayonnaise, sour cream or yogurt, olive oil, mustard, garlic, rosemary, lemon juice, lemon zest, and salt and pepper.

Put a steamer basket in a large saucepan and add about 2 inches of water. Put the potatoes in the steamer basket and steam until tender, about 15 to 20 minutes. Cut into chunks and add the warm potatoes to the dressing in the bowl; toss.

Add the green beans to the steamer and steam until just barely tender, about 2 minutes. Rinse under cold tap water to stop the cooking process, and chop into bite-sized pieces. Mix the beans, green onions, and tuna into the salad, being careful not to break up the potatoes. Cool to room temperature or chill (bring back to room temperature before serving).

To present, line a wide bowl or deep platter with lettuce leaves and arrange the salad on top. Scatter the grape tomatoes and olives around the edge of the salad, pile the chopped egg on top, sprinkle with parsley, and finish with a squeeze of lemon juice.

¼ cup low-fat mayonnaise

¼ cup low-fat sour cream or plain yogurt

2 Tbsp extra-virgin olive oil

2 tsp Dijon mustard

4 cloves roasted garlic (or 1 tsp fresh garlic, puréed in a press)

1 tsp minced fresh rosemary

2 Tbsp fresh lemon juice, plus an extra squeeze to finish

Finely grated lemon zest (about 1 tsp)

Salt and freshly ground black pepper, to taste

2 lb small new red or yellow fingerling potatoes, scrubbed

1 cup fresh green beans, steamed lightly and chopped

2 to 3 green onions, chopped

1 (6 oz) can solid white tuna (packed in water) or sockeye salmon (bones removed), drained and broken into chunks (or ¾ cup leftover diced grilled tuna or salmon)

1 small head butter lettuce, leaves separated, washed, and spun dry

½ cup tiny grape tomatoes, halved

½ cup Niçoise olives

1 hard-cooked egg, chopped

1 Tbsp chopped fresh parsley

GREEN BEAN and POTATO CURRY

This is a simple way to serve green beans in a vegetarian dish. Roti (Indian flat bread) is nice on the side, or serve with rice. This is a mother recipe for any potato and vegetable curry—get creative and substitute cauliflower or other vegetables you have on hand for the green beans. **SERVES 4**.

In a large saucepan, heat the butter over medium-high. Add the cumin seeds and stir until they sizzle and pop. Add the onion and ginger, and cook together for 5 minutes, until the onion is softened and starting to brown.

Stir in the turmeric, dried fenugreek, tomatoes, potatoes, green beans, and water, and combine well. Bring to a boil, cover, reduce heat to low, and braise for about 10 to 15 minutes, until the potatoes are just tender.

Gently stir in the garam masala, chili paste, and cilantro.

2 Tbsp butter or ghee

1 tsp whole cumin seeds

1 onion, chopped
(about 1 cup)

1 Tbsp minced fresh ginger

1 tsp ground turmeric

1 tsp dried fenugreek leaves
(kasoori methi), crushed

2 ripe Roma tomatoes,
seeded and chopped
(about 1½ cups)

2 cups potatoes, cut
into 2-inch pieces

4 cups (1 lb) fresh green or
yellow beans, stems removed

½ cup water

1 tsp garam masala

½ tsp Asian chili paste

1 Tbsp chopped
fresh cilantro

CREAMY CHICKEN and GREEN BEANS on PENNE

This is a simple and homey combination. It makes a nice meal for two with a salad on the side. **SERVES 2.**

In a sauté pan, heat the olive oil over medium-high. Sauté the chicken quickly until browned. Remove from the pan and set aside.

Reduce heat to medium. In the same pan, sauté the onion and garlic until beginning to brown, about 5 minutes.

Stir in the white wine to deglaze the pan, scraping up any browned bits.

Stir in the flour, then slowly add the stock. Bring to a simmer and stir until smooth. Add the green beans, reduce heat to low, cover, and simmer for 5 minutes.

Return the chicken to the pan.

Stir in the sour cream, paprika, and half of the cheese. Add the pasta and cook, stirring until everything is heated through and bubbly. Season with salt and pepper.

Divide between 2 pasta bowls and top with the remaining cheese and the almonds.

2 Tbsp olive oil

1 large boneless, skinless chicken breast (about ½ lb), cubed

1 small onion, chopped (about ½ cup)

1 clove garlic, minced

¼ cup white wine

1 Tbsp all-purpose flour

2 cups chicken stock

3 cups fresh green beans, tops and tails removed, and cut in half if long

½ cup sour cream

½ tsp paprika

1 cup grated Parmigiano-Reggiano, divided

4 cups cooked penne

Salt and freshly ground black pepper, to taste

¼ cup sliced toasted almonds, for garnish

BEETS

Buy

Buy beets in the summer; get small sweet specimens with tender tops—red, yellow, or candy-cane striped Chioggias. Save larger beets for pickling and soups.

Store

Beets are a winter storage crop, so they are available fresh beyond the summer harvest season. At home remove tops, leaving an inch of stem, and store roots in the refrigerator for 3 to 4 weeks. Beet greens are very perishable, so eat them quickly.

Serve

Beet soup or borscht is a classic dish, but new varieties of colorful yellow and striped Italian Chioggia beets have put beets at the center of high-end plates, whether it's whole roasted baby beets, paper-thin slices or spiral-cut ribbons, or lightly pickled beets. To reduce bleeding, cook beets whole and unpeeled, then slip off the skins before serving.

Don't Waste It!

- To roast beets, wash well, wrap loosely in foil, and roast at 400°F for 45 to 60 minutes, until easy to pierce with a sharp knife. Peel and toss with butter or balsamic vinegar.

- Use a spiral slicer to cut beets into thin, curly "pasta" to lightly steam or serve raw in salads.

- Toss hot cooked beet slices with a combination of sugar and red wine vinegar and set aside to cool for a quick pickle.

- Combine raw peeled beets with apples, almond milk, and ginger, and blend for a healthy purple smoothie.

- Dress cooked and shredded red beets and chopped onion with a sweetened vinegar and Dijon dressing.

- Slice roasted yellow beets into wedges and toss with some baby greens, toasted walnuts, crumbled blue cheese, and walnut oil vinaigrette for a sophisticated salad.

- Mix cooked cubed red beets with lemon juice, sour cream or yogurt, and dill for a colorful (fuchsia) side salad.

- Use the beet greens, too—shred and sauté with garlic like you would spinach or chard and add to pasta dishes, or season with balsamic vinegar as a side dish.

- Slow-cook red onions with balsamic vinegar until thick and syrupy and toss with diced roasted beets for a warm side dish or condiment (best if chilled overnight and reheated).

COOL PINK SIP

Sour cream turns this cool beet broth pure pink. Fun to sip cold from a coffee cup or shot glass to start a summer soiree. **SERVES 4.**

Preheat the oven to 425°F. Arrange the beets and onions in a roasting pan. Drizzle with the olive oil and season with the salt and white pepper. Roast for about 45 minutes, stirring occasionally, until the beets and onions are tender. Cool.

Peel the beets and grate using a box grater (or a food processor). Chop the onions and combine with the beets in a saucepan. Add the water, vinegar, and sugar, and bring to a boil. Simmer for 3 minutes, then remove from heat and let cool.

Whisk in the sour cream and chill for several hours or overnight. Purée in a blender or food processor if a smooth soup is desired.

Adjust the seasoning and serve topped with dill.

2 lb beets, scrubbed but unpeeled

2 red onions, quartered

¼ cup extra-virgin olive oil

1 tsp salt

White pepper, to taste

4 cups water

2 Tbsp vinegar

1 Tbsp granulated sugar

½ cup sour cream

Chopped fresh dill, for garnish

ROASTED BEET and WATERCRESS SALAD with GORGONZOLA SAUCE

This composed salad is basically a stacked mini terrine of sliced roasted beets and onions, glued together with a creamy blue cheese sauce. Chefs often use ring molds to keep their stacked creations corralled—you can use a biscuit cutter or small clean tin, with both ends removed, that's about the same size as your beets. Look for a variety of red, pink, and yellow heirloom beets to make this salad stunning. **MAKES 8 INDIVIDUAL SALADS.**

Preheat the oven to 425°F. Arrange the beets and onions in a roasting pan. Drizzle with the olive oil and season with the salt and pepper. Cover pan tightly with foil.

Roast for about 45 minutes, until the beets and onions are tender. Cool. Peel the beets and slice thinly into a bowl. Slice the onions and place in a separate bowl. Drizzle the reduced balsamic over both the beets and the onions, toss to combine, and set aside.

To make the Gorgonzola sauce, heat the olive oil in a saucepan and toast the chopped walnuts for 2 minutes. Transfer to a bowl to cool, then stir in the rosemary, balsamic vinegar, and salt.

Combine the cheese and cream in a blender or food processor and whirl until smooth. Add to the walnut mixture and stir to combine.

To serve, place a small dab of the Gorgonzola sauce on each of 8 salad plates. Top with some sliced beets, a dab of sauce, some red onions, sauce, and more beets, forming a stack. To make this easier, use a ring mold (or a small tin with both ends removed).

Top each stack with a dollop of sauce and a tiny bouquet of watercress leaves. Arrange walnut halves around the edge of each plate, interspersed with drops of reduced balsamic vinegar.

3 lb red, striped Chioggia, and/or yellow beets of equal size, trimmed

2 red onions, quartered

¼ cup extra-virgin olive oil

1 tsp salt

½ tsp freshly ground black pepper

2 tsp reduced balsamic vinegar, plus extra for garnish

2 cups watercress leaves, washed and spun dry (about 2 bunches watercress, stems removed)

½ cup toasted walnut halves

Gorgonzola sauce:

1 Tbsp extra-virgin olive oil

½ cup finely chopped walnuts

1 tsp minced fresh rosemary

1 Tbsp balsamic vinegar

½ tsp salt

6 oz soft Gorgonzola cheese (or substitute Boursin)

½ cup heavy cream

BEST BORSCHT

This classic beet soup is an old family recipe and makes a meal in itself. Make a vegetarian version, or start with beef or pork soup bones or spareribs to make a meat broth base. This makes a big batch, but it freezes well. **SERVES 6-8.**

In a large soup pot, combine the beets, carrots, onion, garlic, cabbage, potato, tomatoes, and water or stock. Bring to a boil over high heat, then reduce the heat to low, cover the pot, and simmer the soup for 1 hour.

Remove the beets from the soup, slip off and discard the skins, and chop or grate the beets. Return the beets to the soup. Stir in the beans, lemon juice or vinegar, sugar, and paprika, and return to low heat. Cover and simmer for 15 minutes.

In a small bowl, whisk together the flour, salt and pepper, and cream or sour cream. Add a few tablespoons of hot stock from the soup and mix well, then whisk the cream mixture into the soup to thicken it. Heat through but do not boil or the soup will curdle. Stir in the fresh dill and serve immediately.

3 medium beets, scrubbed but unpeeled

⅔ cup diced carrots

1 medium onion, minced

2 cloves garlic, minced

2 cups finely shredded green or purple cabbage

1 large Yukon Gold potato, peeled and cubed

1 (14 oz) can tomatoes, puréed

8 cups water or beef stock

1 cup cooked small white beans (or canned white beans, rinsed and drained)

3 Tbsp fresh lemon juice or red wine vinegar

1 Tbsp granulated sugar

½ tsp paprika

2 Tbsp all-purpose flour

Salt and freshly ground black pepper, to taste

½ cup heavy cream or sour cream

2 Tbsp chopped fresh dill

BERRIES

Buy

Strawberries should be red right to the green hull with no white shoulders and no soft spots. They are perishable, so buy them locally in season and look for organic sources. It's the same with raspberries and blackberries—ripe berries don't ship well so find a local source. Blueberries are easier to ship but are tastiest in season. Look for plump, clean berries with no mold or soft spots.

Store

Berries will keep for only a couple of days in the fridge. Don't wash berries until you're ready to eat them, and even then just give them a quick rinse if required. Set strawberries, blackberries, and raspberries in a single layer on a paper-towel-lined plate and plan to eat immediately. Or freeze berries in a single layer, then transfer to freezer bags.

Serve

Berries can be baked into pies and crisps but are really best eaten fresh or with ice cream. To improve slightly underripe strawberries, slice and toss with a drizzle of reduced balsamic vinegar.

Don't Waste It!

- Slice strawberries and toss with a little sugar and Cointreau or fruit brandy, then spoon them over a bowl of vanilla ice cream.

- Add sliced strawberries or blueberries to a spinach salad with candied walnuts or pecans.

- Mash fresh raspberries on buttered toast.

- Make raspberry vinegar by boiling 1 cup white wine vinegar and pouring it over 2 cups raspberries in a clean jar. Macerate at room temperature for 3 days, then strain and sweeten lightly with honey.

- Make a sauce with blueberries, blackberries, or saskatoons, shallots, port, balsamic vinegar, and thyme to serve over seared duck breasts or grilled lamb.

- Create a cool strawberry gazpacho: in a blender, whirl together 1 pound strawberries with a small brioche, a little orange juice, sugar, raspberry vinegar, and fresh tomato, then add ¼ cup olive oil to emulsify. Strain and serve cold in small cups.

- Combine blueberries, blackberries, or saskatoon berries with sliced apples for pies and crisps.

- Whirl fresh berries into fruit smoothies or shakes.

- Dip whole perfect strawberries in dark chocolate, then lay them on a parchment-lined plate for 30 minutes in the refrigerator to set.

- Add blueberries or raspberries to muffin and pancake batter.

- Combine chopped fresh fruit like peaches and melon with strawberries, blueberries, blackberries, and a little sugar for a fruit salad. Top with a dollop of lemon yogurt for dessert.

MIXED BERRY SHORTCAKE

Buy strawberries and blueberries when they're in season and available from local farms. Frozen berries can be substituted, but don't use imported off-season fruit. SERVES 6.

In a bowl, combine the berries with the apple juice and sugar, and let stand at room temperature.

Preheat the oven to 425°F.

In another bowl, stir together the all-purpose flour, whole-wheat flour, ground pecans or walnuts, brown sugar, salt, baking powder, and baking soda. Cut in the butter with a pastry cutter to form coarse crumbs (or combine everything in a food processor and pulse until crumbly).

Add the yogurt and vanilla and stir, just to combine.

Gather the biscuit dough together (handle it lightly) and place on a lightly floured surface. Pat into a round, about 1 inch thick. Cut into 6 wedges, or use a glass or cutter to make 2-inch rounds. Brush each biscuit with a little milk and sprinkle with granulated sugar.

Line a baking sheet with parchment paper and set the biscuits on the sheet, about 1 inch apart. Bake for 10 to 15 minutes, until golden.

Cool slightly on a rack.

Cut the biscuits in half horizontally. Place the bottom half of each biscuit on a dessert plate. Top with some of the berry mixture and some of the whipped cream. Place the second half of the biscuit overtop and garnish with more berries and cream.

2 lb fresh berries (strawberries, blueberries, raspberries, saskatoons), sliced, about 8 cups total

¼ cup apple juice or berry liqueur

¼ cup granulated sugar

Biscuit:

½ cup all-purpose flour

½ cup whole-wheat flour

¼ cup ground pecans or walnuts

½ cup packed brown sugar

½ tsp salt

2 tsp baking powder

1 tsp baking soda

¼ cup butter

½ cup plain yogurt

½ tsp vanilla extract

Milk, for brushing

Granulated sugar, for sprinkling

1 cup heavy cream, whipped with a touch of sugar (or vanilla yogurt)

BLUEBERRY SOUR CREAM TART

Sort of a cross between a pie and a creamy cheesecake, this super-easy summer tart is always a hit. Make it when fresh blueberries are in season, or use fresh strawberries, rhubarb, raspberries, or even chopped peaches. SERVES 6–8.

Arrange an oven rack in the middle position and preheat the oven to 375°F. Butter a 9-inch springform pan.

Use a food processor to make the crust. Combine the flour, sugar, and baking powder in the food processor. Whirl to combine. Add the cubes of butter and pulse a few times until the butter is broken up into tiny pieces and the mixture is mealy. Add the egg and vanilla and pulse the mixture a few more times, just until the pastry comes together.

Pat the crust into the prepared pan, pressing it evenly along the bottom and up the sides an inch or so.

For the filling, whisk together the sour cream, sugar, egg yolks, flour, and vanilla. Spread the blueberries evenly into the crust. Pour the cream filling evenly over the berries and shake the pan so that everything evens out. Bake for 1 hour, until the top is set and lightly browned. Chill and release from the springform pan before slicing into wedges.

Crust:

1½ cups all-purpose flour

½ cup granulated sugar

1½ tsp baking powder

½ cup cold butter, cut into cubes

1 egg, lightly beaten

1 tsp vanilla extract

Filling:

1 cup sour cream

½ cup granulated sugar

2 egg yolks

2 Tbsp all-purpose flour

1 tsp vanilla extract

4 cups blueberries (fresh or frozen)

MINI CHEESECAKE BITES

Make these no-bake cheesecakes in small, ½-cup canning jars (to transport easily on a picnic) or in small glasses. **MAKES 12 SERVINGS**.

In a bowl, whip the cream with the icing sugar and vanilla until stiff. Chill.

In another bowl, beat the cream cheese until smooth. Fold in the whipped cream, one-third at a time, to lighten the cheesecake mixture.

Divide the cookie crumbs evenly between 12 (½-cup) canning jars (or glasses). Top each with an equal portion of the cheesecake filling and a layer of fruit. Top the jars with lids and refrigerate for up to 24 hours before serving.

2 cups heavy cream

½ cup icing sugar

1 tsp vanilla extract

2 (8 oz) packages cream cheese, softened

1½ cups graham cracker or ginger cookie crumbs

1 to 2 cups blackberries, raspberries, or chopped peeled peaches

BROCCOLI

Buy

Get green broccoli or purple sprouting broccoli (related to kale) with heads that are tightly packed and brightly colored, with no yellowing leaves or cracked hollow stems. Smaller stems signal younger, tender florets. Broccoli rabe has smaller stems and no real heads—it's a great green vegetable to quickly sauté with garlic.

Store

Keep it in a perforated plastic bag in the refrigerator and eat quickly—old broccoli loses its sweet flavor.

Serve

Add broccoli to curries or purée it into creamy broccoli soup. Top grilled or steamed broccoli with cheese sauce, hollandaise, or grated Parmesan; blanch quickly, and season with garlic, miso, and sesame oil; or just grab and munch straight out of the fridge.

Don't Waste It!

- Simmer up some cheese and wine for a creamy fondue in which to dip cubes of French bread and broccoli florets.
- Stir-fry your broccoli with ginger, garlic, slivers of steak, and oyster or soy sauce for speedy beef and broccoli.
- Toss leftover cooked broccoli with hot cooked chunky whole-grain pasta, olive oil, and Parmesan.
- Fry cubed pancetta or bacon until crispy, then add broccoli and garlic, cook until tender, and finish with a squeeze of lemon juice.
- Blanch a head of chopped broccoli, toss with a little olive oil and a cup of mixed Romano and Gruyère cheeses, then place under the broiler until bubbly and brown.
- Make a big bowl of Asian noodle soup, with chicken broth, soy sauce, ginger, garlic, slivered carrot, and broccoli.
- Pile steamed broccoli, crispy bacon, and cheddar cheese onto a hot baked potato for a speedy lunch.
- Purée cooked broccoli, chopped garlic, salt and pepper, and 1 cup heavy cream in a food processor for an almost instant sauce to pour over hot macaroni.

BROCCOLI FRITTATA

This is another standard recipe that will work with whatever leftover vegetables, herbs, or cheeses you have in the fridge or freezer. You can even use frozen hash brown potatoes to speed up the prep. **SERVES 4.**

Preheat the broiler.

In a large sauté pan that you can use in the oven, heat the oil over medium-high. Sauté the potatoes, onion, garlic, and red pepper for 5 to 10 minutes. When the potatoes begin to brown, reduce the heat to medium and stir in the Italian seasoning and salt and pepper.

Meanwhile, in a bowl or measuring cup, whisk the eggs until well beaten.

When the potatoes are tender, add the chopped broccoli and stir to distribute evenly in the pan. Pour the beaten egg overtop, stirring lightly and lifting the edges to allow the uncooked egg to run underneath the frittata as it begins to firm up and set. When it's nicely browned on the bottom, and the edges are cooked (this will take about 10 minutes), sprinkle the cheese evenly over the frittata and place the pan in the oven under the broiler. Cook for about 2 minutes, until the cheese is melted and the frittata is cooked through.

Remove from the oven and set aside to cool for a minute or two before slicing into wedges to serve.

2 Tbsp olive oil

2 yellow-fleshed potatoes, peeled and diced

1 onion, chopped

2 cloves garlic, chopped

½ cup diced red bell pepper

½ tsp Italian seasoning

½ tsp salt

½ tsp freshly ground black pepper

6 eggs

1 cup cooked chopped broccoli

1 cup grated cheddar, Gruyère, or Gouda cheese

SAVORY BROCCOLI, CHEDDAR, and BACON SCONES

Savory scones are another "mother recipe" for bits of leftover cooked veggies, cheese, and protein. Add almost any leftover vegetables (grilled peppers, roasted butternut squash, chopped broccoli, caramelized onions, or chopped spinach) or meats (crumbled cooked sausage or bacon, minced ham, or salmon), along with some herbs, green onions, and cheese, to these basic buttermilk scones for the perfect portable breakfast or lunch. **MAKES 8 LARGE SCONES**.

Preheat the oven to 350°F. Line a baking sheet with parchment paper.

In a food processor, combine the all-purpose flour, whole-wheat flour, baking powder, salt, and butter. Pulse until the mixture resembles coarse crumbs, then transfer to a bowl.

Stir the broccoli and bacon into the flour mixture along with the green onion, herbs, and cheese. Add just enough cream to make a soft dough (depends on how wet the vegetable mixture is), stirring with a fork until the mixture just comes together. Don't work the dough too much—the less you handle it, the flakier your scones will be.

Dump the dough out onto a floured work surface and knead gently, then pat lightly into a rectangle about 1½ to 2 inches thick. Cut into 4-inch squares, then cut the squares crosswise into triangles (or make round scones with a 3-inch biscuit cutter). Set the scones on the prepared baking sheet. Using a pastry brush, brush the tops lightly with extra cream, and sprinkle with seeds.

Bake for 20 to 25 minutes, until golden, then transfer to a rack to cool slightly. Serve warm with butter.

1 cup all-purpose flour

1 cup whole-wheat flour

2 Tbsp baking powder

1½ tsp salt

½ cup unsalted butter, chilled and cut into cubes

½ cup chopped cooked broccoli

¼ cup crumbled cooked bacon

1 green onion, minced

1 Tbsp chopped fresh herbs (dill, basil, oregano, etc.)

1 cup grated aged cheddar (or Gruyère, Gouda, crumbled blue cheese, feta, etc.)

⅓ to ½ cup half-and-half or buttermilk, plus more for brushing

Poppy seeds or sesame seeds, for sprinkling

> **TIP**
> Think about complementary and classic combinations for the scones when you survey what you have in your fridge—red pepper with oregano and cheddar cheese; spinach with dill and feta; chopped prosciutto or cooked Italian sausage with basil and Parmesan; caramelized onions, cheddar, and thyme; etc. Or just get creative!

CABBAGE

Buy

Look for bright, heavy heads with tight green leaves for shredding, or looser, wrinkled heads of milder Savoy cabbage for salad rolls or vegetable wraps, and flatter heads for cabbage rolls. Chinese and napa cabbage are milder for stir-fries.

Store

Store in a cool place (2 to 3 weeks in the crisper of your refrigerator). Shredded cabbage can be salted to ferment into sauerkraut and kimchi, and whole cabbages can be pickled in salted brine (1 cup sea salt per gallon of water) for 6 weeks, then frozen.

Serve

Cabbage is a hardy vegetable grown around the world and is a staple ingredient for peasant dishes—everything from cabbage rolls and choucroute to Chinese stir-fries and Korean kimchi.

Don't Waste It!

- Shred cabbage and layer with sea salt in a large crock or food-grade plastic pail. Place a weighted plate on top to keep the cabbage submerged in the liquid that will result; keep it in a cool place and soon you will have sauerkraut for choucroute.

- To make cabbage rolls, combine ground pork with rice and sautéed onions and garlic, roll it up in blanched cabbage leaves, and simmer for an hour or two in tomato juice.

- Slowly simmer sliced cabbage in butter, olive oil, and a couple of cups of chicken broth for 15 minutes, until tender.

- Brown chopped bacon and onion together, then add shredded red cabbage, red wine vinegar, a clove, a bay leaf, a bit of sugar, and a chopped peeled apple. Cover and braise on low heat to serve with pork sausages or duck.

- Fast-fry shredded cabbage in a wok with canola oil, sambal oelek, salt, sugar, ginger, and soy sauce, then toss with cooked Shanghai noodles or ramen.

- Bulk up any vegetable soup with some shredded cabbage or sauerkraut—it's especially good in soups with sausage and white beans.

- Shredded cabbage is the classic addition to Baja fish tacos. Shred red and green cabbage and toss with salt, lime juice, and chopped cilantro for authentic flavor.

- Make a classic coleslaw: mix shredded cabbage, apple, carrot, and chopped green onion with mayonnaise, sour cream, mustard, and a little sugar and cider vinegar. Season with celery salt, dill, and salt and pepper.

COLCANNON

This traditional Irish dish is related to champ (potatoes mashed with green onions) but with the addition of cabbage or kale—cabbage's wilder, coarser relative and the latest superfood. Serve it alongside lamb shanks braised in dark Irish ale. **SERVES 6.**

6 medium potatoes (russet or Viking), peeled and quartered

3 cups shredded cabbage or finely chopped kale

1 large yellow onion (or a bunch of green onions), chopped

2 cups water seasoned with 1 tsp salt

¼ cup heavy cream

¼ cup butter

Freshly ground black pepper, to taste

In a large heavy saucepan, layer the vegetables: half of the potatoes, half of the cabbage, and half of the onion, then repeat. Pour the salted water overtop. Cover the pan and bring to a boil over medium-high heat. Reduce the heat to low and simmer, tightly covered, for 1 hour.

Drain well and use a potato masher to mash everything together, forming a chunky purée. Stir in the cream and butter. Season with pepper.

> **TIP**
> Any leftover colcannon can be made into small patties and sautéed in olive oil or bacon fat to serve with your breakfast eggs.

SALMON with SWEET and SPICY CHINESE CABBAGE

This simple salmon dish makes a delicious meal when served alongside some steamed basmati rice. SERVES 2.

Preheat the oven to 450°F. Line a baking sheet with aluminum foil or parchment paper.

Whisk together the oyster sauce, soy sauce, brown sugar, garlic, and lime juice. Pour over the salmon fillets and marinate for 15 minutes. Remove the fish from the marinade, reserving the marinade.

Set the fillets on the prepared baking sheet. Brush with a little reserved marinade. Bake until just cooked through, about 10 minutes for a 1-inch-thick piece, just until the fish begins to flake. Remove from the oven and let rest for 2 minutes.

While the salmon is baking, prepare the salad. In a mixing bowl, combine the cabbage, carrots, bell pepper, and green onions, and toss. In a small bowl, whisk together the ginger, olive oil, sesame oil, rice vinegar, lime juice, sugar, chili sauce, and salt and pepper. Pour the dressing over the mixed vegetables and toss again. Refrigerate until ready to serve.

Arrange some cabbage salad in the centers of 2 plates. Top each with a salmon fillet. Sprinkle with sesame seeds.

2 Tbsp oyster sauce

2 Tbsp soy sauce

1 tsp brown sugar or honey

1 clove garlic, minced

1 tsp fresh lime juice

2 skinless salmon fillets, each about 5 oz and 1 inch thick

Toasted sesame seeds, for garnish

Cabbage salad:

3 cups shredded cabbage (use Chinese or napa cabbage)

¾ cup shredded carrots

1 small red bell pepper, seeded and slivered

2 green onions, sliced

1 tsp grated fresh ginger

¼ cup olive oil

1 Tbsp sesame oil

2 Tbsp rice vinegar

1 Tbsp fresh lime juice

1 Tbsp granulated sugar

1 to 3 tsp sweet red Thai chili sauce or Asian garlic chili paste (to taste)

Salt and freshly ground black pepper, to taste

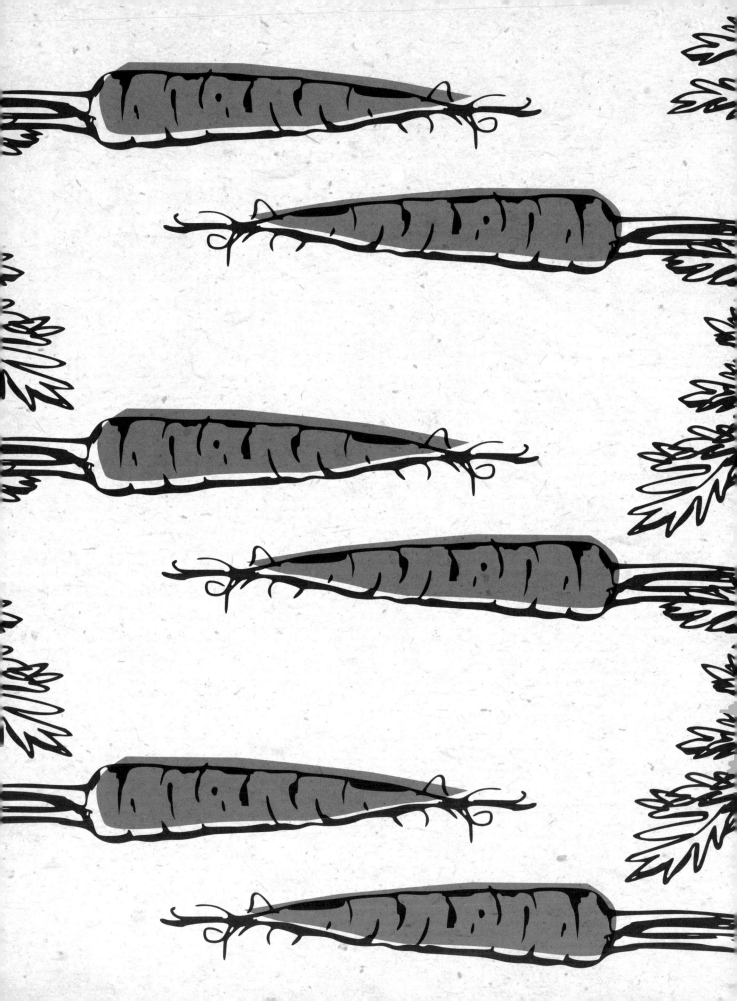

CARROTS

Buy

Look for long, straight, crisp, organic carrots (bagged "baby" carrots are just old carrots turned into rounded bits by a machine) or high beta-carotene red carrots at the market. If the tops are on, and look fresh, the roots are, too.

Store

Remove tops before storing and keep carrots in a plastic bag in the coolest part of the refrigerator for up to 2 weeks (keep away from apples and potatoes—their gases make carrots bitter). For longer storage, try packing carrots tightly into cleaned large milk cartons and sealing them shut.

Serve

Whether chopped into soups and stews, added to cakes and steamed holiday puddings, or simply cut into sticks for vegetable trays, sweet carrots are a staple in the kitchen and, like other orange vegetables, are extremely good for you. If organic, just scrub and eat, healthy skin and all. Steamed carrots taste better than boiled carrots.

Don't Waste It!

- Peel carrots, slice into coins, and toss with a mixture of melted butter and honey, then roast on a parchment-lined baking sheet for 30 minutes. Season with fresh chopped rosemary or thyme.

- Shred carrots to add color to green salads or cabbage slaw.

- Toss steamed carrots with butter, maple syrup, and mustard.

- Purée carrots with apples and ginger for healthy smoothies.

- Roughly mash boiled carrots and potatoes, then season with chopped onions and ginger that have been sautéed in butter.

- Start almost any soup or stew with a classic mirepoix of finely chopped onion, carrot, and celery.

- Buy a spiral cutter and make ribbons of carrot "spaghetti" that you can simply salt or lightly pickle to serve on sandwiches like the classic Vietnamese bánh mì sub sandwich.

- Fresh clean carrot tops can be chopped and combined with other greens in salads.

- Combine shredded carrots, beets, and apples with a little mayo for a sweet side salad.

- To make simple spiced carrot sticks, bring a brine of water, cayenne, coriander seeds, and salt to a boil, pour over the carrot sticks, and cool, then drain and serve.

- Toss whole steamed carrots with chermoula, a Moroccan pesto-like condiment made with olive oil, lemon zest, cilantro, parsley, garlic, cumin, coriander, ginger, and thyme.

ROASTED CARROT SESAME HUMMUS

A creamy, nutty carrot spread to serve as a dip with pita bread, crackers, or crudités. (Pictured on page 163.) **SERVES 4–6.**

Combine all of the ingredients in a blender or food processor and whirl to a chunky or smooth purée.

4 medium carrots, roasted (see Tip)

1 cup cooked chickpeas (or canned chickpeas, rinsed and drained)

⅓ cup tahini

¼ cup extra-virgin olive oil

¼ cup water

2 Tbsp fresh lemon juice

1 tsp Asian chili paste

2 large cloves garlic, chopped (about 1 Tbsp)

1 Tbsp chopped fresh cilantro

1 tsp dried mint

¼ tsp ground cumin

¼ tsp ground coriander

Sea salt, to taste

TIP

To roast carrots, cut into chunks, toss with olive oil and salt, and roast in the oven at 400°F for 20 minutes.

CARROT and CORIANDER SOUP

This is the perfect way to start a dinner party or just use up your fall crop of carrots. A smooth colorful soup, creamy yet low in calories. **SERVES 4–6.**

In a large saucepan over medium heat, melt the butter and sauté the celery, onion, garlic, and ginger for 5 minutes, until tender and fragrant. Add the coriander, curry powder, cilantro stems, and carrots, and cook together for 5 minutes.

Add the stock and bring to a boil over medium-high heat. Reduce heat to low, partially cover the pan, and simmer for 30 to 40 minutes.

Cool the soup slightly, then transfer to a blender or food processor to purée. Return the soup to the pot and reheat. Thin with a little additional stock or water if necessary. Stir in the lemon juice and season with salt.

Ladle into soup bowls and garnish with fresh cilantro leaves.

¼ cup butter

½ cup chopped celery

1 onion, chopped

1 clove garlic, minced

1 Tbsp minced fresh ginger

1 tsp ground coriander

½ tsp curry powder

¼ cup chopped cilantro stems (save the leaves for garnish)

1½ lb carrots, peeled and chopped or shredded

5 cups chicken stock

1 tsp fresh lemon juice

Sea salt, to taste

1 Tbsp chopped fresh cilantro leaves, for garnish

SAIGON SATAY CHICKEN SUBS with CARROT SLAW

The secret to any Vietnamese sub is the crunchy, lightly pickled carrot salad, some sliced cucumber, and a good handful of fresh cilantro leaves. After that it's just mayo, grilled chicken, beef, or pork (think leftovers), a bit of cheese, a good baguette, and a few minutes under the broiler. Buy a commercial satay sauce to make it even faster. **MAKES 2 SUB SANDWICHES.**

Combine the sauce ingredients in a jar or bottle, shake, and refrigerate.

Poach the chicken in boiling water, covered, for about 30 minutes or toss with a little sauce and bake. Once poached, toss the chicken with a little sauce and chill. Alternately, start with chunks of boneless leftover cooked chicken and toss with a little sauce.

Put the carrots in a colander, sprinkle with the salt, and let them drain for an hour to remove moisture. Rinse, pat dry, and combine with the sugar, vinegar, and about 1 cup of water in a container and refrigerate for at least an hour (or up to 3 days) to lightly pickle.

Preheat the broiler.

To assemble the subs, split the baguettes or buns lengthwise and slather one half of each with mayonnaise. Top with chicken and cheese and put on a baking sheet. Broil for 1 to 2 minutes, just to toast the bread and melt the cheese.

Top each sandwich with half of the shredded carrot salad, cucumber strips, onion, chopped chiles, and cilantro. Drizzle each with a few tablespoons of the sauce. Press bread together to enclose filling and wrap in waxed paper to keep everything inside while you eat.

TIP

To create the curly shreds of carrot that take this sandwich into authentic gourmet territory, you'll need a spiral slicer. This handy gadget can turn any hard vegetable—daikon, carrot, beet, potato—into spaghetti-like strands. Perfect for deep-fried potato nests or pickled carrots, beets, or radishes to pile on salads and sandwiches. Search for a spiral slicer in Asian markets and kitchen shops or look for the simple Microplane version.

Sauce:

¼ cup fresh lime juice

¼ cup Asian fish sauce

¼ cup water

2 Tbsp rice vinegar or wine vinegar

1 Tbsp granulated sugar

1 tsp Asian garlic chili paste (or cayenne and garlic powder combined)

1 large boneless, skinless chicken breast (or tender strips of roast or grilled beef), about 6 oz

1 cup matchstick or shredded carrots

1 Tbsp salt

2 Tbsp granulated sugar

¼ cup rice vinegar

2 (6-inch) lengths fresh baguette (or 2 crusty sub buns)

Mayonnaise

Thin slices mozzarella cheese

½ English cucumber, sliced in thin lengthwise strips (use a vegetable peeler)

½ cup finely sliced white onion (½ an onion)

2 to 3 chopped fresh chiles (serrano are good)

Large handful fresh cilantro

CARROT CAKE

For a birthday cake, make this in two or four layers, or bake into cupcakes for individual birthday treats. This is the kind of cake you can bake in a big sheet cake pan and take anywhere (from a church supper to a neighborhood potluck). For a lower-fat cake, substitute applesauce for half of the oil. SERVES 12.

Preheat the oven to 375°F. In a bowl, combine the raisins and Grand Marnier; microwave on high for 1 minute, then set aside to cool.

Combine the flour, baking powder, baking soda, cinnamon, cloves, and nutmeg. In the bowl of an electric mixer, combine the brown sugar, molasses, vanilla, and eggs, and beat until well combined. With the mixer running, slowly add the oil to form a thickened emulsion. Stir in the lemon juice. Add the dry ingredients, in stages, and beat to form a batter. Stir in the prepared raisins, carrots, and pecans.

Oil your baking pan(s)—you can use a 13- × 9-inch sheet cake pan, a 10-inch deep Bundt pan, or two 9-inch layer cake pans (or muffin tins).

Dust with flour, then tip out the excess. Fill the pan(s) two-thirds full with batter to allow for rising during baking. For round or sheet cakes bake for 50 minutes and for a Bundt cake 80 minutes, until a skewer inserted in the center comes out clean. (Cupcakes cook in 20 to 25 minutes.) Cool in the pans on a rack for 1 hour.

To make the frosting, use an electric mixer to cream the cream cheese and butter together until smooth. Add the icing sugar and beat to combine. Beat in the Grand Marnier or vanilla and enough cream or milk to make a spreadable frosting. Use a little more icing sugar to make a stiffer frosting for a layer cake or cupcakes.

For a sheet cake, frost the top and sprinkle with ground pecans, then serve out of the pan. For a layer cake, remove the cakes from the pans. Place the first cake onto a serving plate, and spread evenly with frosting. Place the second cake on top, and frost the top and sides. Press ground pecans around the outside of the cake to finish. For a Bundt cake, add a little more cream to the frosting so you can drizzle it over the top and sides of the cake, then sprinkle the top with ground pecans.

Cake:

½ cup raisins

2 Tbsp Grand Marnier

3 cups all-purpose flour

2 tsp baking powder

1 tsp baking soda

1 Tbsp ground cinnamon

½ tsp ground cloves

½ tsp ground nutmeg

2 cups packed dark brown sugar

¼ cup molasses

1 Tbsp vanilla extract

4 eggs

1¼ cups canola oil

1 Tbsp fresh lemon juice

4 cups finely grated carrots

½ cup chopped pecans

Frosting:

1 (8 oz) package cream cheese (low-fat is fine)

2 Tbsp unsalted butter, softened

1 cup icing sugar

1 Tbsp Grand Marnier or vanilla extract

1 Tbsp heavy cream or milk

Ground pecans

CAULIFLOWER

Buy

Cauliflower is a healthy brassica that's best purchased in winter. You can buy regular white cauliflower, plus new colorful purple and orange varieties. Avoid any with dark spots.

Store

Cauliflower stores well but is sweeter when fresh. Keep whole in a perforated bag in the refrigerator for a week or two. You can also make cauliflower "rice" and freeze it in 2-cup portions.

Serve

Best raw or lightly cooked, cauliflower is versatile, whether you serve it raw with a vegetable dip, steamed with cheese sauce, or roasted with olive oil and sea salt to bring out its sweet flavor.

Don't Waste It!

- To roast, toss florets with olive oil and salt and pepper (or spices like smoked paprika or curry powder), and bake on a baking sheet at 400°F for 35 to 40 minutes, stirring once or twice. Top with grated Parmesan cheese.

- For a satisfying, low-carb side dish, ditch the potatoes and just steam cauliflower until very tender and mash with butter, cream, and salt and pepper.

- Sauté cauliflower florets with caramelized onions, sliced bell peppers, minced garlic, toasted cumin seeds, and turmeric until tender, then stir in a little plain yogurt to finish.

- To make cauliflower "rice," remove leaves and core, then grate or pulse the florets in a food processor until finely chopped. Spread on a baking sheet and bake, flipping once, at 425°F for 15 minutes, or dry fry with a small amount of olive oil and minced onion or garlic in a nonstick pan.

- Remove leaves and cut whole cauliflower into thick "steaks," then brush both sides with olive oil, season with smoked paprika, and grill until tender and charred.

- Serve fresh cauliflower florets with hummus for dipping.

- Combine leftover cooked and chopped cauliflower with flour, baking powder, minced garlic, parsley, grated cheese, and a beaten egg, then fry spoonfuls of batter in oil to make fast fritters.

- For a quick cauliflower soup, sauté onion and garlic in butter, add cauliflower and chicken stock, simmer until tender, then purée with light cream and season to taste.

CAULIFLOWER MAC and CHEESE

Orange cauliflower is perfect in a weekday casserole of cheesy macaroni and cheddar. Add a green salad with chopped tomato and cucumber on the side. **SERVES 4.**

In a large pot over medium, heat the water and cream until starting to boil. Stir in the cauliflower, macaroni, and ¼ tsp of the salt. Simmer for about 15 min, stirring often, or until the macaroni and cauliflower are tender.

In a measuring cup, whisk the flour, mustard, and pepper with the milk until smooth; stir into the macaroni. Return heat to medium; cook, stirring, for 3 to 5 minutes or until sauce is thickened.

Remove from heat; stir in the cheese until melted. Season to taste with the remaining salt.

2 cups water

1 cup heavy cream

2 cups orange or white cauliflower florets

1 cup elbow macaroni

½ tsp salt, divided

2 Tbsp all-purpose flour

1 tsp Dijon mustard or dry mustard

¼ tsp pepper

½ cup milk

3 to 4 cups grated aged or extra-aged cheddar cheese

🌿 FOOD FOR THOUGHT

Recycle unavoidable food waste—composting organic material in your backyard, to feed your food or flower gardens, is preferable to sending it to the landfill, but edible excess food, whether its from your kitchen, your freezer, or your yard, can also go to food banks, emergency shelters, community food pantries, and other food recovery programs.

ROASTED CAULIFLOWER and
MERGUEZ SAUSAGE COUSCOUS

Merguez is a spicy lamb sausage. Roast it alongside the vegetables for this dish, or substitute any leftover grilled spicy sausages. SERVES 4.

Arrange an oven rack in the middle position and preheat the oven to 425°F. Line 1 or 2 baking sheets with parchment paper.

Arrange the cauliflower, onion, red pepper, garlic, and chickpeas in a single layer on the prepared baking sheet(s). Drizzle with the olive oil, season with salt and pepper, and toss to coat. Lay the sausages in the baking sheet alongside the vegetables.

Roast for about 30 minutes, stirring occasionally, until the vegetables are nicely browned and the sausages are cooked through.

Meanwhile, bring the chicken stock to a boil, stir in the couscous, remove from heat, cover, and let stand for 10 minutes. Fluff with a fork and stir in the parsley, paprika, and cumin.

Cut the sausages into bite-sized pieces. Pour the couscous over the roasted vegetables on the baking sheet and combine, stirring up any browned bits.

Transfer to a serving dish and top with the sliced sausage.

1 cauliflower, cut into florets (larger pieces halved)

1 onion, slivered

1 large red bell pepper, seeded and cubed

3 cloves garlic, sliced

1 small (15 oz) can chickpeas, rinsed and drained well

¼ cup extra-virgin olive oil

¼ tsp salt

¼ tsp freshly ground black pepper

4 to 6 merguez sausages

3 cups chicken stock

2 cups couscous

3 Tbsp chopped fresh Italian parsley

1 tsp smoked Spanish paprika

½ tsp ground cumin

CITRUS

Buy

Most citrus fruit is in season in midwinter, so that's the best time to buy California or Florida oranges, Japanese mandarins, and bitter Spanish Seville oranges. Peak season for lemons is later in spring and early summer. Look for smooth skins and heavy fruit; lemons with deep yellow color will be riper and sweeter than greenish fruit. Meyer lemons are sweeter, thin-skinned lemons—a lemon and tangerine cross.

Store

Oranges will keep at room temperature for 2 weeks, while lemons are best refrigerated.

Serve

Citrus flavors, especially lemon, are essential to many dishes, from lemony roast chicken to Chinese lemon chicken or Moroccan chicken tagine with salted preserved lemons. Fresh orange pairs well with beets, black olives, red onions, winter squash, and pork. Lemons are indispensible in the kitchen: a splash of lemon juice makes classic vinaigrettes and mayonnaise, and desserts like lemon meringue pie.

Fill prebaked frozen mini tart shells with homemade lemon curd and top with a dollop of whipped cream and a candied violet for a pretty dessert tray.

Don't Waste It!

- Add a splash of fresh lemon juice just before serving to lift the flavors of almost any soup or stew.
- Make lemony roasted potatoes by tossing halved fingerlings with lemon juice and zest, garlic, and olive oil, and roasting until crisp.
- To make lemon curd, cook ¾ cup fresh lemon juice and ¾ cup sugar with 3 eggs and ½ cup butter, along with 1 tablespoon lemon zest, over low heat, stirring constantly until thick. Chill.
- "Cook" fresh chopped prawns, scallops, and/or white ocean fish (sole, sea bass, grouper, flounder) with lime, lemon, and/or orange juice, chopped chiles, and cilantro for ceviche to scoop up with corn chips.
- Make a lemon quick bread with the finely grated zest and juice of 2 lemons and a handful of poppyseeds.
- Combine a cup of orange juice with a tablespoon each of honey, cider vinegar, and dry mustard, and a splash of hot sauce to marinate chicken for the barbecue.
- Whirl a whole, thin-skinned orange (peel and all) with a 12-ounce bag of fresh cranberries and ½ cup sugar in the food processor for almost instant fresh cranberry sauce. Refrigerate overnight or serve right away.
- Use fresh lemon juice to prevent browning of apples or avocados, once they have been peeled.
- Toss skinless chicken breasts or fillets of sole or pickerel in seasoned flour, brown quickly in butter, then deglaze the pan with fresh lemon juice and pour overtop.
- Use a citrus zester or Microplane grater (a vegetable peeler would also work) to remove the zest from well-washed citrus fruit to add to salads, soups, and desserts.
- Candy blanched strips of citrus peels in a simple sugar syrup until translucent, then roll in coarse sugar or dry to dip in chocolate.
- Dry excess citrus zest and pulverize into citrus "dust" in the blender to use in rubs or to sprinkle over almost anything.

RASPBERRY LEMONADE

This works well with ripe, juicy raspberries, but you can substitute fresh strawberries or even blackberries with delicious results. **MAKES 3 CUPS CONCENTRATE, OR ABOUT 12 SERVINGS OF LEMONADE.**

1 cup water

1 cup granulated sugar

1 cup fresh raspberries

4 large lemons

Fresh mint sprigs, for muddling and garnish

Extra whole raspberries, for garnish

Start by making simple syrup: in a saucepan over medium heat, boil the water and sugar until the sugar has dissolved completely. Cool.

In another saucepan, crush the raspberries with a potato masher, then press through a fine sieve to remove the seeds, capturing all of the fresh juice and pulp in a bowl. Combine the juice and pulp with the cooled simple syrup.

Halve and juice the lemons; strain to remove seeds. Add the lemon juice and lemon pulp—you should have about 1 cup—to the raspberry mixture.

Keep your fruity lemonade concentrate in the fridge, and when you're ready to serve, dilute 4:1 with water. Place a sprig of fresh mint in a tall glass and muddle with a spoon to release the oils. Fill the glass with ice and pour the lemonade overtop. Garnish with whole fresh raspberries.

PRAWN SKEWERS on QUINOA, ORANGE, and AVOCADO SALAD

The tiny grains of quinoa cook in about 10 to 15 minutes and are perfect for pilafs or for salads like this. The grain's bitter natural coating is now removed by mechanical means, but quinoa should be rinsed in a sieve to remove any residual dust. SERVES 4.

Soak 4 bamboo skewers in warm water for 1 hour.

Place the quinoa in a sieve and rinse under running water and drain well.

In a saucepan over medium, heat 1 teaspoon of the olive oil and sauté the garlic, coriander, and cumin for 1 minute. Stir in the orange juice and stock, bring to a boil, cover, and simmer for 1 minute.

Stir in the quinoa, cover, reduce heat to low, and simmer for 15 minutes. Remove from heat and let stand for 10 minutes to steam. Fluff the quinoa with a fork and cool to room temperature or chill.

Peel and chop the avocado and toss with lime juice or lemon juice to prevent browning.

When the quinoa is cool, stir in the red onion, avocado, orange zest and flesh, remaining 1 tablespoon of olive oil, and hot sauce. Stir in the cilantro and season to taste with salt and pepper.

Preheat the broiler.

For the prawn skewers, in a small bowl combine the butter, cumin, coriander, turmeric, salt, and lemon juice.

Thread the prawns lengthwise on the skewers and place in a shallow baking pan in a single layer. Pour the seasoned butter overtop. Place the prawns under the broiler for 5 minutes, until they are pink and nicely glazed (alternately, grill for about 2 minutes per side).

Mound the salad on individual plates and serve each with a prawn skewer alongside.

Salad:

⅔ cup quinoa

1 tsp plus 1 Tbsp extra-virgin olive oil, divided

1 clove garlic, minced

¼ tsp ground coriander

¼ tsp ground cumin

⅔ cup orange juice

½ cup low-fat chicken stock

1 small, ripe avocado

1 Tbsp fresh lime juice or lemon juice

1 small red onion, minced

1 orange, zest finely grated and flesh chopped

1 tsp hot sauce (Tabasco, etc.)

¼ cup chopped fresh cilantro

Salt and freshly ground black pepper, to taste

Prawn skewers:

2 Tbsp melted butter

½ tsp ground cumin

½ tsp ground coriander

½ tsp ground turmeric

½ tsp salt

Juice of 1 lemon (about 3 Tbsp)

1 lb large prawns, peeled and deveined

LEMONY LENTILS

This simple dish of **French Puy lentils (the tiny green or black ones),** seasoned with lemon and olive oil, is perfect alongside grilled fish, poultry, and lamb. **SERVES 4-6.**

* * * * * * * * * * *

In a saucepan, combine the lentils, water, bouquet garni, carrot, and garlic cloves. Bring to a boil and simmer for 20 to 30 minutes, until the lentils are just tender but still firm. Drain the lentils and discard the bouquet garni, carrot, and garlic.

Combine the lemon zest with the lemon juice, mustard, salt, and thyme. Slowly add the olive oil, whisking as you go, to emulsify and thicken the dressing. Season with pepper.

Place the warm lentils in a bowl and toss with the vinaigrette. Stir in the green onions and the red pepper.

1 cup French Puy (or green) lentils, rinsed

3 cups water

Bouquet garni of 1 sprig thyme, 1 sprig rosemary, and 1 bay leaf tied together (or use 1 tsp dried thyme, 1 tsp dried rosemary, and 1 bay leaf in a tea ball)

1 carrot, peeled and quartered

2 cloves garlic

Dressing:

Finely grated zest and juice of 1 lemon (about 3 Tbsp juice)

1 Tbsp Dijon mustard

1 tsp salt

2 tsp chopped fresh thyme (or 1 tsp dried thyme)

¼ cup extra-virgin olive oil

Freshly ground black pepper, to taste

3 green onions, chopped

¼ cup chopped roasted red pepper (from a jar is okay)

> **TIP**
> It's best to use a Microplane grater to remove the yellow zest from a lemon. Otherwise, carefully peel it off with a vegetable peeler and mince until very fine.

LEMON BARS

This is a foolproof recipe for classic lemon squares. Freshly squeezed lemon juice is the secret ingredient. **MAKES 16 SQUARES.**

* * *

Preheat the oven to 350°F. Grease an 8-inch square baking pan.

Combine 1 cup of the flour with the icing sugar, salt, and 1 tablespoon of the lemon zest. Using a pastry blender, cut in the butter until the mixture is fine and crumbly. (Alternately, combine in a food processor and pulse until crumbly.) Press the mixture evenly into the prepared baking pan. Bake for 20 minutes, until lightly golden.

Combine the remaining ¼ cup of flour with the baking powder and set aside. Using an electric mixer, beat the eggs with the sugar until they are doubled in volume. Slowly add the flour mixture, beating until just blended. Stir in the lemon juice and remaining 1 tablespoon of lemon zest. Pour the filling over the warm crust and bake for an additional 20 minutes, until the filling is just set.

Cool squares on a wire rack. Lightly sift a layer of icing sugar over the pan, then cut into small squares to serve.

1¼ cups all-purpose flour, divided

¼ cup icing sugar

Pinch salt

2 Tbsp finely grated lemon zest, divided

½ cup unsalted butter, cut into cubes

½ tsp baking powder

3 large eggs

1½ cups granulated sugar

⅓ cup fresh lemon juice

Extra icing sugar, for dusting

FOOD FOR THOUGHT

The UN's Think.Eat.Save website is filled with inspirational stories and ideas to fuel your zero-waste philosophy, like the one about Original Unverpackt, Germany's first package-free supermarket, in Berlin.

MARMALADE

Use Seville oranges for marmalade if you can find them, or substitute a grapefruit or tangerine for one of the oranges. You'll need about 1½ to 2 pounds of citrus fruit in total. **MAKES 2–3 PINTS.**

3 unpeeled Seville (or Valencia or navel) oranges, scrubbed and quartered

1 large lemon, scrubbed and quartered

4 cups water

4 cups granulated sugar

If you see any seeds in the fruit, remove them and set aside. Using a mandoline or very sharp knife, cut the oranges and lemon, including the peels, in very thin slices. Do this over a bowl to catch all of the juice and pulp. Place the sliced fruit in a saucepan. Put the reserved seeds in a tea ball, or tie them up in cheesecloth, and add to the saucepan. Pour in the water and bring to a boil over high heat. Reduce the heat to medium and simmer for 10 minutes. Remove from heat and let stand, covered, at room temperature overnight.

Discard the seeds. Return the pan to medium heat. Stir in the sugar and bring the mixture to a boil. Boil, over medium heat, for 30 minutes, until the marmalade reaches the jell point (225°F). Skim off any foam. Pour boiling-hot marmalade into hot sterilized ½-pint jars, filling to within ½ inch of the top. Wipe jars clean, top with 2-piece metal lids, screw metal band on firmly, invert for a second, and then cool the jars in an upright position. Store in a cool, dark place, or refrigerate.

CORN

Buy

Buy sweet corn on the cob in season direct from the farm—make sure the husks are fresh and green, not dry, with fresh silk attached. Supermarkets often remove the husk to disguise old corn past its prime. Look for extra-sweet bi-color varieties like peaches and cream.

Store

Buy only as much as you can eat now. Corn begins to lose its sweet flavor the minute it's picked, the sugars turning to starches, so don't store for longer than a day, in the husk, in the refrigerator. Husk, blanch, and chill to freeze when super fresh.

Serve

The classic way to serve fresh corn is steamed or boiled, on the cob, slathered with butter and salt, but sweet corn is also delicious raw in salads, blackened on the grill to add to tomato salsa, or in cornbread, corn pudding, and fritters.

Don't Waste It!

- Cut sweet corn from the cob (stand upright in a big bowl and cut down along the cob), and eat it raw sprinkled on salads (add the cobs to your corn chowder for the most flavorful broth).
- For fresh creamed corn, cut kernels off cobs, scraping well to get all of the milky juice. Then simmer with butter, salt and pepper, a touch of sugar, and a little cream.
- Grill corn in the husk. Just peel back the husk and remove the silk, pull the husk back over the cobs and tie shut, soak in water, then grill.
- Combine raw kernels with cooked black beans, chopped tomatoes, jalapeno, and cilantro for a hearty salsa or salad.
- Grill corn directly over charcoal until it's lightly browned and serve with flavored butters. Try chile pepper, dill, or curry butters.
- Combine puréed corn with mashed potatoes.
- Add fresh corn and cheddar to cornbread batter and deep-fry to make hush puppies.
- Make a succotash of corn sautéed in butter with chopped bell peppers, green onions, and butter beans, seasoned with a little thyme.
- Toss fresh corn kernels with shelled edamame beans, chopped green onion, light soy sauce, lime juice, and sesame oil for an Asian salad.
- Purée 2 cups fresh corn and 2 cups half-and-half in the blender, transfer to a saucepan, heat to boiling, and then simmer for 1 minute. Remove from heat, stir in a can of sweetened condensed milk, chill, and churn in an ice cream maker for a sweet corn dessert.

CHOPPED SALAD with CHICKEN and FRESH CORN

This makes a fabulous luncheon or supper dish in August, when those first cobs of sweet peaches-and-cream corn are ready in the garden. Pick them, ferry them directly to your kitchen, and make this main meal salad. **SERVES 4.**

In a blender or food processor, whirl together the buttermilk, salsa, mayonnaise, mustard, sugar, and cilantro. Season with salt and pepper. Set aside.

Remove the husk and silk from the cobs of corn. Holding the cobs upright on the cutting board, use a sharp knife to remove the kernels, cutting down from the top of the cob to the base. Place the corn kernels in a bowl, along with any of the sweet milky juice that's released.

Preheat the oven to 350°F or heat the barbecue to medium.

Put the chicken breasts on a plate and drizzle with 1 tablespoon of the dressing. Rub all over to coat the chicken. Bake or grill the breasts until just cooked (30 minutes in the oven or about 15 minutes on the barbecue). Set aside to cool and cut into cubes or shreds.

Add the jicama, red pepper, avocado, and tomatoes to the corn in the bowl. Add half of the remaining dressing and toss to coat. Set aside.

In a nonstick pan over medium-high, heat about ½ inch of canola oil. Cut the corn tortillas into thin strips. Add them to the hot oil, a few at a time, and deep-fry until curled and crisp. Drain on paper towels and sprinkle with a little sea salt.

When you're ready to eat, toss the lettuce with just enough of the remaining dressing to lightly coat. Divide the greens among 4 plates. Top each salad with some of the shredded chicken and some of the corn salad. Strew the crispy corn tortilla strips around and serve immediately.

Dressing:

1 cup buttermilk

½ cup spicy tomato salsa

⅓ cup light mayonnaise

½ tsp Dijon mustard

½ tsp granulated sugar

1 Tbsp chopped fresh cilantro

Salt and freshly ground black pepper, to taste

Salad:

4 ears fresh corn

2 boneless, skinless chicken breasts (or 4 thighs)

1 small jicama or young turnip, peeled and diced (¼-inch dice)

1 red bell pepper, seeded and diced

1 ripe avocado, diced

1 cup cherry tomatoes, halved or quartered if larger

Canola oil, for frying

6 fresh corn tortillas

Sea salt, to taste

4 cups shredded Romaine lettuce

CORN CHOWDER

Cream makes this colorful chowder decadent, but evaporated milk makes a creamy soup that is far lower in fat and calories. **SERVES 4.**

In a large pot over medium-low heat, melt the butter. Add the onion, garlic, celery, half of the corn, and salt and pepper. Cover the pot and sweat the vegetables for 10 minutes, until tender.

Cool the mixture slightly, then purée in a food processor and return to the pot. Stir in the oregano, chili powder, cumin, and chicken stock, and bring to a boil. Add the potato, reduce heat to low, cover, and simmer for 10 minutes, just until the potato chunks are tender.

Stir in the cream or evaporated milk, Tabasco, and red pepper and the remaining corn kernels. Return the soup to a boil and cook for 5 minutes, just until the corn is tender. Season to taste with additional salt and pepper if necessary, and serve immediately.

¼ cup butter

1 medium onion, chopped

1 clove garlic, minced

1 stalk celery, chopped

3 cups fresh corn kernels, divided in half

1 tsp salt

¼ tsp pepper

½ tsp dried oregano

Dash chili powder

Dash ground cumin

4 cups chicken stock

1 large yellow-fleshed potato, peeled and diced

1 cup heavy cream or evaporated milk

Dash Tabasco sauce

½ red bell pepper, chopped

CUCUMBERS

Buy

Hothouse English cucumbers have thin skins and fewer seeds, are available year round, and are used for slicing. Field cucumbers are usually knobbier and picked small for pickling. They are found in late summer in markets. Most cucumbers are green, but you may also discover round yellow varieties in Indian markets.

Store

Keep in the crisper in the refrigerator for up to a week, and watch for any soft spots—cucumbers spoil quickly. Cucumbers will be damaged by temperatures below 50°F (10°C) so if you refrigerate, keep them out of the cold spots. There is some science that suggests cucumbers actually keep better at room temperature (but keep them away from tomatoes, melons, and bananas).

Serve

The cucumber is ubiquitous in salads of chopped tomatoes and greens, but may also be paired with strawberries or cooked quickly in butter with cream or yogurt and dill. Many cucumbers are consumed as dill pickles or relish, but they can also end up in gazpacho. Wash cucumbers well before eating as they may be waxed.

Don't Waste It!

- Peel and slice cucumbers, salt, and drain to remove some of the liquid, then toss with a dressing of sour cream, salt and pepper, fresh dill, and a little sugar.

- Thinly slice small cucumbers and radishes and arrange on buttered white bread with a sprinkling of sea salt for pretty, open-faced cocktail sandwiches.

- Chop cucumbers, tomatoes, black olives, green onions, and fresh oregano, toss with red wine vinegar and olive oil, and top with crumbled feta cheese for a classic Greek salad.

- Pack scrubbed small pickling cucumbers tightly into sterilized jars, each with a handful of fresh dill and a clove of garlic, then pour a boiling salt and vinegar brine over them and seal for classic dill pickles.

- Cut mini cucumbers lengthwise into quarters for healthy snacking, or slice into thin ribbons to roll and stuff with tuna salad for lunch.

- For tzatziki, shred a cucumber, toss with salt, and drain in a colander to remove excess moisture. Squeeze, then toss with plain Greek-style yogurt, minced garlic, and a drizzle of olive oil.

- In the blender, purée peeled cucumber with fresh mint, simple syrup, and lime juice. Strain and serve over ice with white rum and club soda for refreshing cucumber mojitos.

- Toss sliced salted cucumbers with sesame oil, rice wine vinegar, sugar, garlic, and chili flakes for a fast Thai-style salad.

- For an exotic raw chutney, combine chopped cucumber, green chiles, cilantro, roasted peanuts, unsweetened grated coconut, lemon juice, and black mustard and cumin seeds.

- Make cucumber ribbons by slicing cucumbers lengthwise with a mandoline or simple vegetable peeler. Coil slices into a vegetable "ring" to encircle salad greens for a chic salad course (a cut halfway through the ribbon at each end lets you lock the ring together).

- Whirl up a classy cold gazpacho soup in the blender with cucumbers, ripe tomatoes, green onion, garlic, sherry vinegar, and olive oil.

- Add refreshing cucumbers to a summer fruit salad of watermelon, mango, and berries.

CUCUMBER and SHRIMP SALAD ROLLS

Look for rice paper in the dried noodle section at your Asian market. It comes in a plastic package, dried and stacked like delicate milky-white wafers, usually embossed with a basket-weave pattern. MAKES 32 PIECES.

Cook the rice noodles in a pot of boiling water for 3 to 5 minutes until tender, then drain and rinse in cold water to chill. Drain well and cut the noodles into 3-inch lengths with kitchen shears. Set aside.

Cut the cucumbers into 3-inch chunks, then slice lengthwise. Stack the slices and cut into thin matchstick pieces. This is known as julienne. If you have a mandoline, use it to make the finest strips.

Cut the carrots into 2-inch lengths and julienne.

Cut the green onions (both the white and green parts) into 2-inch-long pieces and then lengthwise into long slivers.

To assemble the salad rolls, quickly dip a piece of rice paper into a bowl of hot water to soften (work with one piece at a time). Set the rice paper on a cutting board or clean kitchen towel. Layer some of the cooked noodles, cucumber, carrot, green onion, cilantro (and/or Thai basil and/or mint leaves), lettuce, and shrimp along the bottom edge of the rice paper. Fold the sides in over the filling, and roll up tightly. The rice paper will stick to itself to seal the roll. Set aside on a plate and cover with a clean damp towel to prevent the rice paper from drying out and getting too chewy. Continue soaking and rolling until all of the rice paper and filling are used up. Keep the rolls covered with the damp towel, and seal with plastic wrap, then chill before serving.

To make the peanut sauce, whisk the peanut butter, soy sauce, coconut milk, and chili paste together until smooth.

To serve, use a sharp knife to cut each roll into 2 pieces on a sharp diagonal. Arrange the rolls, standing or overlapping on a platter, with a bowl of peanut sauce on the side for dipping.

Salad rolls:

2 oz dried rice noodles

3 small English cucumbers

2 medium carrots, peeled

2 green onions

16 rice paper wrappers, each about 8 or 9 inches in diameter

Fresh cilantro leaves, Thai basil leaves, and/ or mint leaves

2 cups shredded romaine or butter lettuce

½ lb cooked small salad shrimp or crabmeat

Peanut sauce:

¼ cup natural peanut butter

2 Tbsp soy sauce

2 Tbsp coconut milk or water

½ tsp Asian chili paste

TIP

If you can't find rice paper, try this combination as a layered rice noodle salad, topped with cucumber and shrimp, and drizzled with peanut sauce.

CUCUMBER RAITA

The cucumber originated in India and this simple condiment is served with almost every meal, to cool the heat of Indian curries. **SERVES 6.**

Wash the cucumber and cut into small cubes (or shred). Place in a colander, toss with the sea salt, and set aside to drain for 30 minutes. Rinse and squeeze out excess moisture.

In a bowl, combine the yogurt, cumin, and cayenne. Whisk in the chives, cilantro, and mint, then mix in the drained cucumber.

Season with pepper and a splash of lemon juice. Cover and refrigerate. Raita will keep for 1 to 2 days in the refrigerator.

1 medium cucumber

½ tsp sea salt

1 cup plain yogurt

½ tsp ground cumin

⅛ tsp cayenne

2 Tbsp chopped fresh chives

1 Tbsp chopped fresh cilantro

1 Tbsp chopped fresh mint

Black pepper, to taste

Fresh lemon juice

QUINOA SALAD with CUCUMBER and TOMATO

This is a quinoa salad inspired by classic tabouli. Serve it with chicken or fish for a complete meal, or pack it for a healthy lunch. **SERVES 4.**

Place quinoa in a sieve and rinse under running water. Drain well.

Place a saucepan over medium-high heat and add the quinoa, stirring to dry and toast lightly.

Add the water and bring to a boil. Reduce heat to low, cover the pan, and simmer for 15 minutes. Remove from heat and let stand, covered, for 5 minutes. Fluff with a fork. Stir in the lemon juice, lemon zest, olive oil, and garlic. Set aside to cool.

Transfer to a serving/salad bowl. Stir in the tomatoes, cucumbers, parsley, mint, and green onions. Toss well to combine. Season with salt and pepper. Serve at room temperature.

2 cups quinoa

3 cups water or stock

¼ cup fresh lemon juice

1 Tbsp finely grated lemon zest

¼ cup extra-virgin olive oil

1 large clove garlic, minced

1 cup grape tomatoes, halved

2 mini cucumbers, chopped

½ cup chopped fresh Italian parsley

¼ cup chopped fresh mint

3 green onions, minced

Salt and freshly ground black pepper, to taste

FOOD FOR THOUGHT
The average American consumer wastes 10 times as much food as someone in Southeast Asia.

EGGPLANT

Buy

Eggplant or aubergine is a beautiful vegetable—whether you find the fat, shiny deep purple variety, the elegant and thin mauve Asian eggplant, or the pretty green and white globe eggplant. Look for heavy, smooth specimens, with no soft spots, and bright green stems.

Store

Eggplant is quite perishable. Store in a loose bag in the refrigerator for no more than a few days before cooking, away from apples and tomatoes.

Serve

Known for its meaty texture, eggplant is a sponge that soaks up flavor (and oil) so be careful how you cook it. It's best roasted, grilled, or quickly sautéed for pasta sauces, or puréed along with garlic, tomato, and olive oil for dips. Eat the skin, too—it's nutritious.

Don't Waste It!

- Grill sliced eggplant with portobello mushrooms or bell peppers, and layer with cheese and fresh basil in buns or between slices of focaccia, then toast in a panini press.

- Roast whole eggplant with red peppers, onions, and tomatoes, drizzled with olive oil, at 350°F, then peel, cut into strips, and dress with a splash of red wine vinegar and fresh basil.

- Purée roasted eggplant with ginger, onions, sesame oil, cilantro, and soy or hoisin sauce for an Asian eggplant dip to scoop up with prawn chips or serve over Chinese-style crispy fried fish.

- Sauté chopped eggplant with onion, cherry tomatoes, chickpeas, chopped cilantro, and curry power, and serve over basmati rice.

- Brush eggplant slices with oil, season with salt and pepper, and grill alongside peppers and onions, then toss with pasta and cheese.

- Make eggplant "caviar": purée roasted eggplant with chopped green onion, garlic, parsley, olive oil, and a little mayo. Spread on toasted baguette.

- Roast eggplant until blackened and tender, then peel and mash with lemon juice, garlic purée, tahini, cumin, and parsley, to scoop up with pita bread.

EGGPLANT PARMESAN

Start with a fat purple eggplant or two, slice and sauté, then layer like lasagna noodles with shredded cheese and tomato sauce (from scratch or your favorite bottled kind) or even sliced tomatoes—and voila! An easy and elegant vegetarian dinner for four. Just add a green salad. SERVES 4.

In a saucepan over medium, heat the olive oil. Add the garlic and onion and cook together, stirring occasionally, until the onion is tender and beginning to brown. Add the white wine and simmer for 5 minutes, until most of the liquid has cooked away. Stir in the chili paste and tomatoes (crush them through your fingers into the pan or whirl them until smooth in a blender or food processor). Bring to a boil and simmer for 15 minutes until slightly thickened. Season to taste with the sugar and salt. Stir in the basil. Set aside.

Slice the eggplant crosswise into thin, ¼-inch slices. Salt the eggplant on both sides and set in a bowl. Cover with water and let stand for 1 hour to draw out any bitterness. Rinse the eggplant with water and press between paper towels to dry.

Preheat the oven to 350°F.

Place the seasoned flour on a plate. Heat the olive oil in a nonstick pan over medium-high. Dip the eggplant slices in the flour, shaking off any excess, and place into the hot pan. Fry quickly, a few minutes per side, until nicely browned. Do this in batches, using more oil as necessary. Drain on paper towels.

To save time (and calories), you can also grill or broil the eggplant. Heat a gas barbecue to medium and grill the eggplant, brushing both sides with olive oil (it's not necessary to flour the eggplant). It will only take 4 to 5 minutes on each side to cook the eggplant until tender.

In a bowl, combine the Parmigiano-Reggiano and mozzarella cheese.

To assemble, rub a shallow 13- × 9-inch rectangular baking dish (or a 10-inch round shallow baking dish) with olive oil. Spread a thin layer of the tomato sauce in the bottom of the dish. Top with half of the eggplant slices, overlapping to fit, half of the sauce, and half of the cheese. Repeat layers, ending with cheese. Bake for 30 to 40 minutes, until bubbly and lightly browned. Let stand for 10 minutes before cutting.

Sauce:

¼ cup olive oil

2 cloves garlic, minced

1 small onion, minced

½ cup white wine

½ tsp chili paste

1 (14 oz) can plum tomatoes

½ tsp granulated sugar, or to taste

½ tsp salt, or to taste

2 Tbsp chopped fresh basil (or 2 tsp dried)

1 large eggplant (about 1½ lb)

½ cup all-purpose flour, seasoned with black pepper

2 Tbsp extra-virgin olive oil, plus more as needed

1¼ cup finely grated Parmigiano-Reggiano

1 cup shredded mozzarella cheese

CAPONATA

Caponata is a chunky antipasto with roots in Sicily, great to pile on slices of crusty bread or toss with hot pasta and grated Parmesan for a speedy dinner. Make lots of caponata when eggplants, peppers, and squash are available at the market in August, store it in jars or containers, and freeze it for instant eating anytime. MAKES 6 CUPS.

Put the eggplant and zucchini cubes in a colander. Toss with the salt and set in the sink to drain for half an hour. Rinse quickly and pat dry.

In a large sauté pan or Dutch oven over medium, heat the oil. Add the onion, garlic, red pepper, and yellow pepper, and sauté for 5 minutes. Add the eggplant and zucchini cubes and sauté for 5 to 10 minutes, until the mixture is beginning to soften. Stir in the tomatoes, cover the pan, and cook together for 10 minutes. Remove the lid and continue to simmer until the vegetables are very soft and the liquid in the pan has been reduced, about 5 minutes.

In a small bowl, whisk together the brown sugar, tomato paste, and balsamic vinegar. Add to the pan and stir to combine. Mix in the olives. Remove from heat and add the basil. Season with salt and pepper (and a little hot sauce if you like it spicy).

Cool to room temperature and serve. Caponata will keep for a week in a covered container in the fridge, or it may be frozen.

1 eggplant (2 lb), skin on, diced

1 zucchini or other summer squash (1 lb), diced

2 tsp salt

½ cup extra-virgin olive oil

1 large onion, chopped (about 2 cups)

4 large cloves garlic, minced

1 red bell pepper, seeded and chopped

1 yellow bell pepper, seeded and chopped

1 (14 oz) can plum tomatoes, chopped or puréed (or 2 cups chopped fresh tomatoes)

1 Tbsp brown sugar

¼ cup tomato paste

3 Tbsp balsamic vinegar

½ cup air-cured black olives, pitted and chopped

2 to 3 Tbsp chopped fresh basil or rosemary

Salt and freshly ground black pepper, to taste

Hot sauce, to taste (optional)

LAMB MOUSSAKA

This layered casserole of eggplant, potatoes, and meat sauce is a Greek classic and worth the effort it takes to assemble. Reheats perfectly for leftovers. **SERVES 6–8.**

Salt the eggplant slices, and set them in a colander in the sink for 30 minutes to drain. Rinse and pat dry with paper towels.

Preheat the oven to 450°F. Line 2 baking sheets with parchment paper. Arrange the sliced eggplant in a single layer on one sheet, and the sliced potatoes on the other. Drizzle the potato and eggplant lightly with 2 to 3 tablespoons of the olive oil, and season with salt and pepper. Bake for 10 to 15 minutes, until beginning to brown. Remove from the oven and cool.

Reduce the oven temperature to 350°F.

To make the meat sauce, heat 2 tablespoons of the remaining olive oil in a large sauté pan and crumble in the ground lamb. Cook, stirring, for 10 minutes, until the meat is beginning to brown and caramelize. Add the onion, garlic, bell pepper, and carrot to the pan, with a little more olive oil, and sauté for an additional 5 minutes.

Stir in the chopped tomatoes, tomato paste, and wine, then add the bay leaf, oregano, cinnamon, and brown sugar. Bring to a boil, then reduce heat to low and simmer for 20 minutes, until the sauce has reduced and is very thick. Set aside to cool.

For the béchamel, in a saucepan over medium heat, melt the butter and stir in the flour. Cook for 1 minute, then slowly add the milk, whisking until the mixture begins to boil. Season with the nutmeg and simmer for 2 minutes, until thick.

Remove from the heat and stir for 3 minutes to cool slightly. Slowly whisk in the eggs, and stir in 1 cup of the feta.

To assemble, lightly coat a 13- × 9-inch baking dish with olive oil. Arrange the potatoes in the bottom of the dish. Top with ½ cup of the remaining feta, then one-third of the eggplant, overlapping slices to fill the pan. Add one-third of the meat sauce, then another layer of eggplant, feta, meat sauce, and the final layer of eggplant and meat sauce.

Pour the béchamel sauce evenly over the casserole. Bake at 350°F for 50 to 60 minutes, until it is bubbly and golden. Let the moussaka rest for 20 minutes before cutting.

2 large purple eggplants, sliced into ¼-inch to ½-inch slices

2 large red potatoes, peeled and thinly sliced

½ cup olive oil, divided

Salt and freshly ground black pepper, to taste

¾ lb lean ground lamb

1 large onion, minced

3 to 4 cloves garlic, minced

1 medium red bell pepper, seeded and finely chopped

1 carrot, shredded

1 (28 oz) can chopped tomatoes, undrained

2 Tbsp tomato paste

⅓ cup dry white wine

1 bay leaf

1 tsp dried oregano

¼ tsp ground cinnamon

¼ tsp brown sugar

Béchamel:

3 Tbsp butter

3 Tbsp all-purpose flour

1¼ cups milk

Pinch ground nutmeg

2 eggs, beaten

2 cups crumbled Greek sheep-milk feta, divided

QUINOA with ROASTED EGGPLANT and PEPPERS

This makes a great side dish for grilled lamb. For a more substantial main dish, try stirring in some crumbled feta cheese after the grains have steamed. SERVES 4–6.

Preheat the oven to 450°F. Place the eggplant cubes in a colander and sprinkle with the salt. Let stand for 20 minutes to extract bitter juices, rinse, and pat dry.

Place the eggplant cubes in a large bowl with the red and yellow bell peppers and the onion, and toss with 3 tablespoons of the olive oil to coat. Season with salt and black pepper and toss again. Cut the top ¼ inch from the head of garlic, and drizzle a little olive oil over the exposed cloves.

Line a baking sheet with parchment paper. Spread the vegetables in a single layer on the sheet and add the garlic head. Roast, stirring occasionally, until the vegetables are browned, about 30 minutes.

In a large saucepan over medium-high, heat the remaining tablespoon of olive oil. Add the cumin, turmeric, and ginger to the pan. Stir in the roasted eggplant, bell peppers, and onion. Squeeze the roasted garlic out of its skin into the pan. Add the stock and stir to combine. Bring to a boil over medium heat, and stir in the quinoa. Cover, reduce heat to medium-low, and simmer for 10 minutes, until most of the liquid is absorbed. Remove from heat and let stand, covered, for 15 minutes.

Stir in the lemon juice and parsley (plus feta cheese, if using). Serve warm or at room temperature.

1 large purple eggplant, cubed

1 tsp salt

1 red bell pepper, seeded and cubed

1 yellow bell pepper, seeded and cubed

1 large white onion, cubed

4 Tbsp olive oil, divided

Salt and freshly ground black pepper, to taste

1 whole head of garlic

2 tsp ground cumin

½ tsp ground turmeric

¼ tsp ground ginger

2½ cups low-fat vegetable or chicken stock

1 cup quinoa, rinsed in a sieve

1 Tbsp fresh lemon juice

2 Tbsp chopped fresh parsley

½ cup crumbled feta cheese (optional)

GREENS

Buy

A variety of greens from Swiss chard, lettuces, and kale to beet, dandelion, and collard greens are available year round but are best in spring and summer.

Store

Wrap greens in paper towels and store in plastic bags in the refrigerator, away from the coldest corners, for 1 week.

Serve

Fresh mixed greens make great salads when tossed with assertive mustardy vinaigrettes and bacon. They're also tasty sautéed in olive oil with garlic and chili flakes, stir-fried with garlic and ginger, or slivered in soups and frittatas.

Don't Waste It!

- Too much lettuce? Shred it finely and add to boiled green peas along with some chopped green onion or mint, cook for 1 minute, drain, and season with butter and salt and pepper.

- Serve a pesto purée of blanched greens, red pepper, garlic, toasted pecans, and olive oil piled on toasted baguette slices as appetizers.

- Toss hot cooked pasta with olive oil, cooked Italian sausage, black olives, fresh herbs, Parmesan, and ribbons of mixed greens until they wilt.

- Purée spicy greens like watercress and arugula with parsley, garlic, mayonnaise, and a little buttermilk or sour cream and lemon juice, for a quick green goddess dressing or dip.

- Combine leftover sautéed chopped greens with mashed potatoes and butter.

- Brush sturdy greens (kale, arugula, curly endive) with a little olive oil, spread on a parchment-lined baking sheet, and bake at 325°F until crisp. Season chips with sea salt.

- Purée greens (spinach, chard, kale) with apples, apple juice, ginger, and almond milk in a blender for a healthy breakfast smoothie.

- Use a sharp knife to cut hearty greens like kale into fine shreds to add to salads or coleslaw.

- Wrap grilled shrimp and slivered carrots in lettuce cups with a drizzle of chili soy dressing for easy appetizers.

- Make a pesto-like purée of mixed greens, garlic, and olive oil to add to pasta dishes or risotto. Ditto for delicate fresh herbs like basil, cilantro, and parsley. Don't let them go off, just whirl them up in the blender with olive oil for an herb purée you can keep in a jar in the fridge (or freeze in ice cube trays).

KALE CAESAR

Curly kale comes in all kinds of colors but the texture can be tough when raw. Chef's secret? Massage the leaves for several minutes with your hands before dressing the salad to soften and wilt the leaves. **SERVES 3–4.**

2 cloves garlic, crushed

2 tsp finely chopped anchovies or anchovy paste

1 tsp Dijon mustard

1 egg yolk

Juice of half a lemon

1 tsp Worcestershire sauce

3 drops Tabasco sauce

½ tsp freshly ground black pepper

Pinch salt

½ cup extra-virgin olive oil

¾ lb kale, stems removed, sliced

½ cup grated Parmigiano-Reggiano

½ cup homemade croutons (optional)

In a large wooden bowl, whisk together the garlic, anchovies, mustard, and egg yolk. Stir in the lemon juice, along with the Worcestershire sauce and Tabasco sauce. Stir well to combine and season with the freshly ground pepper and salt. Slowly drizzle the olive oil into the dressing, whisking as you go to form an emulsion.

In a separate bowl, massage the kale with a few tablespoons of dressing for a few minutes to break down and wilt the leaves slightly. Add the kale to the remaining dressing and toss to coat. Add the cheese and croutons, if using, and toss again. Serve immediately.

TIP

There is always a small danger of salmonella poisoning with raw eggs, so this salad should not be served to those who are very young or very old or those with compromised immune systems. For safety, never use cracked eggs, and coddle (dip them in barely simmering water for a minute or two) the eggs before using to make sure there are no contaminants on the shells. Here, save the leftover white in a covered container in the refrigerator to add to the eggs in your morning omelet.

WILTED GREENS with RICE

This vegetarian dish is popular during Lent in Greece, when wild spring greens (*horta*) are piled in the markets. Stir in some crumbled feta for a full meal. You can add all of the greens at the beginning of cooking, but reserving half to add at the end helps to keep the color fresh and vibrant. **SERVES 4-6**.

Wash the greens well and remove any tough stems, then stack the leaves, roll, and slice into fine shreds. Set aside.

In a heavy, deep saucepan over medium, heat the olive oil and cook the onions until translucent, about 5 minutes. Add the garlic and cook for 1 minute.

Add the rice and stir to coat with oil. Cook for 2 minutes. Stir half of the greens into the rice. When the greens begin to wilt and cook down, add the water or stock and half of the dill or fennel fronds. Bring to a boil, cover, and reduce heat to low.

Steam until all of the liquid is absorbed, about 20 minutes, adding a little more water if necessary. Stir in the lemon juice, remaining shredded greens, and remaining dill or fennel fronds, and season with salt and pepper and chili flakes.

Pile the rice into a bowl or deep platter. Drizzle with a little more olive oil before serving, and garnish with lemon slices, olives, and crumbled feta, if desired.

2 lb fresh greens (a mixture of fresh spinach, dandelion, mustard, chard, arugula, and/or sorrel)

⅓ cup extra-virgin Greek olive oil

1½ cups minced onions

2 cloves garlic, minced

1 cup long-grain rice

1 cup water or vegetable stock

¼ cup chopped fresh dill or fennel fronds, divided

Juice of 1 lemon (about 3 Tbsp)

Salt and freshly ground black pepper, to taste

⅛ tsp crushed red chili flakes, or to taste

Lemon slices, for garnish

Black kalamata olives, for garnish

Crumbled feta, for garnish (optional)

TUSCAN GREENS and BEANS SOUP

Too many greens in the garden? Make a pot of this rustic Italian soup. In Italy, home cooks never waste the rinds of expensive Parmesan—they add them to soup at the beginning of cooking for flavor, and discard before serving. **MAKES 8 CUPS, ENOUGH FOR 6–8 SERVINGS.**

Place the beans in a bowl and cover with cold water. Place in the fridge to soak overnight. (Or quick soak them in a pressure cooker: bring the beans and enough water to cover generously to full pressure, then remove from heat and let stand until pressure drops naturally.) Drain.

Halve the leeks lengthwise, wash thoroughly, and slice thinly. In a large saucepan over medium, heat the oil, add the leeks, and sauté until softened. Add the garlic and tomatoes, and cook for 2 minutes. Add the drained beans and bay leaf to the pot with the stock or water.

Bring to a boil over high heat. Reduce the heat to medium-low, partially cover, and simmer for 45 to 60 minutes, until the beans are tender.

Discard the bay leaf. Remove 1 cup of the soup and purée in the blender until smooth, then return to the pot. Add the greens to the hot soup and heat through, stirring just until the greens wilt.

Stir in the rosemary and balsamic vinegar. Season with the chili paste and the salt and pepper.

Top each serving with a little basil pesto and some shavings of Parmigiano-Reggiano (using a vegetable peeler).

2 cups dried white beans (see Tip)

3 large leeks (white and pale green parts only)

¼ cup extra-virgin olive oil

3 cloves garlic, minced

4 ripe Roma tomatoes, seeded and chopped

1 bay leaf

8 cups low-salt chicken stock or water

3 cups fresh kale, chard, spinach, or beet greens, washed well and chopped

2 tsp minced fresh rosemary

1 Tbsp balsamic vinegar

1 tsp Asian chili paste, or to taste

Salt and freshly ground black pepper, to taste

1 Tbsp basil pesto, for garnish

Shavings of Parmigiano-Reggiano, for garnish

TIP

You can also use 2 small cans of white beans for this soup. Rinse and drain them well before adding to the soup, and reduce the liquid to 6 cups and the simmering time to 20 minutes.

MUSHROOMS

Buy

You'll find cultivated white, brown, shiitake, and portobello mushrooms at grocery stores. Look for wild mushrooms such as morels, chanterelles, pine mushrooms, and truffles at seasonal markets. If you're buying wild mushrooms, make sure they are from a reputable source—mistakes can be deadly. You can also buy many mushrooms dried, from Chinese mushrooms to morels and porcini (also known as cèpes).

Store

Keep mushrooms in a paper bag in the refrigerator. Don't wash them, just brush off any dirt or debris. Dry mushrooms in a dehydrator for longer storage (especially morel and porcini).

Serve

Mushrooms make creamy soups and sauces, tasty toppings for steaks, and "meaty" additions to vegetarian fare.

Don't Waste It!

- Sauté chopped mushrooms in butter with garlic and finish with a splash of Madeira or heavy cream to serve on steak or pile on toasted baguette.

- Make a mushroom gravy by sautéing onions, garlic, and sliced mushrooms in butter and olive oil, then finishing with a little flour, red wine, tomato paste, and stock. Add a spoonful of sour cream and a little paprika to make a sauce for noodles or polenta.

- Sauté mushrooms in butter and fold into scrambled eggs with chives, for breakfast.

- Pulverize dried mushrooms to a powder in a blender or coffee grinder (a good way to use the mushroom bits from the bottom of the bag) to dust over steaks, chicken, or chops before grilling, or add to cream sauces. You can also infuse warm olive oil with mushroom powder—just strain it well before bottling.

- Brush whole portobello mushrooms with olive oil and grill until tender to serve as vegetarian burgers.

- Soak dried shiitake mushrooms in boiling water to hydrate, then braise with 2 tablespoons each of sugar, mirin, and soy sauce.

- Stuff large white mushrooms with crabmeat, cream cheese, and chives, and broil until bubbly. Save the mushroom stems for sautés and soups.

WILD MUSHROOM and POTATO BISQUE

With exotic wild mushrooms, a little potato for body, and just a touch of fresh cream, this mushroom soup is worlds away from the supermarket staple, and healthier, too. For a fancy presentation, sauté some extra chopped mushrooms with garlic in butter and spoon over each portion to garnish. **SERVES 4.**

In a medium-sized pot over medium, heat the oil and sauté the onion and garlic until softened. Add the potatoes and mushrooms, and continue to cook until the mushrooms begin to give up their moisture, about 5 minutes. Add the stock, bay leaf, thyme, and tomato paste, and bring to a boil.

Cover the pot, reduce heat to low, and simmer the soup for 30 minutes. The potatoes should break down and thicken the soup.

Stir in the cream and heat through. For a silky smooth bisque, purée half or all of the soup in a blender (or use an immersion hand blender). Season with salt and pepper.

1 Tbsp olive oil

1 small onion, minced

2 cloves garlic, minced

¾ lb Yukon Gold potatoes, peeled and grated

1 cup finely chopped wild and domestic mushrooms (brown, oyster, shiitake, portobello, morel, cèpe, etc.)

4 cups homemade chicken stock or vegetable stock

1 bay leaf

¾ tsp minced fresh thyme

1 Tbsp tomato paste

½ cup heavy cream

Salt and freshly ground black pepper, to taste

✿ FOOD FOR THOUGHT

According to the book *Waste: Uncovering the Global Food Scandal*, the world's nearly one billion hungry people could be lifted out of malnourishment on less than a quarter of the food that is wasted in the US, UK, and Europe.

STUFFED PORTOBELLOS

These are great as an appetizer or as part of a tapas meal of small but substantial bites. **SERVES 4.**

* * * * * * * * * * * *

Preheat the oven to 400°F. Butter a baking dish.

Remove the stems from the mushrooms. Use a spoon to scrape the brown gills out of the base of the mushrooms. (Save the stems for the soup pot, but discard the gills.)

Sauté the shallots in the butter until tender, then mix with the mashed potatoes, cream, and cheese. Season with salt and pepper.

Brush the mushrooms on both sides with melted butter. Spread the pesto over the inner surface of each mushroom, then stuff with the potato filling. Brush tops of the potato mounds with more melted butter.

Set the mushrooms in the prepared baking dish, and bake for 10 to 15 minutes until golden. Cut into wedges to serve.

2 large portobello mushrooms (about 1 lb)

2 shallots, minced

2 Tbsp butter

1 cup leftover cold mashed potatoes (or fresh or dried bread crumbs)

¼ cup heavy cream or milk

½ cup grated Parmigiano-Reggiano

Salt and freshly ground black pepper, to taste

Melted butter, for brushing

1 Tbsp basil pesto

ONIONS

Buy

Onions may be yellow, white, or red, and they come in a variety of sizes, from massive Spanish onions to tiny pearl onions (which are great for pickles). In summer, fresh onions have thin, tight skins, while storage onions are stronger, with papery husks. Some hybrids, like Vidalia, Maui, or Walla Walla, are sweeter. Avoid soft or sprouted onions.

Store

Keep your onions in a cool, dark, dry place, away from potatoes. Yellow onions store better than white or red onions.

Serve

Onions are essential to almost any dish, and they can also be enjoyed alone, grilled on skewers, pickled, or slowly caramelized in butter or olive oil.

Don't Waste It!

- Slice onions and caramelize slowly in olive oil until golden and sweet. Store in a jar in the fridge. Use caramelized onions (AKA onion jam) on pizza, on sliced baguette for appetizers, tossed with pasta, or on sandwiches and burgers.

- To make raw onions mellow for salads or burgers, slice thinly and soak in ice water for 10 minutes, then drain.

- Slice red onions and soak them in a vinegar-and-sugar solution for a quick refrigerator pickle that can be used on sandwiches and burgers.

- Slow-cook chopped red onions in butter with a splash of balsamic vinegar and some chopped thyme until they melt into a marmalade. Goes great with pork terrines or cheese plates.

- Roast small whole onions until browned and caramelized, and add to braised beef stews or lamb dishes.

- Slice sweet white Vidalia onions, brush with olive oil, and season with salt, then grill or broil on high heat until softened and lightly charred. Serve on steaks or burgers, or chop and mix with cilantro, honey, and lime for salsa.

- Braise meats (think pork shoulder or beef pot roast) with lots of sliced onions and red wine or beer.

- To make classic onion soup, slowly sauté 4 slivered onions with a little garlic and a bit of sugar in butter until browned and caramelized, then add good-quality beef stock and a healthy splash of sherry, and simmer. Top each bowl with toasted bread and grated Gruyère, and broil until bubbly.

SPICY ONION FRITTERS

This is a home-style version of the popular Indian restaurant snack known as pakoras. You can fry other sliced vegetables in this batter, too—try matchstick pieces of eggplant or sweet potato or sliced cauliflower. **SERVES 4–6, AS AN APPETIZER.**

Place the onions in a large bowl. Add the cumin seeds, coriander, cumin, paprika, salt, chili powder, and garam masala, and toss to coat. Set aside for 15 minutes, until the onions release their juices.

Drizzle with the butter. Add the chickpea flour, rice flour, and baking soda. Use your hands to combine and mix everything together.

You should have a loose mass that's sticky but fairly dry (you don't want a batter—the coating should just hold the onions together). Add a little water if necessary, or more flour.

In a wok over medium-high, heat the canola oil. Working in batches, gently drop the onions a spoonful at a time into the hot oil forming loose patties. Turn several times in the oil until golden brown. Drain on paper towels and keep warm in an oven heated to 200°F while you fry the rest of the fritters.

Serve fritters while hot with chutney for dipping.

You can cook these ahead of time and recrisp in an oven heated to 400°F for 5 to 10 minutes.

3 large onions, peeled and thinly sliced

1 tsp whole cumin seeds

1 tsp ground coriander

1 tsp ground cumin

1 tsp paprika

1 tsp salt

½ tsp chili powder

½ tsp garam masala

1 Tbsp melted butter or ghee

2 cups chickpea flour

1 cup rice flour or all-purpose flour

¼ tsp baking soda

¼ cup water (if required)

1 cup canola oil, for frying

Chutney, for dipping

ONION TART

Warm, rich puffed pastry topped with creamy cheese and sweet caramelized onions. Pour a fresh young Riesling and enjoy alongside this Bavarian-style snack. (Find puff pastry in the frozen foods section of the supermarket.) **MAKES 24 PIECES.**

1 package frozen puff pastry

2 Tbsp butter

2 large white onions, slivered

3 cloves garlic, minced

1 Tbsp chopped fresh thyme

1 cup white wine

Salt and white pepper, to taste

4 oz goat cheese, crumbled

4 oz cream cheese

½ cup sour cream

Thaw the puff pastry overnight in the refrigerator or on the counter for 1 hour.

In a large skillet over medium-low heat, melt the butter. Add the onions and garlic and sauté slowly until golden, about 30 minutes. Add the thyme, wine, and salt and pepper. Simmer until the liquid has evaporated. Set aside.

Preheat the oven to 350°F. Grease a 13- × 9-inch baking sheet.

Roll the puff pastry into a thin sheet, large enough to cover the baking sheet. Place the pastry on the prepared baking sheet and set aside.

In a food processor, combine the goat cheese, cream cheese, and sour cream, and whirl until smooth, scraping down the sides as necessary.

Spread the cheese mixture evenly over the pastry with a spatula. Then scatter the caramelized onions evenly overtop, pressing down lightly into the cheese.

Bake until golden, about 15 to 20 minutes. Cut into squares and serve while warm.

FOOD FOR THOUGHT

"Eat what you buy, buy what you need, and use your power as customer and citizen to demand that the businesses you buy from also stop wasting food." —Tristram Stuart, UK author and global food-waste activist

PEACHES

Buy

Best when tree-ripened in summer and purchased from farmers' markets. Avoid supermarket imports and greenish fruit—peaches should be red with a yellow or white background color. There are clingstone (early) and freestone peaches. The latter release their stones easily so are best for canning or cutting. Soft fruit is heavily sprayed so choose organic peaches whenever possible.

Store

Peaches are perishable and should be handled gently. To speed ripening, store at room temperature for 2 days in a paper bag. Keep ripe fruit for up to 1 week in the refrigerator. Blanch, peel, and toss with lemon juice to freeze. Cook with sugar to preserve as jam.

Serve

The only time to eat peaches is in summer. Eat them like an apple over the sink or sliced over ice cream and shortcake. Wash to rub off the fuzz. Peaches are also perfect in pies and crumbles, on their own or with apples and raspberries.

Don't Waste It!

- Caramelize butter and sugar in a sauté pan, then add sliced peaches and strawberries or pitted cherries. Warm through for 2 minutes, sprinkle with vanilla or brandy, and serve warm.

- Cook chopped peaches with sugar and lemon juice until thick, ladle into canning jars, and process preserves for 10 minutes in a boiling water bath.

- Add peaches to fresh tomato salsas with chiles and cilantro.

- Slice ripe peaches into a bowl, sprinkle with a little sugar to release the juices, marinate with a little sweet dessert wine (late harvest Riesling or ice wine), and serve in parfait glasses, alone or with a small scoop of vanilla or raspberry gelato.

- Combine peaches with milk or frozen yogurt for decadent peach shakes.

- Drizzle sliced peaches with honey and grill over high heat to caramelize, then serve warm over ice cream.

- In a glass bowl (or individual glasses), layer cubes of white cake with sliced peaches, fresh raspberries, and lemon yogurt for a fast peach trifle.

- Slice fresh peaches into a pretty bowl and drizzle with a little liquid honey, then serve topped with fresh raspberries.

- Cut peaches in half and remove the pits. Set peach halves in a baking dish and drizzle with a mixture of melted butter, vanilla, brown sugar, and brandy, then broil to caramelize and serve with a dollop of sweetened mascarpone and crumbled amaretti cookies.

- Poach peeled peaches in a white wine syrup flavored with lavender, then serve chilled.

PEACH SANGRIA

Make this peachy sangria for your next patio party and serve it in red wine glasses, with a few slices of marinated fruit in each glass. MAKES ABOUT 12 CUPS.

1 lemon

1 orange

2 peaches, slivered

½ to ¾ cup Triple Sec or other orange-flavored liqueur

2 bottles fruity red or white wine

Ice

2 to 3 cups soda water or lemon-lime soda (like Sprite or 7-Up)

Lime wedges, for garnish

Scrub the lemon and orange, then thinly slice, rind and all, into rounds using a very sharp knife or mandoline (the slicing blade on a good food processor works, too). Place the citrus fruit into a vessel large enough to hold about 3 quarts. Add the peaches, orange liqueur, and wine, and let the sangria steep for several hours (refrigerate if you have space).

When your guests arrive, add the ice and soda water to chill and dilute to taste.

PEACH KUCHEN

This simple coffee cake—a biscuit crust filled with fruit and topped with a sweet crumble—has German roots. Another "mother" recipe for your repertoire, it's easy to adapt to apples, plums, and other tree fruits. **SERVES 8.**

Preheat the oven to 350°F.

In a bowl, toss the peaches with the maple syrup. Set aside.

In another bowl, combine the flour, baking powder, and salt. In large bowl, use an electric mixer to cream together the butter and sugar until fluffy, then beat in the egg. Add the dry ingredients, alternating with the buttermilk, and blend well.

For the topping, mix the sugar, flour, ginger, lemon zest, butter, and nuts in a bowl and, using a fork or your hands, combine to form a crumbly mixture.

Butter a 10-inch springform pan. Spread two-thirds of the batter evenly in the pan and arrange the peach slices in a pattern overtop. Dot the remaining batter over the fruit, leaving spaces between spoonfuls of batter. Sprinkle with the topping.

Bake for 45 to 55 minutes, until the kuchen is nicely browned and a toothpick inserted in the center comes out clean. Cool on a wire rack in the pan for 30 minutes.

Release from the springform pan to serve. Cut into wedges and serve warm with ice cream or frozen yogurt.

4 large peaches, peeled and sliced

¼ cup maple syrup

2½ cups all-purpose flour

2 tsp baking powder

¼ teaspoon salt

¼ cup butter, softened

½ cup granulated sugar

1 large egg

⅔ cup buttermilk

Topping:

½ cup granulated sugar

⅓ cup all-purpose flour

1 tsp ground ginger

Finely grated zest of half a lemon

¼ cup butter

½ cup chopped pecans or hazelnuts

PEACH RASPBERRY CRISP

Make this crisp in summer when peaches and raspberries are in season—or try it with plums or apricots and fresh ginger (as long as you start with 6 cups of fruit, anything goes). SERVES 6-8.

Combine the sugar, cinnamon, nutmeg, brandy, and honey, and mix well. Toss with the peaches and let marinate for 1 hour, until the fruit releases its juices.

Preheat the oven to 350°F. Butter a shallow baking dish.

Sprinkle the peaches with the flour and combine well. Gently fold in the raspberries and pour the mixture into the prepared baking dish (or layer the berries with the peaches as you pour).

For the topping, combine the flour with the brown sugar and butter, mixing to form coarse crumbs. Stir in the oats, almonds, salt, and cinnamon. Scatter the crumble over the fruit.

Set the baking dish on a baking sheet to catch any juice that may run over. Bake for about 45 to 55 minutes, until bubbling and golden brown. Serve the crisp warm with vanilla ice cream or lemon yogurt.

¾ cup granulated sugar

½ tsp ground cinnamon

¼ tsp ground nutmeg

3 Tbsp brandy, Calvados, or Grand Marnier

2 Tbsp honey

6 large peaches, pitted and sliced

3 Tbsp all-purpose flour

2 cups raspberries (or substitute cranberries or chopped rhubarb)

Topping:

¼ cup whole-wheat flour

¼ cup packed brown sugar

3 Tbsp butter, softened

¼ cup rolled oats

¼ cup sliced blanched almonds

Pinch salt

½ tsp ground cinnamon

Tub gourmet vanilla ice cream or lemon yogurt

PEACH MELBA TRIFLE with SHERRIED CUSTARD

Make this trifle in a large, straight-sided glass bowl for a dramatic presentation, or layer it in individual parfait glasses. SERVES 8.

To make the raspberry sauce, press the thawed raspberries through a sieve set over a saucepan to extract the juice and pulp, and remove the seeds. Set the fruit purée over medium heat and stir in the sugar and cornstarch. Cook, stirring constantly, until boiling and thick. Remove from heat and cool (may be made 2 days in advance).

To make the custard, start with a saucepan that has been rinsed out with hot water but not dried—this prevents the milk solids from sticking to the bottom of the pan. Heat the milk until bubbles begin to form around the edges. Do not boil. Beat the egg yolks with the sugar and cornstarch until smooth, and slowly whisk into the hot milk. Cook over medium heat, whisking constantly, for 3 to 5 minutes or until the custard has boiled for about 1 minute and is quite thick. Remove from heat and place in a bowl. Stir in the sherry and vanilla. Cool slightly, then cover with plastic wrap, placing the wrap directly on the surface of the custard, and refrigerate up to 2 days.

Line an 8-cup glass trifle bowl or individual dishes with a layer of pound cake or ladyfingers. Sprinkle a little sherry over the cake, and top with a quarter of the custard. Arrange about a third of the peaches overtop, making sure you press some of the pieces close to the glass. Drizzle with a third of the raspberry sauce.

Repeat the layers of cake, sherry, custard, peaches (reserving a few slices for garnish), and raspberry sauce, ending with a layer of cake, sherry, and custard. Cover the trifle tightly with plastic wrap and refrigerate at least 4 hours or overnight.

Before serving, whip the cream with the sugar to sweeten it. Use the whipped cream, reserved peach slices, and mint leaves to garnish the trifle.

Raspberry sauce:

1 (10 oz) package frozen unsweetened raspberries, thawed

¼ cup granulated sugar

2 tsp cornstarch

Custard:

3 cups milk or half-and-half

4 egg yolks

½ cup granulated sugar

¼ cup cornstarch

¼ cup sweet sherry

1 tsp vanilla extract

1 pound-cake, thinly sliced, or 2 packages soft ladyfingers, halved

½ cup sweet sherry

3 cups canned peaches (about 12 peach halves), drained and sliced, or fresh peaches, poached in sugar syrup and sliced

1 cup heavy cream

2 Tbsp granulated sugar

Mint leaves, to garnish

PEARS

Buy

Buy pears when underripe and wait until the stem end is slightly soft before eating (Bartlett pears will turn yellow when ripe, but D'Anjous remain green). There are several varieties of pears: early golden Bartletts, the most common domestic pear; elegant brown Boscs with their tapered necks; and D'Anjous, which are buttery (though the flesh can be a bit granular when underripe). The Asian pear is a round pear, native to China and Korea, fragrant, crisp, and best eaten raw. Handle pears carefully, as they bruise easily.

Store

Pears are sold green and actually ripen better off the tree. Pick mature but green fruits and give them 5 to 7 days to ripen, in a warm spot (they will ripen faster if placed in a paper bag with an apple). If you have a windfall of pears and need to store them for more than a couple of weeks, keep them at 30°F (-1°C) to 45°F (7°C) and 85 percent humidity for up to 3 months—a cool garage is perfect. Choose pears that are ripe but still very firm for canning.

Serve

A perfectly ripe pear is juicy and buttery, a great snack to eat raw. Pears are also easy to substitute for apples in pies, crumbles, strudels, and tarts.

Don't Waste It!

- Add sliced pears to a tossed green salad with candied walnuts and blue cheese.
- Slice pears and wrap in strips of prosciutto for easy appetizers.
- Serve sliced pears on a cheese plate with blue cheese, Parmesan, Brie, and walnuts.
- Sauté pears in butter with brown sugar and chopped preserved or candied ginger to serve warm over ice cream.
- Peel pears, leaving stems intact, and remove the core from the bottom with a small melon baller. Poach for 10 minutes in simple syrup (made from 1 part sugar, 3 parts water) and a little vanilla or in light red wine flavored with sugar, cinnamon, cloves, and lemon peel.
- For free-form individual pear tarts, wrap wedges of peeled pears loosely in rounds of puff pastry, season with cinnamon, brown sugar, and a drop of almond liqueur, and bake in an oven heated to 400°F until brown.
- Top pizzas or flatbreads with sliced pears and Brie or Gorgonzola, bake until cheese is bubbly, and finish with fresh arugula.
- Combine pears with cranberries or rhubarb for seasonal fruit pies and crumbles.
- Cut ripe pears in quarters and season with a little ground black pepper.
- Cook pears down to a butter or sauce with sugar, cinnamon, and cloves, then purée using a food mill, to freeze or can in jars. Fruit butter is simply sauce that has been reduced and thickened further (you can use a slow cooker to prevent scorching). To can, process quart jars of pear sauce or butter in boiling water for 20 minutes.
- Simmer diced pears with simple syrup, port, star anise, cinnamon, and chopped dried apricots, cherries, and figs for a warm fruit compote to serve over cake.

PEAR and AVOCADO SALAD

Combine as many fresh lettuces and greens from the market or garden as possible for this big green salad. Use leaf lettuce, baby turnip greens, watercress, nasturtium, and romaine for flavor and texture contrasts. Pea shoots can often be found at Asian markets. **SERVES 6.**

To make the dressing, whirl the orange juice, oil, lemon juice, and salt and pepper in a blender to emulsify, or combine in a small jar and shake like crazy. Set aside.

Wash the greens well in a sink full of cold water and spin-dry in a salad spinner. If not using right away, pack loosely in a plastic bag with a piece of paper towel, seal, and refrigerate for several hours or overnight. This will ensure your salad is crisp.

If you're serving immediately, core the pear and slice it very thin, leaving the skin on, and then cut the slices into flat batons or 1-inch squares. Peel the avocado, and cut into thin slices or slivers. Toss the avocado with the lemon juice to prevent it from discoloring.

Pick out a large, pretty salad bowl and fill it with the mixed greens. Top with the pea shoots (if using), green onions, and pine nuts. If you're taking it somewhere, stop at this point and finish assembling just before serving. When you're ready to serve, add the pear and avocado, drizzle with the dressing, and toss.

Dressing:

¼ cup orange juice

¼ cup extra-virgin olive oil

1 tsp fresh lemon juice

Salt and freshly ground black pepper, to taste

Salad:

8 cups mixed salad greens

1 ripe pear (regular or Asian)

1 ripe avocado

1 tsp fresh lemon juice

2 cups pea shoots (optional)

3 green onions, minced

⅓ cup toasted pine nuts

PEAR MINCEMEAT

When you have a peck of pears, make this yummy mincemeat to fill tarts or give away to friends over the holidays. Totally vegan, too. MAKES 5 CUPS.

In a large saucepan, combine the pears, apple, lemon zest and juice, orange zest and juice, dried cranberries, raisins, brown sugar, cinnamon, nutmeg, ginger, and salt. Bring to a boil over medium heat.

Reduce heat to medium-low, cover, and simmer for 1 hour, until mixture is thickened.

Remove the lid and continue to simmer for 10 minutes to thicken further. Stir in the walnuts and cognac, and cook for 5 minutes.

Spoon the mincemeat into hot, sterilized half-pint jars, leaving ½ inch of headspace. Seal the jars with 2-piece lids and refrigerate, freeze, or process in a boiling water bath for shelf storage.

2½ lb pears, peeled, cored, and chopped

1 green apple, peeled, cored, and chopped

Finely grated zest and juice of 1 lemon

Finely grated zest and juice of 1 orange

½ cup dried cranberries or currants

1 cup golden raisins

½ cup packed brown sugar

1 tsp ground cinnamon

1 tsp ground nutmeg

¼ tsp ground ginger

Pinch salt

½ cup chopped walnuts or pecans, toasted

½ cup cognac or pear brandy

← TIP

Use a heavy, covered canner for processing preserves. If you don't have a proper canner (with a wire lifting insert), place a metal rack in the bottom of a stockpot. Seal filled jars with metal lids and rings, closing until just "fingertip" tight. Carefully lower the jars into boiling water using a jar lifter until they are all submerged in a single layer. When submerged, the jars should be covered by about 1 inch of boiling water. Cover the pot. When the water returns to a full, rolling boil, start timing—process for 10 minutes. Lift the processed jars from the water and set on a folded towel on the counter to cool. You will hear the lids pop down as the preserves cool, proof of a proper seal.

PEPPERS

Buy

Sweet red, orange, green, and yellow bell peppers from hothouse growers are available year round; hot peppers from farmers' markets can be found in late summer, along with less common sweet pale yellow or lavender varieties. Select smooth specimens.

Store

Keep peppers in the crisper. Green peppers last longer than other colors. Roast peppers on the barbecue (or under a gas broiler) until blackened, then cool in a covered bowl or plastic bag, peel, and store in olive oil or freeze in containers.

Serve

Sweet bell peppers make colorful additions to salads when raw. Add to stir-fries and stews or stuff with rice. Roasted bell peppers are tasty additions to sandwiches, pasta, or pizza. Peppers that you've roasted and frozen are great for making into salsa.

Don't Waste It!

- Dice several red bell peppers and simmer with balsamic vinegar and salt for about 30 minutes, until the vinegar is reduced to a glaze, then toss with a little olive oil and black pepper for a colorful condiment.
- Purée about 8 roasted and peeled peppers with caramelized onion, fresh thyme, chicken stock, and a little hot sauce for a creamy pepper soup.
- Top pizza with tomato sauce, mozzarella, and roasted red peppers, then finish with fresh arugula.
- Add roasted red peppers to hummus: Combine drained canned chickpeas with a slug of olive oil, garlic, lemon juice, tahini, cayenne or smoked paprika, and about 1 cup of roasted red peppers, then purée in the food processor and serve with pita bread.
- Cut bell peppers into thick rings, sauté in butter until beginning to brown on both sides, then crack an egg into each ring and cook until the whites are done and the yolks are still soft. Perch on a piece of toast.
- Stir-fry slivered red and yellow bell peppers with black bean sauce.
- Stuff hot jalapeno chiles with cubes of Monterey Jack cheese, then dip in beaten egg, roll in bread crumbs, and fry in hot canola oil until crisp.
- In a low oven (or dehydrator), dry hot chiles until crisp and crumble to make chili flakes.
- Combine roasted peppers with extra-virgin olive oil and minced garlic for an antipasto to pile on toasted bread.
- Purée roasted peppers with goat cheese, minced garlic, olive oil, and fresh basil, thyme, and rosemary for a tasty dip.

GRILLED STEAK FAJITAS

For an interactive dinner, serve the grilled steak and peppers with all of the garnishes in bowls on the side and let your guests make their own fajita wraps. **MAKES 12 FAJITAS, SERVES 6.**

To make the marinade, combine the canola oil, lime juice, hot pepper, garlic, green onion, tequila, cumin, and cilantro in a food processor and whirl until smooth.

Place half of the marinade in a zippered plastic bag with the steak. Put the remaining marinade in a bowl with the red, green, and yellow peppers and the onion and toss to coat. Set both aside at room temperature to marinate for 30 minutes.

Heat the barbecue to high. Using a perforated barbecue grill pan, stir-fry the peppers and onion in batches on the grill until starting to char. This will take 10 to 15 minutes. Grill the steak for 6 to 8 minutes per side, then set aside for 10 minutes to allow the juices to set.

Marinade:

3 Tbsp canola oil

Juice of 2 limes (about ¼ cup)

1 small hot pepper, minced

1 clove garlic, minced

1 green onion, minced

2 Tbsp tequila

½ tsp ground cumin

¼ cup chopped fresh cilantro

Filling:

1½ lb round or flank steak

2 red bell peppers, seeded and sliced into strips

1 green bell pepper, seeded and sliced into strips

1 yellow bell pepper, seeded and sliced into strips

1 white onion, slivered

Meanwhile, make the chipotle mayo. In a food processor or blender, whirl together the mayonnaise, garlic, lime juice, and chipotle chile until smooth, and then stir in the cilantro, if using.

Carve the rested steak into thin strips across the grain. Pile the steak in the center of a serving platter and surround it with the grilled vegetables.

Serve with the chipotle mayonnaise, whatever toppings you like, and warm tortillas on the side.

Chipotle mayonnaise:

½ cup mayonnaise

1 clove garlic, minced

1 tsp fresh lime juice

1 canned chipotle chile in adobo sauce

1 Tbsp chopped fresh cilantro (optional)

Suggested toppings:

Grated cheese (jalapeno jack, cheddar, mozzarella blend)

Fresh tomato salsa and/or tomatillo salsa

Fresh guacamole

Chimichurri (see p. 268)

Sour cream

Lime wedges

12 warm flour tortillas

MOUHAMMARA

This Syrian red pepper and walnut spread is simple but addictive. It may take a trip to a Middle Eastern grocer for pomegranate molasses, but the results are worth it. Serve with sliced baguette or pita bread, and make extra to freeze (and give away in little jars as hostess gifts). If you have a stash of frozen roasted red peppers, they'll work well here. Or you can buy roasted peppers in a jar. **MAKES 2 CUPS**.

3 Tbsp extra-virgin olive oil

1 small onion, minced

3 cloves garlic, minced

⅔ cup ground walnuts

4 red bell peppers, roasted and peeled

2 hot red peppers, roasted and peeled

3 Tbsp fresh lemon juice (from 1 lemon)

1 Tbsp pomegranate molasses

Ground cumin, for dusting (optional)

In a saucepan over medium-low, heat the oil. Add the onion and garlic, cover, and sweat for 15 minutes until very tender.

Add the walnuts to the pan, increase the heat, and toast for 3 minutes, stirring constantly.

Transfer to a food processor along with the red bell peppers, hot peppers, lemon juice, and pomegranate molasses, and purée until smooth.

Chill the purée overnight. To serve, spoon into a bowl, drizzle with more olive oil, and dust lightly with cumin if desired. Serve with pita bread.

RISOTTO-STUFFED BELL PEPPERS

This is a hearty main dish of halved bell peppers filled with cheesy Italian sausage risotto. These stuffed peppers are perfectly portable and easy to reheat in a microwave. They freeze well, too. Vegetarians can substitute soy protein or a can of lightly mashed chickpeas for the ground meat. **SERVES 4–6.**

Slice the sausage casings lengthwise to release the sausage meat.

In a sauté pan over medium heat, crumble the sausage meat and cook until nicely browned. Break it up with a fork as it cooks. Set the sausage aside in a large bowl.

In a saucepan, bring 2 cups of salted water to a boil. Add the rice, cover, and reduce heat to low. Simmer for about 20 minutes, until the water is absorbed and the rice is tender.

Remove from heat and let stand, covered, for 10 minutes to steam. Add the rice to the bowl with the cooked sausage. Stir to combine and cool.

Stir in the cheese, parsley, garlic, salt and pepper, and eggs. Combine until well mixed, then add just enough bread crumbs to bind the mixture.

Place the pepper halves on a plate, cut side up, and sprinkle lightly with salt. Press the stuffing firmly into the peppers, mounding slightly.

In a large nonstick pan over medium, heat the olive oil and cook the peppers, skin side down, for 6 minutes. Flip so that the filling side is down and cook for another 8 to 10 minutes, until the tops are nicely browned and the filling is cooked through.

Serve immediately with a little warm tomato sauce and grated Parmigiano-Reggiano overtop of each stuffed pepper. (Or reserve the tomato sauce and cheese and refrigerate and reheat later.)

½ lb fresh spicy Italian sausages

1 cup Arborio or other Italian risotto rice

¾ cup grated Italian cheese mix (or a 50/50 mix of mozzarella and Parmesan)

2 Tbsp chopped fresh Italian parsley

2 cloves garlic, minced

½ tsp salt

¼ tsp freshly ground black pepper

2 large eggs, lightly beaten

⅓ cup fresh or dried bread crumbs

4 large red or yellow bell peppers, halved, seeds and ribs removed

2 Tbsp extra-virgin olive oil

Plain tomato sauce (canned is fine), warmed, for garnish

Grated Parmigiano-Reggiano, for garnish

POTATOES

Buy

Potatoes come in so many different shapes, sizes, colors, and types that you need to choose the right potato for the job—dry fluffy russets for baking or gnocchi, waxy reds for potato salads, buttery yellow Sieglinde and blue heirlooms for colorful mashes, French fingerlings to steam for fancy dinners. Choose firm potatoes without cuts or blemishes; skin should be smooth, not wrinkled, with no green tinges and no sprouting (if your potatoes are sprouting, it's time to plant them).

Store

New potatoes are dug young, when the skins are still thin, so they are not meant for storage. Potatoes that have been harvested after the top of the plant dies down can be stored for several months in a cool, dark, dry place. When exposed to light, potatoes turn green—cut all green portions away as they are bitter and toxic.

Serve

Potatoes can be boiled, steamed, mashed, fried, or baked, and are the starch of choice for many meals. For rustic mashes, buy organic potatoes; don't peel—simply scrub, steam, and mash. For guilt-free fries, cut potatoes into wedges, toss with a little oil, and bake.

Don't Waste It!

- For breakfast, slice cold leftover boiled potatoes and sauté in hot bacon fat or butter until golden brown.

- Steam skin-on baby potatoes until just barely tender, rub with olive oil, press to break the skin and lightly crush, then bake at 450°F for 20 minutes, or until crispy. Season with flaky sea salt.

- Grate 3 large raw potatoes and mix with 2 beaten eggs, a minced onion, and salt and pepper. Shape into 4-inch pancakes, and fry in canola oil for 5 minutes per side until brown and crisp.

- Combine leftover mashed potatoes with a can of salmon, an egg, a spoonful of flour, and a chopped green onion, then make patties and fry them in olive oil or butter until golden on both sides.

- Stuff leftover baked potatoes: cut in half and spoon out cooked potato. Combine potato with sour cream, cooked broccoli or spinach, cooked bacon, chopped green onion, and grated cheese, then fill skins and rebake at 350°F until hot and bubbly, about 15 minutes.

- Mash boiled potatoes, yams, and carrots. Sauté an onion with fresh minced ginger in lots of butter and mix into the mash.

- Cut baby potatoes in half, toss with olive oil, and bake until crisp and brown, then use, like toasts or crackers, as the base for toppings like smoked salmon, sour cream and caviar, or bacon jam.

- Slice potatoes, layer with sliced onions and cheese in a casserole dish, cover with broth or cream, and bake at 350°F into a bubbly gratin.

- When you have leftover baked potatoes, recycle the skins as tasty snacks: brush skins with butter, top with chopped crisp bacon, green onions, and grated cheese, and bake at 400°F until bubbly. (Use the flesh of the potatoes in potato breads, potato pancakes, gnocchi, or soups.)

- Use leftover mashed (or boiled) potatoes in homemade pasta, in gnocchi, and in pancakes—just combine with an egg and some flour for the dough. You could even use it for the outside of perogies.

- Fry up your leftover potatoes with ham or bacon for a crispy hash to serve with eggs.

POTATO SALAD

When you have leftover cold boiled potatoes, make potato salad. Waxy red potatoes are best for salads as they keep their shape. For a more substantial salad, add a few hard-cooked eggs, chopped. Instead of the shelled peas, you can use chopped edible-podded peas (snap or snow peas) or lightly steamed green beans, cut into small pieces. **MAKES 6 SERVINGS.**

Cut cold leftover potatoes into cubes.

In a bowl, whisk together the mayonnaise, sour cream, mustard, dill, lemon juice, and salt and pepper. Add the potatoes to the bowl, then gently fold in the celery, green onions, radishes, and peas, being careful not to break up the potatoes.

Serve immediately or chill for several hours.

2 lb new red potatoes, scrubbed and boiled

¼ cup low-fat mayonnaise

¼ cup low-fat sour cream or plain yogurt

2 tsp Dijon mustard

1 Tbsp chopped fresh dill (or 1 tsp dried dill, in a pinch)

1 Tbsp fresh lemon juice

Salt and freshly ground black pepper, to taste

½ cup finely chopped celery

2 to 3 green onions, chopped

6 radishes, sliced

½ cup freshly shelled green peas, in season

POTATO GNOCCHI

The trick to perfect fluffy gnocchi is in the potato—use only dry white baking potatoes. You should also try to handle the dough as little as possible. Classic sauces to toss with the hot gnocchi are basil pesto cut with a little cream, browned butter with sage and Parmesan, or Gorgonzola sauce—just simmer cream with blue cheese. Or simply serve with tomato sauce, or with butter and fresh herbs. **SERVES 4.**

4 white baking potatoes (about 1 lb)

⅔ cup all-purpose flour, plus more if needed

1 tsp salt

Preheat the oven to 400°F. Puncture the potatoes with a fork and bake them for about 30 to 40 minutes, until they're soft. Cool slightly and peel while hot.

Put the potatoes through a food mill or ricer (you can also mash, but don't use a food processor).

Spread the potato out on a work surface to cool, then sprinkle with the flour and salt. Work the flour into the dough, just until it comes together, then very gently knead to make a smooth, soft, and slightly sticky dough. If you knead the gnocchi too much, you risk incorporating too much flour, which will equal heavy, not ethereal, dumplings.

On a floured surface or large cutting board, roll or pat the dough into a rectangle, about 1 inch thick. Cut into 1-inch strips, then lightly roll each strip into a rope and cut into 1-inch dumplings. (At this point you can boil a test dumpling to make sure you've incorporated enough flour that it won't fall apart.)

Roll each dumpling lightly along a ridged wooden gnocchi paddle or the back of a fork (this is optional but gives the gnocchi their classic ridges) and round the ends. Place the dumplings on a lightly floured baking tray in a single layer and cook immediately or refrigerate for up to 24 hours. You can also freeze them on the tray for later use (package in plastic bags once frozen and use within 2 months).

Boil the gnocchi in salted water, a few at a time, stirring gently so that they don't stick together. When they float to the surface, boil them for about 30 seconds longer, then lift them out of the water using a slotted spoon. Toss with pesto, melted butter and herbs, or another sauce before serving.

> **TIP**
> If you find that your gnocchi disintegrate in boiling water, you may not have used enough flour, or you may be boiling the water too hard. Simmer gently until they float.

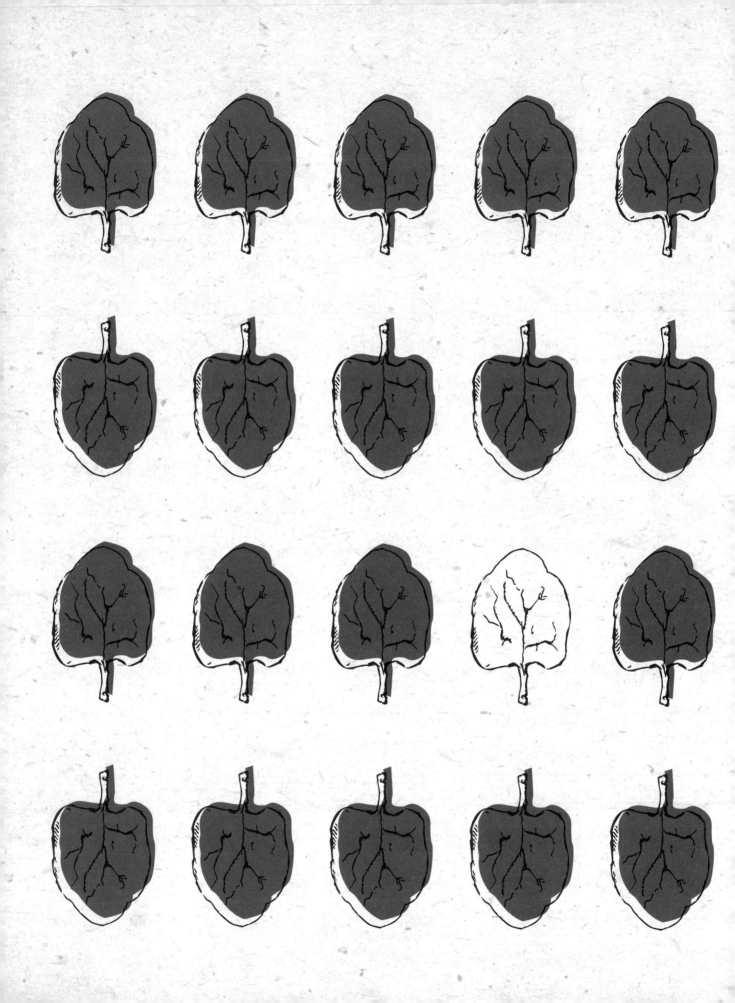

SPINACH

Buy

Whether it's baby spinach, available year round, or larger, crinkly bunches of spinach from the farmers' market, leaves should be dark and crisp, never yellowing.

Store

Remove twist ties from bunches, then wrap lightly in paper towel and place in a perforated plastic bag to store in the crisper. To wash field spinach, which can be gritty, fill the kitchen sink with water, swish the spinach, and lift it out, leaving the sand behind, then whirl in a salad spinner to dry before refrigerating.

Serve

Spinach is a versatile green that goes from salads to sautés. It's perfect to use as a colorful base for serving grilled chicken or fish, to purée in a smoothie or sauce, or to wilt into a hot pasta dish.

Don't Waste It!

- Sauté fresh baby spinach with a little butter, olive oil, and 1 tablespoon of Indian curry paste, then finish with ¼ cup of heavy cream.
- Add several cups of shredded spinach to a hearty Italian vegetable soup made with carrots, celery, potatoes, tomatoes, and white beans.
- Toss fresh spinach leaves with slivered red onion, sliced pears, toasted pecans, and blue cheese, and a simple vinaigrette.
- Combine cooked spinach with grated Gruyère and Parmesan, minced garlic and shallots, beaten eggs, and chervil. Fry the mixture like an omelet, in olive oil, until brown on both sides, for a first course or to serve cold as an appetizer or snack.
- Quickly sauté fresh baby spinach with olive oil, butter, garlic, and a splash of orange juice until it just wilts and turns bright green. Season to taste with salt and pepper.
- Add a big handful of shredded spinach to hot cooked chunky pasta, dressed with garlic, olive oil, and Parmesan. Toss to wilt.
- Combine chopped cooked spinach with beaten egg, ricotta, chopped parsley, grated mozzarella, and Parmesan to fill cooked cannelloni or large shell pasta (or roll in fresh eggroll wrappers). Then top with tomato sauce and cheese, and bake at 350°F until bubbly.
- To quickly cook spinach to use in other dishes, simply wash and steam in a skillet, with just the water that clings to the leaves, for a couple of minutes, until the spinach wilts and turns bright green. Squeeze out excess water and chop.
- Purée cooked spinach with other green vegetables (green onions, celery, peas) and some garlic, and then thin with stock and cream for a fast spring soup.

GREEN BREAKFAST SMOOTHIE

Fresh spinach or baby kale works perfectly in this healthy breakfast drink. This delicious green smoothie is also great for kids! MAKES ABOUT 4 CUPS.

Combine all of the ingredients in a powerful blender (like a Vitamix) and purée for 2 minutes until bright green and smooth.

2 apples, cored

2 cups baby spinach

5 pieces frozen peach or pineapple

1 Tbsp chopped fresh ginger

1 cup pure fresh-pressed apple juice

½ cup almond milk

Juice of half a lemon

VEGETARIAN SPINACH and RICOTTA LASAGNA

Start with oven-ready lasagna noodles and this vegetarian dish comes together quickly, even on a weeknight. SERVES 6.

Preheat the oven to 350°F.

Pour 1 cup of the tomato sauce into a 13- × 9-inch lasagna pan to cover the bottom. Place 3 or 4 lasagna noodles side by side over the sauce (the noodles should be close together but not touching, as they will expand as they cook).

In a sauté pan, heat the olive oil and sauté the onion and garlic until they are soft and just beginning to brown. Stir in the chopped spinach and heat through. Season with salt and pepper.

Layer the cooked spinach mixture evenly over the noodles in the pan. Top with 3 or 4 more noodles and 1 cup of the sauce.

In a bowl, beat the egg. Add the white pepper, nutmeg, ricotta cheese, and ½ cup of the Italian cheese mixture. Mix well and spread evenly over the noodles and sauce.

Top with 3 or 4 additional noodles. Pour the remaining 1 cup of sauce overtop. Sprinkle evenly with the remaining grated cheese.

Bake for 40 to 45 minutes, until the noodles are tender and the cheese is lightly browned on top. Let the lasagna stand for 10 minutes before cutting.

1 (24 oz) jar good-quality tomato sauce (about 3 cups), divided

1 box oven-ready lasagna noodles (9 to 12 noodles)

2 Tbsp olive oil

1 medium onion, chopped

1 clove garlic, minced

1½ cups cooked spinach, about 2 lb fresh spinach (or 1 [10 oz] box frozen spinach, thawed and squeezed to remove excess moisture)

Salt and freshly ground black pepper, to taste

1 large egg

Pinch white pepper

Pinch ground nutmeg

2 cups ricotta cheese

1½ cups grated Italian cheese mixture (mozzarella and Parmesan), divided

TIP

Make sure you read the label when buying tomato sauce— look for natural, low-fat versions made with tomatoes and vegetables, with no hydrogenated oils, and no excess sugars or preservatives.

BACON and TOMATO RISOTTO with SPINACH

This technique turns basic risotto into an electric-green treat that's not only colorful but also delicious. Quickly blanching and cooling is the secret to locking the bright green color into spinach, herbs, and other greens, whether you're making a quick sauté or a pesto. Make sure to buy good-quality, artisan-style bacon from your local butcher for this dish. **SERVES 4.**

Bring a large pot of water to a boil. Place the spinach in a sieve and submerge it in the boiling water for 10 seconds. Remove immediately and submerge in a bowl of ice water to chill. When cooled, drain and squeeze the spinach to remove any excess moisture.

In a blender, combine the cream and spinach and blend until smooth. Set aside.

In a large sauté pan over medium, heat the olive oil and sauté the onion, garlic, and bacon until the onion is soft and the bacon is crisp.

Add the rice and stir for 1 minute to toast the rice, then add the wine and simmer until it has been absorbed. Add the chicken stock, a ladleful at a time, stirring until it is absorbed by the rice.

Continue adding stock until the rice is almost al dente (tender but a bit chewy), then stir in the spinach purée.

Bring back to a low simmer, stirring until all of the liquid has been absorbed. The risotto should be creamy and a little loose.

Stir in the Parmigiano-Reggiano and cherry tomatoes. Season with salt and pepper and serve immediately.

4 cups baby spinach, well washed, divided

⅓ cup heavy cream

2 Tbsp olive oil

1 small onion, minced

2 cloves garlic, chopped

4 thick slices double-smoked bacon, chopped

1 cup Arborio rice

¼ cup white wine

4 cups chicken stock, warmed

½ cup grated Parmigiano-Reggiano

1 cup cherry tomatoes, quartered

Salt and freshly ground black pepper, to taste

TOMATOES

Buy

Best when vine-ripened in summer, though less flavorful hothouse versions are available year round. Heirloom tomatoes come in all shapes, sizes, and colors and often have the best flavor.

Store

Stored at room temperature, tomatoes will ripen—put them in the fridge only when fully ripe. Freeze tomatoes whole, unpeeled, in zippered plastic bags. When you want to use them for soups or sauces, run frozen tomatoes under hot water and the skins will pop right off. Or cook with basil and salt, and seal in jars to can. Use the oven or a dehydrator to dry Romas.

Serve

Tomatoes are standard in every mixed green salad, essential in tomato salsa and Italian bruschetta, and important components in soups, stews, pasta sauces, and pizza. Or just broil with cheese for breakfast.

Don't Waste It!

- Cut Romas into quarters, discard seeds, arrange on a parchment-lined baking sheet, season with olive oil and salt and pepper, and oven roast at 300°F for about 1 hour until chewy.

- Spear cherry tomatoes with baby bocconcini that have been rolled in basil pesto and olive oil for instant appetizers.

- Chop fresh tomatoes and combine with olive oil and chopped fresh garlic and basil, then pile on toasted bread for classic bruschetta.

- Slice tomatoes, arrange on a platter, and season with sea salt, a drizzle of your best olive oil, and balsamic vinegar. Strew around some chopped fresh herbs and serve.

- Toss chopped fresh cherry tomatoes with hot pasta, olive oil, fresh basil, pressed garlic, and Parmesan.

- Slather a pizza shell or pita bread with basil pesto, top with chopped tomatoes and mozzarella, and bake at 400°F until bubbly.

- Make fresh pico de gallo with chopped fresh tomatoes, minced white onion, chopped jalapeno, salt, lime juice, and chopped cilantro, to scoop up with tortilla chips or add to fish tacos.

- For a fast fresh tomato sauce, sauté onion and garlic in olive oil until browned, deglaze with a splash of white wine, add 3 cups chopped fresh or canned tomatoes, some basil pesto, and salt and pepper. Simmer for 10 minutes. Add sautéed meatballs or fresh Italian sausage to up the ante, and toss with hot cooked pasta.

- Cut up a variety of small and large red and yellow tomatoes, drizzle with olive oil and salt and pepper, and roast at 400°F for about 25 minutes, then toss with cooked couscous or quinoa.

- Cut medium tomatoes in half horizontally, arrange cut side up on a baking sheet, drizzle with olive oil, season with salt and pepper, minced garlic, and parsley, and bake at 400°F for 25 minutes. Serve with eggs for breakfast.

- Boil 12 large Roma tomatoes with 12 seeded serrano chiles, 2 sliced onions, and 8 garlic cloves for 30 minutes. Purée with 1 cup beer, simmer for 30 minutes, and season with salt and lots of chopped cilantro. For pasta, grilled chicken, or burritos.

- For a quick chilled tomato soup, purée 12 ripe tomatoes, remove and discard the seeds and skins, and thin the pulp with tomato juice. Season with salt and pepper, sugar, and lime juice, and serve topped with a little fresh herb and tomato relish.

FRESH TOMATO TART on a CORNMEAL CRUST

This contemporary tart is inspired by those served in the south of France. Use a variety of colorful heirloom tomatoes and try a sprinkling of herbes de Provence (or some fresh chopped rosemary, lavender, and thyme) for added authenticity. To speed up the process, use a precooked flatbread base. SERVES 6.

For the tart shell, combine half of the flour with the yeast and water. Let stand for 5 minutes to proof. Add the remaining flour, cornmeal, olive oil, honey, and salt. Knead with enough extra flour to make a smooth, elastic dough. Form the dough into a ball, rub with olive oil, and set aside for 1 hour, covered, to rise.

Preheat the oven to 450°F.

Punch the dough down and roll into a rectangle. Sprinkle an oblong baking sheet with cornmeal and fit the dough into the pan, rolling and crimping the edges. Prick the surface all over with a fork. Bake for 10 minutes. Reduce heat to 350°F and bake for another 10 minutes, until golden. Set aside.

Overlap the tomato slices on a deep platter or dish and season with salt and pepper. Set aside for 1 hour. The salt will leach some of the liquid from the tomatoes. Remove the tomatoes with a slotted spoon and arrange over the tart crust. Discard the liquid.

Preheat the broiler. Combine the olive oil, garlic, basil, and parsley, and sprinkle overtop of the tomatoes. Sprinkle with the cheese. Place the tart under the broiler until the cheese begins to bubble and brown. Cut the tart into squares and serve warm or at room temperature.

Tart shell:

1½ cups unbleached flour

2 tsp active dry yeast

¾ cup warm water

¾ cup cornmeal

1 Tbsp olive oil

1 Tbsp honey

½ tsp salt

Topping:

8 medium to large heirloom tomatoes, sliced (aim for a variety of colors)

Salt and freshly ground black pepper

3 Tbsp extra-virgin olive oil

3 cloves garlic, minced

¼ cup chopped fresh basil

2 Tbsp chopped fresh parsley

¾ cup finely grated Parmigiano-Reggiano and/or Asiago cheese

SPICY HOMEMADE SALSA

There's no better bonding exercise than a day of slaving over a hot stove to create pretty jars of homemade preserves. Make salsa in September, when the farmers' market is overflowing with cheap and delicious flats of ripe Roma tomatoes and multi-colored hot and sweet peppers. Worth the work. **MAKES ABOUT 8 CUPS OF SALSA. (YOU CAN EASILY DOUBLE OR TRIPLE THE RECIPE, THOUGH.)**

In a large, nonreactive pot (stainless steel is the best), combine the tomatoes, banana peppers, onions, jalapeno chiles, cider vinegar, red and yellow bell peppers, garlic, tomato paste, sugar, salt, paprika, and oregano. Bring to a boil over medium-high heat, stirring often to prevent the salsa from sticking and burning on the bottom. When the mixture is boiling, reduce the heat to medium-low. Continue to simmer for 1 to 2 hours, until the salsa is thickened to your liking. Remember, you want it to be scoopable, not runny.

Remove from heat and stir in the cilantro. Add enough Asian chili paste to make the salsa as hot as you like it. Peppers have different levels of heat, depending on how they have been grown, so you may need to adjust the recipe.

When you're satisfied with the flavor and texture, prepare your jars. Use 1-cup canning jars with 2-part metal lids. Wash the jars and lids well and rinse in boiling water. Using a wide-mouthed funnel, ladle the salsa into the jars, leaving ¼ inch of head space at the top to allow for expansion. Wipe the edges of the jars with a clean cloth, center the lids on top, and tighten the screw bands. They should just be "fingertip" tight.

Place the jars in a canning kettle filled with boiling water. The water must be a couple of inches above the tops of the jars. Return the water to a rolling boil and process the salsa for 20 minutes.

Lift the jars from the water using tongs, and cool on a folded kitchen towel on the counter. The lids should pop and snap down as the salsa cools, indicating that the jars are properly sealed and safe. Salsa will keep in a cool dark place for 1 year or more. Refrigerate after opening.

> **✎ TIP**
> Decide how chunky you want your salsa, then chop the tomatoes, peppers, and onions in a uniform dice (I like a ¼-inch or so). Wear gloves while chopping hot peppers and never touch your eyes.

8 cups chopped ripe Roma tomatoes (about 3 lb)

4 cups chopped banana peppers (medium hot), seeds removed

2 cups chopped onions

1 cup chopped fresh jalapeno or serrano chiles, seeded

1 cup apple cider vinegar

½ cup chopped red bell pepper

½ cup chopped yellow bell pepper

4 cloves garlic, minced

1 (5½ oz) can tomato paste

2 Tbsp granulated sugar

1 Tbsp salt

2 tsp Hungarian paprika

2 tsp dried oregano

½ cup chopped fresh cilantro

2 tsp Asian chili paste, or to taste

WINTER SQUASH or PUMPKIN

Buy

There are many varieties of winter squash and pumpkin, from small pie pumpkins to bulbous turban squash, yellow spaghetti squash, buff butternut, and green-skinned acorn. Choose a squash that's heavy for its size, with a stem that's dry but intact and a dense but dull, matte skin with no cracks or soft spots. Favorites for sweetness: sweet dumpling and carnival. For cubes, the large neck of butternut.

Store

Squash and pumpkins keep well for 2 to 3 months (some even longer) in a cool dark place, around 55°F (13°C) with 60 percent humidity (a cool basement). If you have a bumper crop to store, wipe the outsides with a vinegar solution, dry well, wrap loosely in paper, and keep on an open shelf to allow air circulation.

Serve

Squash and pumpkin are versatile, turning up in classic dishes from creamy squash soup to main courses and desserts. Think about squash for curries, gnocchi, risotto, and vegetable mashes, too.

Don't Waste It!

- Cut sweet butternut squash into sticks to serve raw.
- Poke holes in a whole unpeeled squash with a fork or skewer, then wrap in plastic to microwave (or foil to bake in the oven) until tender. Discard seeds and season the flesh with butter and salt and pepper.
- Slice small pumpkins or squash into rings or wedges, toss with oil, sugar, cinnamon, and salt, and bake until tender.
- Swap half of the oil in your favorite carrot cake recipe with puréed pumpkin to reduce the fat.
- For a frozen pumpkin dessert, purée cooked pumpkin with softened vanilla ice cream or frozen yogurt, then fill a crushed gingersnap crust, and freeze.
- Add cooked and puréed pumpkin to tomato sauce to make it creamier.
- Add spaghetti squash "noodles" to chicken broth.
- Cut firm delicata squash into sticks, toss with olive oil, and bake at 400°F for oven fries.
- Brush small acorn squash halves with butter and cinnamon and bake, then serve warm, filled with maple walnut ice cream.
- Combine leftover squash with leftover potatoes (boiled or mashed) and other cooked veg (carrots, Brussels sprouts), cook in olive oil, mashing, to create a hash that's nicely browned and crisp to serve as a side with breakfast eggs.
- Use cooked butternut squash or pumpkin in cookies and muffins.
- Halve small squash (sweet dumpling or carnival), remove seeds, and fill with stuffing made with bread or rice and cheese, then bake until tender.

CREAMY COCONUT SQUASH SOUP ~

Here's a rich, colorful soup to start a special dinner, or simply serve it in a big bowl for lunch. A great way to make healthy and inexpensive winter squash both exotic and addictive. **SERVES 6.**

In a soup pot over medium, heat the oil and sauté the red pepper, shallots, garlic, and ginger for 3 minutes, or until softened. Stir in the fish sauce, sugar, chicken stock, chili paste, and white pepper, and bring to a boil.

Add the squash to the pot, cover, and simmer until tender, about 20 minutes.

Using a slotted spoon, transfer the solids to a food processor and purée until smooth. Return the purée to the liquid in the pot and add the coconut milk. Bring to a boil, then remove from the heat and stir in the lime juice. Season with salt and pepper.

For the lime ginger cream, in a small bowl, whisk together the sour cream, lime juice, lime zest, and ginger.

Serve the soup with a dollop of the cream and garnish with a little chopped cilantro.

1 Tbsp canola oil

½ red bell pepper, seeded and finely chopped

2 shallots, minced

1 large clove garlic, minced

2 tsp minced fresh ginger

2 tsp Asian fish sauce

2 tsp granulated sugar

3 cups chicken stock

½ tsp Asian garlic chili paste (sambal oelek)

Pinch white pepper

2 cups peeled and cubed butternut squash

1½ cups light coconut milk (1 [14 oz] can)

2 tsp fresh lime juice

Salt and freshly ground black pepper, to taste

Chopped fresh cilantro, for garnish

Lime ginger cream (optional):

⅓ cup sour cream

1 tsp fresh lime juice

1 tsp finely grated lime zest

½ tsp minced fresh ginger (use a garlic press to release the juice)

PUMPKIN CUSTARD

This is like pumpkin pie, but without the crust and all of the extra work and calories. Bake in little custard cups for individual holiday desserts. **SERVES 6–8.**

¾ cup granulated sugar

3 Tbsp water

1 cup half-and-half

1 cup evaporated skim milk

2 Tbsp dark rum

Pinch salt

3 large eggs

1½ cups cooked puréed pumpkin or canned pumpkin purée (not pie filling)

⅓ cup packed brown sugar

1 tsp cornstarch

½ tsp ground cinnamon

½ tsp ground ginger

½ tsp ground mace

Whipped cream, to top

In a heavy skillet over medium, heat the granulated sugar and water, stirring, until the sugar dissolves. Increase the heat and boil without stirring until the mixture turns golden brown, swirling the pan occasionally and using a wet pastry brush to rinse any sugar from the sides of the pot. This should take about 10 minutes.

Working quickly, pour the caramelized sugar into an ungreased 8-cup round soufflé or baking dish, swirling to coat. Set aside to allow the sugar to harden. You can also do this in 6 or 8 individual ovenproof soufflé molds, for individual desserts.

Preheat the oven to 350°F.

In a heavy saucepan over medium heat, bring the half-and-half, evaporated milk, and rum to a boil. Remove from heat and stir in the salt.

In a large bowl, whisk together the eggs, pumpkin, brown sugar, cornstarch, cinnamon, ginger, and mace to blend well. Gradually whisk in the hot milk mixture.

Pour the custard into the prepared baking dish. Place the dish in a larger baking pan filled with 2 inches of hot water. Bake the custard for about 1 hour, until set and puffed. Remove from the water and cool. Cover with plastic wrap and chill overnight.

Before serving, run a knife around the edge of the dish and invert the custard onto a rimmed plate. The caramel sauce should form a pool around the custard. Cut into wedges and serve with a little sauce spooned over each piece and a dollop of whipped cream on the side.

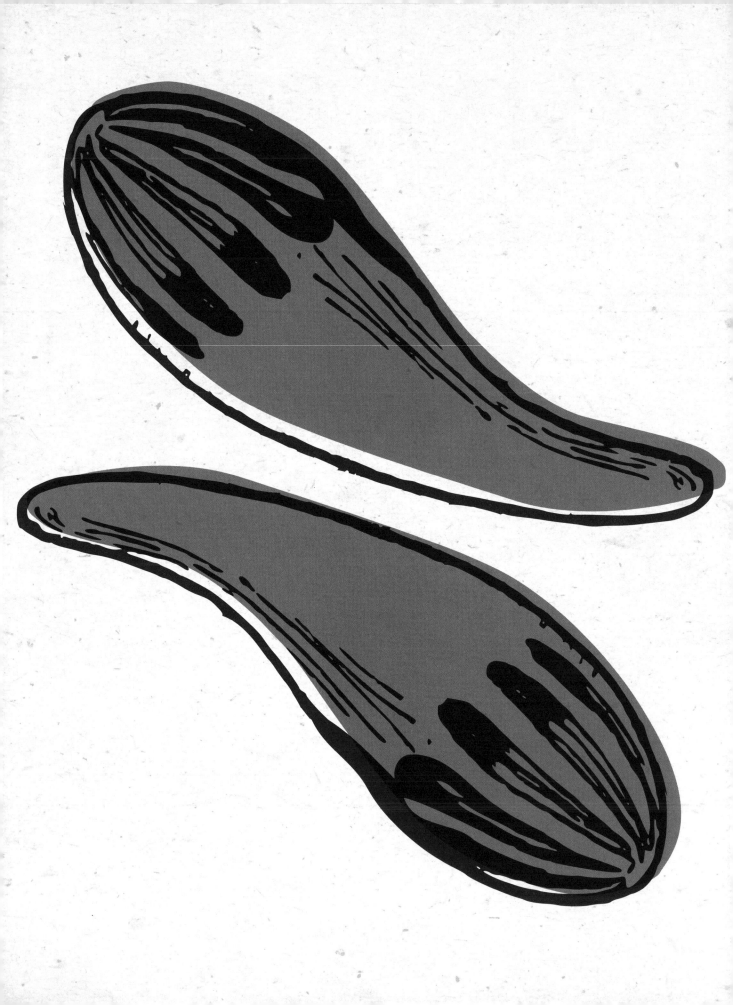

ZUCCHINI

Buy

Perishable summer squash, like zucchini, grows large but should be purchased when small and young in summer. Usually dark green but may be yellow or pale green.

Store

Refrigerate for up to 4 days. Shred and freeze in measured portions to add to breads or cakes.

Serve

Zucchini is a fresh, sweet summer squash that takes well to grilling and roasting, soaks up flavor, and marries well with other Mediterranean ingredients, from tomatoes to eggplant. You can even serve it raw.

Don't Waste It!

- Combine shredded zucchini and shredded potatoes with minced onion, egg, and bread crumbs, then fry in oil to make savory zucchini fritters. Serve with sour cream and chives.

- Sauté grated zucchini in butter until tender, about 5 minutes, then toss with cooked short pasta, chopped fresh mint, and salt and pepper.

- Cut zucchini into slices, brush with olive oil, season with salt and pepper, and grill until tender.

- Like carrot cake, zucchini spice bread is an easy way to use up excess squash. Grate your zucchini and freeze in 1-cup or 2-cup portions to add to your recipes.

- Slice zucchini, salt, and squeeze to remove some of the liquid, then layer with noodles, cheese, and tomato sauce in your favorite lasagna recipe.

- Slice small zucchini and toss with salt. Let stand for 15 minutes, then squeeze out excess liquid. Add rice vinegar, sugar, sesame oil, garlic, and chopped chiles for a fast Asian pickle.

- Use a vegetable peeler to create long, thin zucchini ribbons, then sauté with garlic and olive oil to toss with pasta.

- Substitute zucchini for cucumbers in your hamburger relish or pickle recipes.

- Chop zucchini into small cubes and add raw it to potato or pasta salads for color and crunch.

- Oversized zucchini? Slice into 2- to 3-inch chunks and hollow out. Sauté chopped onions, garlic, and Italian sausage meat (removed from casings) until brown, then mix with bread crumbs, a little broth, and grated mozzarella cheese. Stuff zucchini chunks, top with tomato sauce, and bake at 350°F for 30 minutes.

ZUCCHINI GRATIN

In summer, serve this fresh vegetarian dish warm or cold. **SERVES 4.**

❧ ❧ ❧ ❧ ❧ ❧ ❧ ❧ ❧ ❧ ❧ ❧ ❧

In a sauté pan over medium-high, heat 2 tablespoons of the olive oil. Add the onion and cook for about 10 minutes, until soft and beginning to brown. Reduce heat to low, cover the pan, and sweat for 10 minutes. Remove the lid and sprinkle the onion with the sugar. Continue to cook, stirring, until the onion is nicely caramelized. Set aside.

Preheat the oven to 350°F.

Drizzle 1 teaspoon of the olive oil into a shallow gratin dish, and arrange a third of the zucchini in the dish, overlapping in concentric circles. Top with half of the caramelized onion. Add half of the tomatoes, a third of the minced garlic, a little thyme and salt and pepper, and about ¼ cup of the bread crumbs.

Repeat the layers. Add a final layer of zucchini, season with the remaining garlic and thyme and a little salt and pepper, and top with ½ cup of the bread crumbs and the remaining 1⅔ tablespoons of olive oil.

Bake for 1 hour. Drain any excess liquid, top with cheese, if using, and bake for another 20 to 30 minutes, until bubbling and browned.

4 Tbsp olive oil, divided

1 large onion, thinly sliced

½ tsp granulated sugar

3 lb small zucchini, sliced

6 ripe Roma tomatoes, thinly sliced

6 cloves garlic, minced

1 tsp chopped fresh thyme

Salt and freshly ground black pepper, to taste

1 cup fresh or dried bread crumbs

Optional toppings:

1 cup grated Gruyère cheese

½ cup grated Pecorino cheese

SPICY ZUCCHINI and ONION FRITTERS

These Indian-inspired appetizers are easy to make, and you can add any fresh vegetables to the tasty pakora batter (slivered carrots, potatoes, cauliflower, etc.). SERVES 4.

Combine the chickpea flour, baking powder, cumin, coriander, cayenne, turmeric, salt and pepper, and cilantro. Add the zucchini, onion, and jalapeno chiles to the dry ingredients, tossing to coat.

Drizzle in a little of the water, mixing with your hands, just until the batter comes together enough to hold the vegetables into a loose mass (you don't want a runny batter; it should be quite dry).

Heat the oil in a wok over medium. When the oil is sizzling (about 350°F), add the battered vegetables, a small handful at a time. Cook in batches to ensure the oil remains hot. Cook the fritters slowly, until golden brown (if the oil is too hot, they will be gooey in the center). Drain the fritters on paper towels and keep warm in an oven heated to 200°F.

Serve hot with chutney.

1 cup chickpea flour

½ tsp baking powder

½ tsp ground cumin

½ tsp ground coriander

½ tsp cayenne

½ tsp ground turmeric

Salt and freshly ground black pepper, to taste

2 Tbsp chopped fresh cilantro

1 medium zucchini, cut into julienne strips

1 medium onion, cut into thin slivers

2 fresh jalapeno chiles, seeded and chopped

¼ to ½ cup water

2 cups canola oil, for frying

Coriander chutney, for dipping

FAT-FREE CHOCOLATE ZUCCHINI CAKE

Here's a great way to hide zucchini and make a tasty cake that's fat-free, too. SERVES 8.

Preheat the oven to 350°F. Coat a Bundt pan with nonstick spray.

Sift the all-purpose flour, cake flour, and baking soda together in a bowl. Stir in the cocoa powder, cinnamon, and salt.

In another bowl, whisk together the prune purée, sugar, corn syrup, and vanilla. Add to the dry ingredients. Stir in the grated zucchini. In a separate bowl, beat the egg whites until stiff. Fold them into the batter to lighten the mixture.

Pour the batter into the prepared pan. Bake for about 1 hour and 15 minutes, until a tester inserted in the center of the cake comes out clean.

1½ cups all-purpose flour

⅔ cup cake or pastry flour

2 tsp baking soda

1 cup cocoa powder

2 tsp ground cinnamon

1 tsp salt

1 cup prune purée (or prune baby food) (see Tip)

1⅔ cups granulated sugar

¾ cup corn syrup

1½ tsp vanilla extract

1 lb grated zucchini

2 egg whites

TIP

To make prune purée, combine 1⅓ cups pitted prunes with 6 tablespoons water and process until smooth in a food processor.

STAPLES

BACON

Buy

Ironically, now that bacon has become the food that goes with everything, buying it in bulk is really not the way to go. Instead find a good artisan butcher who specializes in all things pig and get some double-smoked bacon, sliced to your specifications. Or buy rolled Italian pancetta or Canadian back bacon (which is cut from loin, not pork belly). Avoid commercially packaged bacon that is filled with sugar, nitrites, and other chemicals. Look for local pork from ethically raised pastured pigs and you'll have tastier bacon and sausages.

Store

Good bacon is smoked so it has a fairly long shelf life, but if you get a few pounds from your butcher, divide it into 4- to 6-strip packages and freeze (a vacuum-packaging system is your friend).

Serve

Of course, bacon goes with eggs for breakfast, but it's also perfect in sandwiches, on burgers, added to pasta dishes, or crumbled over salads and soups.

Don't Waste It!

- Pour hot bacon fat (drippings) into a small glass jar or bowl to store in the refrigerator. Use bacon fat for frying potatoes.

- Use the center cut of your bacon for breakfast strips; cut off the ends and chop them up for flavoring stews and soups.

- Wrap beef steaks (like filet mignon) in bacon before grilling.

- Sauté chopped bacon with greens like kale or chard.

- Make bacon jam by cooking bacon until crisp, caramelizing chopped onions in the bacon fat with a little garlic and brown sugar, then combining with the reserved crumbled bacon. Store in a jar in the fridge.

- For white bean or lentil soup, start by sautéing smoky bacon or pancetta, chopped onions, carrots, and garlic. Add stock and beans or lentils, then simmer until tender and finish with chopped fresh rosemary or thyme and a splash of balsamic vinegar.

- Make a Bloody Mary or Caesar cocktail with bacon-infused vodka, and garnish with a piece of crispy bacon.

- Wrap chicken breasts in bacon and brush with a mixture of maple syrup and Dijon mustard before grilling.

- Brush bacon with maple syrup and bake at 400°F on a rack on a baking sheet, brushing with extra maple syrup to glaze.

- Make a toasted BLT on whole-wheat toast with a slather of mustard mayo, shredded lettuce, crispy side or back bacon, and sliced ripe tomatoes. Top with aged cheddar, melting it under the broiler.

- In a large pot over medium-high, sauté chopped bacon with minced garlic and shallots. Add fresh mussels in the shell, raise heat to high, and steam for 2 to 3 minutes. Finish with a glug of heavy cream and some chopped Italian parsley.

STONE SOUP

Making stone soup with just a little of this and a little of that is the classic story of cooking with leftovers. This soup starts with basic bacon and leftover tomato sauce. **SERVES 4–6.**

In a deep sauté pan over medium heat, cook the bacon until it begins to brown, then add the onion and garlic, and cook until tender. Drain off any excess fat and add the tomato sauce and chickpeas to the pan. Cover, reduce heat to low, and simmer for 15 minutes.

Meanwhile, in a large saucepan, bring the water to a boil and cook the pasta until al dente, about 3 to 5 minutes.

Add the sauce to the pasta pot (with the water) and stir to combine. Bring back to a boil and simmer for 15 minutes, adding more water if necessary.

Season with pepper and top each serving with a little grated Parmigiano-Reggiano.

½ lb bacon, cut into ¼-inch pieces

1 small onion, minced

4 cloves garlic, puréed

1 cup plain tomato sauce

1 (19 oz) can chickpeas, rinsed and drained

12 cups water

1 lb small soup pasta (macaroni, ditali, orzo, etc.)

Freshly ground black pepper, to taste

Grated Parmigiano-Reggiano, for garnish

FOOD FOR THOUGHT

We may waste far more food today than in previous generations because food is cheaper and more plentiful in First World countries than ever before. In 1961, food costs were 19 percent of household expenditures in the US—by 2008 that number dropped to hit an all-time low of 5.6 percent. At the same time, food waste increased by 77 percent.

WARM POTATO SALAD with BACON and MUSTARD DRESSING

Serve this warm potato salad in the fall with grilled chicken and apple sausages or alongside a baked ham. Make sure to use waxy red potatoes—they will hold their shape and toothsome texture, while other varieties will fall apart in the pot. **SERVES 4–6.**

Sauté the bacon until crisp. Remove from the pan and drain off all but 1 tablespoon of fat. Set the bacon aside.

Sauté the onion in the bacon fat until it starts to become translucent. Add the garlic and cook for 1 minute. Set aside.

In a large bowl, whisk together the mayonnaise, olive oil, vinegar, mustard, brown sugar, dill, and black pepper.

Cook the potatoes in boiling water until just barely cooked. Drain well. Return the pot to the stove over low heat and add the potatoes to dry well. (You can also toss the potatoes with a little olive oil and roast them at 400°F for about 45 minutes or until tender.)

Add the warm potatoes to the dressing. Toss to coat well, then stir in the sautéed onion and garlic and reserved crispy bacon. Serve warm.

6 slices double-smoked bacon, chopped

½ cup minced red onion or shallots

2 cloves garlic, minced

¼ cup mayonnaise

2 Tbsp olive oil

2 Tbsp apple cider vinegar

2 Tbsp grainy mustard

1 Tbsp brown sugar

2 tsp minced fresh dill

¼ tsp freshly ground black pepper

2 lb baby red potatoes, cut into 1-inch pieces

BREAD and FLATBREAD

Buy

Find a good baker and buy artisan loaves—chewy baguettes, sourdough white, or whole-grain and olive breads. For flatbreads like pita or naan, look for a local baker who makes them fresh, as frozen are rarely the same.

Store

To keep the crust crisp, artisan loaves should be stored in a paper bag. Some foil over the cut end will keep it fresh longer. Sliced bread freezes very well in a plastic bag (you can remove as much as you need) but don't refrigerate bread, as it will go stale faster. Freeze crusts and ends of loaves to use later in bread puddings, croutons, and stuffings. A good fresh artisan sourdough lasts longer than a commercial loaf without getting moldy. Use flatbreads immediately (they have a short shelf life) or seal in plastic, removing all the air, and freeze.

Serve

Offer bread and butter with soups and salads, use to make sandwiches, or just toast and enjoy with your morning eggs. Refresh slightly stale bread by reheating it for a few minutes in the oven. Use flatbreads for wraps of grilled kabobs and leftovers, or for dipping with curries and hummus.

Don't Waste It!

- Make a grilled cheese sandwich with bread that's not perfectly fresh. Add roasted peppers, portobello mushrooms, eggplant, black olive tapenade, pesto, or thin slices of prosciutto ham.
- Brush bread with olive oil, cut into cubes, season, and bake into crisp croutons to toss with Caesar salads or add to soup.
- Turn stale bread into crumbs in the food processor and freeze to use in stuffings or as topping for casseroles.
- Slice bread, brush with olive oil, and toast in the oven for crostini to top with bruschetta, tapenade, cheese, or hummus.
- Make rouille with bread crumbs, saffron, cayenne, garlic, egg yolks, and olive oil. This mayonnaise-like emulsion is great added to bouillabaisse.
- For maple French toast, beat eggs with cream or milk, a spoonful of maple sugar, and vanilla, then soak slices of white or raisin bread in the egg mixture, fry in butter to brown, and place in an oven heated to 350°F for 10 minutes to puff. Dust with icing sugar and serve with maple syrup.
- For breakfast muffins, cube day-old bread, soak in beaten eggs and milk, toss with grated cheese, chopped ham, and pepper, pack into paper-lined muffin tins, and bake until golden.
- Up-cycle a day-old crusty artisan loaf by making a classic muffuletta sandwich: cut the whole loaf in half, remove some of the interior bread, then layer with tapenade, sliced salami, prosciutto, roasted peppers, sliced cheese, olive oil, and fresh basil, then wrap well in foil, press under a weight in the fridge for a few hours, and cut into wedges for a picnic.
- Make personal pizzas with flatbreads: top with tomato sauce or pesto, a little sausage and/or veggies, and cheese, and bake at 400°F until bubbly.
- Cut pitas halfway around their circumference using kitchen shears, open like a pouch (with 2 flaps), and fill with falafels, leftover meat, lettuce, tomatoes, and garlicky yogurt sauce. Tuck one flap inside, over and around the filling, then tightly roll, with the other flap on the outside.

SAVORY BREAD PUDDING with SALMON and GREENS

This is classic comfort food and a mother recipe that works with all kinds of leftovers. As long as you have cheese, eggs, milk, and fresh herbs, feel free to use any other cooked vegetables, meats, or fish that you have on hand. Make it the night before and bake it for brunch, or whip it together after work for a fast family dinner with salad on the side. **SERVES 4.**

In a large nonstick sauté pan over medium, heat the olive oil and slowly cook the onion until soft and caramelized. This will take 30 minutes. Add the garlic halfway through cooking.

In a large bowl, toss the caramelized onion with the bread cubes, dill, and spinach. Mix in 1½ cups of the grated cheese.

Whisk together the eggs, milk, and salt and pepper. Pour this mixture evenly over the bread cubes and stir until most of the egg mixture has been soaked up by the bread.

Preheat the oven to 350°F. Lightly rub a deep, 8-inch round or oval casserole dish with olive oil. Layer half of the bread mixture in the dish. Break the salmon into chunks and spread evenly on top, then finish with the remaining bread cubes. Sprinkle with the remaining ½ cup of cheese.

Bake the casserole, uncovered, for 45 minutes, until the pudding is golden brown and crisp on top. Cool for 5 minutes before serving.

2 Tbsp olive oil

1 medium onion, chopped or thinly sliced

2 cloves garlic, minced

4 cups (2-inch) bread cubes (slightly stale French bread is the best)

2 to 3 Tbsp chopped fresh dill

3 cups chopped fresh spinach or chard

2 cups grated cheese (Gruyère, Gouda, Fontina, etc.), divided

4 eggs, lightly beaten

1 cup milk

½ tsp salt

½ tsp freshly ground black pepper

1 (7½ oz) can sockeye salmon, drained

PANZANELLA

This Italian bread salad combines roasted peppers and tomatoes with a red wine vinaigrette—lots of juicy stuff to keep cubes of toasted focaccia tasty and tender. You can also make this with day-old pita bread, torn into pieces, and substitute fresh mint and parsley for the oregano and basil, and you'll have Lebanese-style fattoush. **SERVES 6–8.**

Preheat the oven to 400°F.

In a large bowl, toss the red and yellow peppers, onion, and garlic with 2 tablespoons of the olive oil. Line a baking sheet with parchment paper and scatter the peppers, onion, and garlic around in a single layer. Season with salt and pepper.

Put the bread cubes on a second baking sheet, drizzle with 2 tablespoons of the olive oil, and season with salt and pepper.

Place both pans in the oven and cook for 10 to 15 minutes, moving the pans around and stirring the contents, until the bread cubes are nicely browned and the vegetables are starting to brown and caramelize, even slightly char.

In a large salad bowl, combine the roasted vegetables with the tomatoes. Whisk the remaining 4 tablespoons of oil with the red wine vinegar (or lemon juice) and mustard to form a vinaigrette and add it to the vegetables. Set aside for at least 10 minutes.

About 30 minutes before serving, add the toasted bread to the salad bowl, along with the oregano and basil, and toss to combine. Season with salt and pepper to taste.

1 red bell pepper, seeded and cut into large cubes

1 yellow bell pepper, seeded and cut into large cubes

1 small red onion, slivered

4 cloves garlic, halved

½ cup olive oil, divided

Sea salt and freshly ground black pepper, to taste

1 loaf plain focaccia bread, cut into ½-inch cubes (about 4 cups)

4 cups cherry tomatoes, halved or quartered

2 Tbsp red wine vinegar or fresh lemon juice

1 Tbsp Dijon mustard

2 Tbsp roughly chopped fresh oregano

2 Tbsp roughly chopped fresh basil

PITA CHIPS

Before your pita bread gets stale, make these simple chips. Tastier than commercial chips, they are also low in fat. Switch up the herbs and spices to create different flavor profiles (Tex-Mex, Cajun, Asian), depending on what you're dipping into. **MAKES 2 LARGE BAGS OF CHIPS.**

½ cup extra-virgin olive oil

3 cloves garlic, puréed in a press

2 packages pita bread (a mix of white and whole-wheat makes a nice contrast)

Variety of dried herbs and spices, like basil, oregano, thyme, cayenne, paprika, celery salt (see Tip)

Combine the olive oil and garlic in a bowl and let stand for 15 minutes. Preheat the oven to 400°F.

Separate each pita into 2 rounds (cut around the edges with kitchen shears). With a pastry brush, lightly brush the rough sides of the bread with the garlicky olive oil. Cut into wedges (or tear into chips for a more rustic look) and arrange on baking sheets, rough side up. Sprinkle with herbs and spices.

Bake for 3 to 4 minutes, watching carefully—these will go from golden brown to burnt very quickly. Cool and keep in sealed bags at room temperature.

TIP

Some spice combos work better than others. Try something traditional like Italian basil, oregano, and pepper, or something more exotic, like cumin, coriander, and chili powder or Chinese five-spice, ginger, and chili powder. A light dusting of cayenne adds sparkle to any combination.

Pita Chips pictured with Roasted Carrot Sesame Hummus (p. 62) and Chimichurri (p. 268).

CURRIED ROTI WRAPS

You'll find vendors selling rotis on the street in the Caribbean. These wraps make a perfect fast meal when you have leftover potatoes in the fridge. You can buy roti or paratha bread from the freezer section at your local Indian grocery store. You can also make these wraps with extra-large flour tortillas from the supermarket. Rotis are made for moving and carrying. It's a to-go lunch or dinner. **SERVES 4.**

In a large nonstick skillet over medium-high, heat the oil. Add the onion and fry for 5 to 10 minutes, until it is just beginning to brown. Add the garlic, curry powder, cumin (if using), and mustard seed (if using), and cook together until fragrant, about 2 minutes. Stir in the hot sauce.

Add the cooked potatoes to the pan and stir to coat them well with the spices. Cook together for 5 minutes to heat through. Add the salt. If you're using chickpeas or cauliflower, add them now and heat them up. Add the lime juice and stir in the cilantro.

Divide the filling among the tortillas, piling it in the center. Fold each roti like a square envelope—bottom up, sides in, top down—then wrap in waxed paper and/or foil for easy eating.

2 Tbsp canola oil

1 large onion, chopped (about 2 cups)

2 cloves garlic, minced

1 Tbsp curry powder

½ tsp ground cumin (optional)

½ tsp whole mustard seed (optional)

1 tsp hot sauce

1 lb red potatoes, cooked and cubed

⅛ tsp salt

1 cup cooked chickpeas (or canned chickpeas, rinsed and drained) or chopped, cooked cauliflower (optional)

Squeeze fresh lime juice

2 Tbsp chopped fresh cilantro

4 extra-large flour tortillas (or roti or paratha), very fresh

FRUITY BREAD and BUTTER PUDDING with CARAMEL SAUCE

This is the perfect recipe to use up leftover Italian fruit bread or panettone after the holidays. Raisin bread will work, too, but panettone, with its brioche background, anise, and peel, makes a richer pudding. SERVES 6.

In a saucepan over medium heat, combine the milk, cream, vanilla, orange, and fennel seeds, and bring to a boil. Remove from heat and set aside to infuse for 20 minutes.

Preheat the oven to 350°F.

In a bowl, whisk the sugar, eggs, and yolks together until light and fluffy. Strain the infused warm milk into the bowl, whisking continuously. Discard the orange pieces.

Cut the bread into ¼-inch slices, then cut each slice on the diagonal. Arrange the slices, overlapping, in a shallow oval baking dish, making 2 or 3 rows. Pour the milk mixture evenly overtop, pressing the bread into the custard so that it soaks up most of the liquid.

Place the baking dish in a roasting pan, and fill the roasting pan with about 1 inch of hot water (this is called a bain-marie—it keeps the pudding moist and creamy as it bakes).

Bake for about 30 minutes, until the pudding is just set in the middle. Let cool in the water bath.

Meanwhile, in a small saucepan over medium heat, boil the sweetened condensed milk with the cream until it turns a caramel color. This will take about 15 minutes. Stir it regularly to make sure it doesn't burn. Remove from heat and stir in the Grand Marnier, if using.

Serve the bread pudding warm or slightly chilled, drizzled with the warm caramel sauce.

2 cups milk

2 cups heavy cream

1 tsp vanilla extract

½ orange, chopped, including peel

½ tsp fennel seeds

1 cup granulated sugar

4 eggs

4 egg yolks

1 loaf panettone fruit bread or raisin bread, a little dry

Caramel sauce:

1 can sweetened condensed milk

½ cup heavy cream

1 Tbsp Grand Marnier (optional)

CANNED FISH

Buy

From tuna and salmon to baby shrimp, smoked salmon, anchovies, crabmeat, and sardines, canned fish is a pantry staple. Look for "wild caught" salmon (otherwise it's farmed); sockeye is premium. For tuna, premium is that labeled "solid white." Look for cans that are BPA-free (a common lining in tins) or buy "pouched" fish in BPA-free foil packages. The finest salmon and tuna is cold-packed (packed raw) in tins before processing, retaining all of the fish's natural juices and oils, but most is precooked before canning with oil or water added. Make sure to buy fish that's canned at high pressure in a tin (retort cooking) for food safety. Only use a pressure canner for canning at home.

Store

Keep your canned fish in a cool, dry place, and eat within 2 years. Once opened, refrigerate and consume within 2 days. Discard dented or rusting cans.

Serve

Canned tuna and salmon are perfect for tuna melts, cheesy noodle casseroles, cold fish salad sandwiches, and dips. Sardines, packed in oil or tomato sauce, make great snacks on Melba toast or crackers. Crabmeat goes into crab dip, seafood sauces, and casseroles; canned clams into chowder and pasta dishes.

Don't Waste It!

- For a fast tuna casserole, combine a good-quality macaroni and cheese mix with canned tuna, frozen peas, and chopped green onions.

- Make a creative tuna salad with good mayo, shredded carrot, and chopped fresh dill.

- Make a lemony aioli with lemon zest, Dijon mustard, egg yolks, lemon juice, and olive oil. Drizzle over canned tuna on toasts for easy appetizers.

- Combine a can of solid white tuna with canned white beans, roasted red pepper, sundried tomatoes, black olives, red onion, sour cream, Dijon, and mayo. Serve on a bed of bitter greens.

- Add a can of Italian tuna packed in olive oil to a fresh tomato sauce of chopped tomatoes, garlic, black olives, capers, basil, and green onion. Toss with hot chunky pasta like fusilli.

- Combine a can of smoked salmon with some low-fat cream cheese, dollops of mayo and horseradish, and some chopped green onions and fresh dill, for a dip or to roll up in flour tortillas and cut into pinwheels.

- Brown chopped leftover boiled potatoes and onions in butter, simmer with a glug of heavy cream, then toss with chunks of sockeye salmon and minced green onion for a decadent breakfast hash.

- Combine a can of sockeye salmon with leftover mashed potatoes and chopped green onion, then form into patties and fry in butter for crispy salmon cakes.

- Mix a can of sockeye salmon with a fresh salsa of chopped tomatoes, avocado, red onion, jalapeno, cilantro, lime juice, and olive oil to fill pita pockets.

- Make an omelet or quiche with canned salmon, beaten eggs, green onion, parsley or dill, roasted red peppers, and smoked mozzarella.

- Combine a can of baby shrimp with mayo and dill and stuff into halved avocados.

- Brush sliced baguette with olive oil, toast in a hot oven, and top with chopped tomato, minced garlic, chopped basil, and minced anchovies.

- Mash minced anchovies and combine with sweet butter to spread on toasts.

PAN BAGNAT

This sandwich recalls the south of France. Start with good-quality canned fish, and augment with leftovers. I especially like to make this when I have cold grilled eggplant and zucchini. **SERVES 4**.

Cut the bread or buns open. Combine the garlic, olives, basil, and olive oil. Spread over the cut sides of the bread.

Drain the anchovies and soak in cold water or milk for 5 minutes to remove excess salt. Pat dry.

Layer the onion, tomatoes, red pepper, and zucchini or eggplant (if using) over one half of the bread portions and top with the tuna and anchovies.

Add the top cuts of bread to form a sandwich (or sandwiches), wrap tightly in plastic wrap, and press (using a cutting board weighted with food), refrigerated, overnight.

Slice the baguette into 3-inch pieces to serve, or serve the buns cut in half.

1 baguette or 4 crusty buns

6 cloves garlic, minced

10 black olives, minced

1 Tbsp chopped basil
(or use basil pesto)

¼ cup olive oil

1 (2 oz) can flat fillets
of anchovies

1 small red onion, slivered

2 tomatoes, thinly sliced

1 large red bell pepper,
roasted and peeled (or
from a jar), cut into strips

2 small zucchini or 1 small
eggplant, slices brushed
with olive oil, grilled,
and chilled (optional)

1 (5 oz) can water-
packed tuna

KILLER CLAM CHOWDER

This makes a big batch of soup. With the red and green garnish of red pepper and parsley, it makes a nice addition to a Christmas Eve feast. It is also delicious as a simple everyday dinner. **MAKES 12 CUPS.**

In a saucepan over medium heat, combine ½ cup of the butter with the flour, and cook, stirring, for about 5 minutes to make a smooth roux.

Slowly add the fish stock to the roux, whisking as you add the liquid to prevent lumps.

In a separate soup pot over medium-low heat, melt the remaining ¼ cup of butter and sauté the carrots, onion, celery, and garlic, stirring until the vegetables are soft but not browned. Add the potatoes, thyme, and cayenne, and sauté for 5 minutes.

Add the base (the mixture of roux and stock) to the pot of sautéed vegetables. Lower the heat to low, and simmer for 20 minutes, stirring often to prevent scorching.

Add the half-and-half, and heat through. Stir in the clams and heat through but don't boil—the clams will get tough if you boil them. If your soup is too thick, thin it with some of the reserved clam juice. Adjust the seasoning with salt and white pepper.

Ladle the chowder in shallow soup plates and, for a festive touch, sprinkle on a pinch of red pepper and parsley. Serve the chowder with plenty of French bread.

¾ cup butter, divided

½ cup all-purpose flour

10 cups fish stock or bottled clam juice

½ cup chopped carrots

1 cup chopped onion

½ cup chopped celery

¾ tsp chopped garlic

2 cups diced peeled potatoes

1 tsp chopped fresh thyme

⅛ tsp cayenne

2 cups half-and-half

1 cup drained canned baby clams, juice reserved

Salt and white pepper, to taste

Finely chopped red bell pepper, to garnish (optional)

Minced parsley, to garnish (optional)

ROTINI with TUNA TAPENADE

Take a tin of Italian tuna in olive oil and whirl it with olives for tuna tapenade. Nothing could be simpler served with toasted baguette as an appetizer, but it's also awesome tossed quickly with any short pasta. Look for tiny tins of tuna packed in olive oil at Italian markets. **SERVES 4**.

In a food processor, combine the olives and garlic, and pulse until chopped but still chunky. Add the oil, tuna, mustard, hot sauce, and lemon juice. Pulse again to combine.

Process for a few seconds. The tapenade should be partly pasty and partly coarse. Add the lemon zest and parsley and pulse just to combine. Refrigerate.

Cook the rotini in a pot of boiling water until al dente; drain well. Toss the hot pasta with the tapenade and Parmigiano-Reggiano. Serve immediately.

1 cup pitted green olives (use the kind that are stuffed with anchovies if you can)

1 Tbsp minced garlic

2 Tbsp olive oil

1 (3½ oz) can tuna packed in olive oil

1 tsp grainy mustard

½ tsp hot sauce

Juice and finely grated zest of half a lemon

2 Tbsp chopped fresh parsley

¾ lb rotini or other short pasta

1 cup grated Parmigiano-Reggiano

SPICY CORN FRITTERS with SALMON and DILL

Make these savory corn cakes small and top with sour cream, chunks of canned wild salmon, and a sprig of fresh dill for appetizers. Or try adding the flaked salmon to the fritter batter, and serving the fritters alongside eggs for breakfast. **MAKES ABOUT 36 COCKTAIL-SIZED FRITTERS.**

Bring a pot of water to a boil and add the ears of corn. Cover and remove from heat. Let stand for 5 minutes. Drain the corn and cool, then cut the kernels from the cobs. Discard the cobs. (Skip this step if using canned. For frozen corn, thaw in a sieve under cold water.)

Place the corn kernels in a bowl with the jalapeno chiles, chipotle chile, red pepper, green onions, and garlic.

In food processor, combine the eggs, flour, cornmeal, baking powder, salt, milk, and yogurt, and whirl until smooth. Add the vegetables and pulse just to mix. Stir in the cilantro and black pepper. Let stand at room temperature for 30 minutes.

In a nonstick frying pan over medium, heat the canola oil. Working in batches, spoon a few dollops of the batter into the oil. Make the fritters each about 1 to 2 inches in diameter for appetizers, or larger if serving as a side dish. Cook, turning once, until golden on both sides. Drain on paper towels and keep warm. Repeat with the remaining batter.

To serve, top each fritter with a dollop of sour cream, a bit of salmon, and a sprig of dill.

Corn fritters:

3 ears fresh corn, shucked (or about 2 cups canned or frozen corn kernels)

2 fresh jalapeno chiles, seeded and minced

1 chipotle chile, chopped

1 red bell pepper, seeded and chopped

6 green onions, chopped

2 cloves garlic, minced

2 eggs

1 cup all-purpose flour

½ cup cornmeal

1 tsp baking powder

1 tsp salt

1 cup milk

¼ cup plain low-fat yogurt

3 Tbsp minced cilantro

Freshly ground black pepper, to taste

2 Tbsp canola oil, for frying

Topping:

½ cup sour cream

1 (7½ oz) can wild plain or smoked salmon, drained, bones removed

Sprigs fresh dill

CHEESE

Buy

Buy cheese from a good cheese-monger, one that has whole cheeses and will cut you a wedge from a wheel. Ask to taste a sample. Don't buy too much: for a party platter, offer 1 to 2 ounces of cheese per person.

Store

While most cheese is sold wrapped in plastic, quality cheese will actually keep, and age, better in your refrigerator if you wrap it in parchment or waxed paper and then loosely in a plastic bag, and store it in the cheese drawer, the warmest part of the fridge. It's possible to freeze hard cheese, but it will then be crumbly and only useful for cooking. You can cut blue or green mold away on hard cheeses, but when you see yellow or pink spots on soft cheese, or smell ammonia, it's spoiled and should be discarded.

Serve

Whether you buy a big block of aged cheddar, a double package of sliced provolone, or a chunk of Parmesan, you can save money by buying cheese in bulk. Just don't let it go to waste. Remember, a grating of authentic Italian Parmesan goes well over any pasta dish, is essential in risotto, and adds flavor to broccoli or asparagus. You can even try tossing some with your popcorn.

Don't Waste It!

- Make a sauce with 1 tablespoon of butter, 1 tablespoon of flour, ½ cup of beer or cider, a dash of dry mustard, and a dash of Worcestershire. Stir in 1 to 2 cups of grated cheese (this is the time to clean out the fridge and make a mix), then pour the sauce over thick slices of toast, and broil until brown. Top with a dash of paprika.

- Sprinkle grated cheese over sheets of puff pastry (from the supermarket freezer), then slice into long strips, twist, and bake for tasty cheese-straw appetizers.

- Slice a baguette into ½-inch slices, slather with goat cheese, and place under the broiler until melted and bubbly. Serve 2 or 3 of these warm cheese toasts over individual salads of mixed greens.

- When you buy expensive Parmigiano-Reggiano, don't discard the rind. Save these hard bits and use them to flavor pots of minestrone soup, as Italian nonnas have for generations.

- Put a piece of blue cheese and a slice of fresh fig on a bit of toasted baguette and drizzle with wildflower honey or reduced balsamic syrup for an instant appetizer.

- Like bacon, cheese goes with almost anything: grate it into a salad, over any pasta dish, over steamed vegetables, into an omelet, or into a toasted panini sandwich.

- When there are bits of various cheeses in the fridge, grate, melt with a little white wine, season with a dash of nutmeg, and serve as a cheese fondue for dipping French bread and steamed broccoli.

- Shred or crumble leftover cheeses (feta, cheddar, goat), mix with a little cream cheese and butter, roll into balls, then roll in toasted nuts and spices to make creative cheese-ball appetizers.

- Serve a traditional ploughman's lunch with bread and butter, green salad, chutney, and a few slabs of farmhouse cheddar.

CHEESY SHORTBREADS

These crackers are great on their own as a snack or served with more cheese. **MAKES ABOUT 36 COCKTAIL CRACKERS.**

In a food processor, combine the butter, cheese, flour, baking powder, nuts, hot sauce, and salt and pepper, and pulse just until the dough comes together.

Dump the dough onto a sheet of parchment paper or plastic wrap, form it into a log that's 2 inches in diameter, and roll up in the parchment or plastic wrap, twisting the ends to enclose. Chill the dough for at least 2 hours or freeze.

When you're ready to bake the shortbread, preheat the oven to 350°F, and line a baking sheet with parchment paper. Using a sharp knife, slice the roll of dough into ⅛-inch to ¼-inch slices and lay the slices on the baking sheet. Bake for 12 to 15 minutes, until the shortbreads begin to color around the edges. Cool on a wire rack.

½ cup cold butter, cut into cubes

1 cup grated cheese (½ Parmigiano-Reggiano, ½ aged cheddar or Stilton)

⅔ cup all-purpose flour

¼ tsp baking powder

½ cup finely ground nuts (pecans, almonds, or walnuts)

Dash hot sauce

½ tsp salt

½ tsp black pepper

CREAMY MAC and CHEESE

Real macaroni and cheese doesn't come out of a box. It starts with a simple cream sauce that's combined with grated cheese. Use aged cheddar or shred up a combination of hard cheeses you have left over in the fridge, even add leftover cream cheese or blue cheese for a gourmet twist, and use any short pasta you have in the pantry. **SERVES 2–4.**

Bring a large saucepan of water to a boil. Add the pasta and cook until al dente, about 8 to 10 minutes. Drain well.

In another pan over medium-high heat, melt the butter and when it's bubbling, stir in the flour. Cook, stirring, for about 2 minutes, until the flour just begins to brown, and slowly whisk in the milk, making sure that the sauce is smooth. Add the cream and simmer until bubbly, then whisk in the mustard and hot sauce. Remove from heat and add the cheese, a handful at a time, stirring just until melted. Season with salt and pepper.

Add the pasta to the sauce, return to the stove, and heat through over medium-low heat. Serve immediately.

3 cups elbow macaroni or other short pasta

2 Tbsp butter

1 heaping Tbsp all-purpose flour

1 cup milk

½ cup heavy cream

½ tsp Dijon mustard

¼ tsp hot sauce

2 cups grated aged cheddar (or combination of cheddar, Monterey Jack, Swiss, Pecorino Romano, or Parmigiano-Reggiano)

Salt and freshly ground black pepper, to taste

⚮ TIPS

For a more virtuous dish, try using 1 (13 oz) can of evaporated milk instead of the milk and cream. It makes a low-fat yet amazingly silky sauce for mac and cheese.

Turn your mac and cheese into something more substantial by adding leftovers to the mix. Cooked vegetables (think broccoli, roasted peppers, sautéed mushrooms, caramelized onions) can be folded in with the sauce. Or consider adding a tin of drained tuna or salmon, some chopped cooked chicken or Italian sausage, minced green onions and chopped spinach, or even a scoop of fresh tomato salsa.

CRISPY INSIDE-OUT GRILLED CHEESE

This is a delicious way to use up two kinds of cheese—presliced provolone or mozzarella and Havarti or Butterkase (butter cheese)— at once and enjoy all of the various flavors of cooked cheese, both gooey and creamy and crispy and brown. Simply the best grilled cheese sandwich you'll ever make. **MAKES 1 SANDWICH**.

2 slices bread (from an oval loaf of sourdough or light rye)

1 Tbsp mustard (Dijon, honey, grainy, whatever you like)

1 thick chunk Havarti or butter cheese

1 dill pickle, sliced paper thin (optional)

2 thin, large cheese slices (the oval slices of packaged mozzarella or provolone work perfectly for this technique)

Slather 2 slices of bread with mustard (if you really like mustard, you can spread it on both sides of each slice).

Cut the Havarti into ¼-inch to ½-inch slices, trim to fit, and place between the slices of bread, mustard sides out. If you like, add a few slices of dill pickle between the bread and cheese for added flavor.

Stick a slice of the second kind of cheese to the mustard on the outside of each slice of bread (you're aiming for a slice of cheese that is approximately the same size and shape as the slices of bread).

Heat up a smooth-sided sandwich press and place the sandwich in the press. Press the lid down and cook until the cheese on the outside is crisp and the cheese on the inside is soft.

Enjoy your sandwich while it's hot and crisp on the outside and gooey on the inside.

SMOKED CHICKEN and PEACH QUESADILLAS

Slivers of sweet juicy peaches are perfect with smoky chicken and salsa in these grilled quesadillas, to serve as appetizers or as a summer lunch with salad on the side. Make sure you don't overfill the tortillas (or they'll be sloppy, not crisp). Also, remember to watch the tortillas closely on the grill as they can burn quickly. Learn this technique and with some salsa, cheese, and cilantro, you will be able to recycle all kinds of leftovers, from sliced ham and pulled pork to roasted peppers, cooked black beans, and avocados, into tasty snacks. **MAKES ABOUT 30 WEDGES.**

10 flour tortillas

¼ cup olive oil

1 cup spicy tomato salsa (homemade or from a jar)

1 large, ripe freestone peach, cut into thin slivers

6 thin slices smoked chicken or turkey, slivered

¼ cup chopped fresh cilantro

2 cups grated Monterey Jack or mozzarella cheese

To make perfect quesadillas, learn this technique: Using a pastry brush, very lightly coat one side of a tortilla with oil. Lay the tortilla, oiled side down, on a plate. Spread a thin layer of salsa over the tortilla, to the edges, and top with a few slivers of peach, some slivers of smoked chicken or turkey, and a smattering of chopped cilantro. Sprinkle evenly with cheese. Top with a second tortilla, brush the tortilla lightly with oil, and press down with a spatula to seal the layers.

Continue to make quesadillas in this manner (you can just stack them up on the plate as you go). Remember to fill the quesadillas sparingly—too much filling is counterproductive, as your quesadillas will be soggy and difficult to eat. They should be a little gooey, but crisp.

Heat the barbecue to medium-high and, using a wide spatula, carefully transfer the quesadillas to the grill in batches. Cook on one side for 2 to 3 minutes, until it starts to brown and melt together, then quickly flip to cook the second side.

Repeat until all of the quesadillas are crispy on the outside and cooked through. Watch carefully so they don't burn.

Set the grilled quesadillas aside on a cutting board for a few minutes to cool before cutting into wedges. Serve immediately.

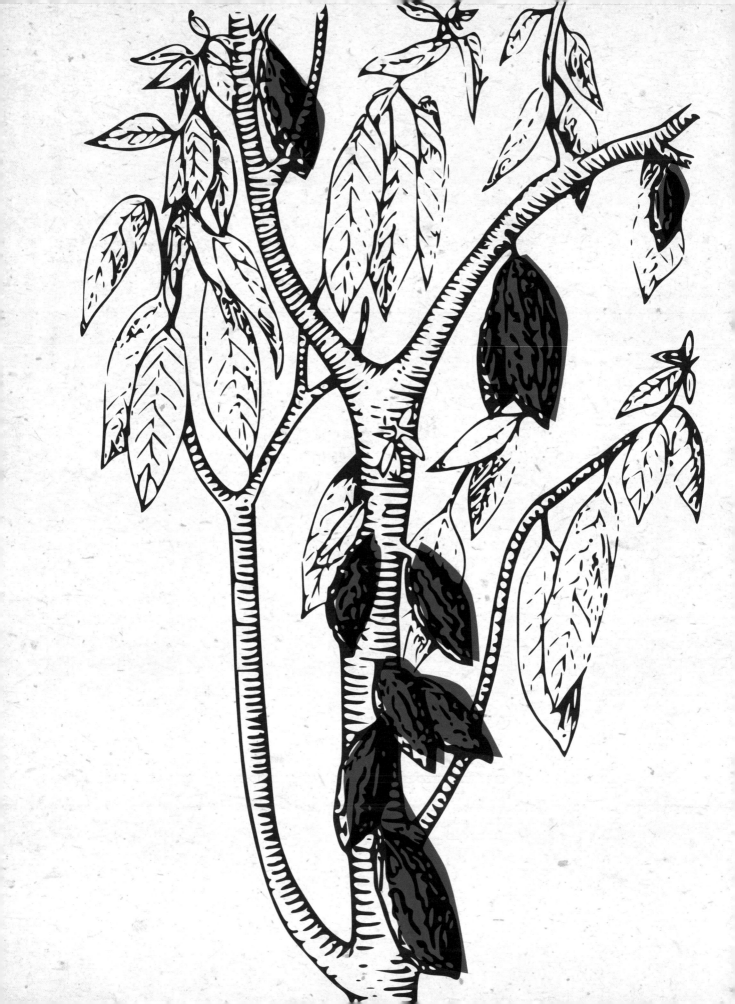

CHOCOLATE

Buy

Only buy real chocolate (containing cocoa butter, cocoa mass, or chocolate liquor, and some small amounts of sugar and lecithin), with at least 60 percent cacao. Milk chocolate will contain a lower percentage of cacao, and white chocolate is really only cocoa butter and sugar. When it comes to cocoa powder, or cocoa solids, look for Dutch-process cocoa.

Store

Store chocolate in a dark, dry place, away from strong smelling foods. Never refrigerate chocolate. Chocolate can develop a chalky white "bloom" because of temperature variations in storage—it's not beautiful but it won't affect the flavor. Store cocoa powder in a dark, airtight container (like the tin it comes in) for up to 2 years.

Serve

Chocolate is great served on its own—have a tasting of artisan bean-to-bar samples—or added to desserts, from cakes and cookies to mousses and tarts. You can also add bitter chocolate to savory sauces—think Mexican mole, cocoa-rubbed ribs, or spicy beef chili. Serve eating chocolate at room temperature for best flavor, texture, and aroma.

Don't Waste It!

- Make easy chocolate pudding by whisking milk into a mixture of cocoa powder, sugar, and cornstarch, and simmering until thickened. Add vanilla to taste and chill.

- For chocolate ganache, heat heavy cream just to boiling and stir in chopped high-quality chocolate, just until melted.

- For simple chocolate syrup, mix equal parts cocoa powder, sugar, and water in a saucepan and boil for 1 minute, then remove from heat and add a splash of vanilla. Refrigerate.

- Melt 4 ounces semisweet baking chocolate with an equal amount of smooth peanut butter and a tin of condensed milk for a warm, nutty chocolate sauce.

- Dip fresh strawberries or cherries in melted quality chocolate to coat, then set aside to allow the chocolate to harden.

- Combine chopped chocolate with instant coffee and top with near-boiling milk, stirring to melt the chocolate. When cool, combine in a blender with vanilla ice cream and blitz for mocha milkshakes.

- For simple chocolate sundaes, place a graham wafer in the bottom of a cereal bowl, drizzle with chocolate sauce, and top with a scoop of chocolate chunk ice cream, some marshmallow cream topping, and crumbled graham wafers.

- Stuff a chunk of dark chocolate into your croissants before baking for pain au chocolat.

- Make Mexican hot chocolate by melting special spiced Mexican chocolate (flavored with cinnamon and vanilla) into hot milk or water.

- Add shaved dark chocolate and cocoa to your pancake or waffle batter.

- Combine melted dark chocolate with salted pretzel pieces, heap onto a parchment-lined pan, and chill, for fast clusters.

CHICKEN in MOLE NEGRO

Chocolate is the secret ingredient to black mole. This recipe is inspired by the moles of Oaxaca. After you've made the mole paste, simply add broth to make the mole sauce. Use to braise chicken, as in this dish, or simply serve the sauce over grilled chicken or fish. **SERVES 6-8**.

Remove the veins and seeds from all of the varieties of chiles. Reserve the seeds. Toast the chiles in a hot, dry pan until puffed and softened, about 30 seconds to 1 minute. Be careful not to burn them. Place the chiles in a bowl (you should have about 4 to 5 cups of chiles, depending on their sizes), cover with hot water, and soak for 30 minutes. Drain, reserving the liquid.

If you like, turn on your oven's exhaust fan, and toast a handful of the chile seeds until they're completely blackened. Adding this chile "charcoal" to the sauce is traditional and adds to the black color.

In the same pan as you cooked the chiles, toast the cloves, cinnamon, peppercorns, oregano, and thyme over medium-high heat until the spices are aromatic (1 minute or less), then pour into a bowl to cool. Once cooled, grind the spices using a spice mill or mortar and pestle.

Heat the oven to 425°F and on a baking sheet, toast the sesame seeds, pumpkin seeds, almonds, and bread until browned, about 10 minutes. Set aside to cool.

On another baking sheet, drizzle the onion and garlic with 1 tablespoon of the canola oil. Add the tomatoes and roast in the oven until brown, about 45 minutes (if using canned tomatoes, skip this step). Cool.

In a blender or food processor, grind the toasted seeds and nuts and the chile seeds, if using, then add the bread and pulse to form crumbs. Add the spices and pulse to grind, then add the hydrated chiles, raisins, and plantain, and about 1 cup of the reserved soaking liquid. Blend until very smooth. Scrape out and set aside.

Don't clean the blender but add the roasted onion, garlic, and tomatoes. Blend until smooth. Add a little stock if necessary.

Mole paste:

4 mulato chiles

4 pasilla chiles

4 ancho chiles

1 small chipotle chile (dried or canned)

2 whole cloves

1 tsp ground cinnamon

¾ tsp black peppercorns

¾ tsp dried oregano

½ tsp dried thyme

¼ cup sesame seeds

¼ cup shelled pumpkin seeds

¼ cup raw almonds

1 slice white bread (or 1 fresh corn tortilla)

1 white onion, sliced

4 cloves garlic

4 Tbsp canola oil, divided

4 ripe Roma tomatoes (or 2 cups canned tomatoes, puréed)

2 Tbsp raisins

½ very ripe plantain, sliced

2 oz Mexican chocolate, chopped

2 Tbsp brown sugar

½ tsp salt

In a large Dutch oven over medium-high, heat the remaining 3 tablespoons of canola oil and add the tomato purée. Cook, stirring, until it's a thick, dark paste, about 10 minutes. Add the nut and spice purée, chocolate, brown sugar, and salt. Continue cooking, stirring, for 10 to 15 minutes, until you have a very dark, thick, almost black mass.

Your mole paste is now complete. Place it in the refrigerator to chill overnight. (You should have about 6 cups of mole paste—use 3 cups for this chicken dish and freeze the rest.)

The next day, continue with the sauce. In a large saucepan over medium-high heat, slowly whisk the stock into the mole paste and bring to a boil.

Cut the chicken thighs into large chunks, add to the sauce, cover, and simmer for 1 hour until tender and thick, adding more stock if necessary. Shred the chicken and serve over rice or roll up in tortillas.

It's traditional to sprinkle a few toasted sesame seeds overtop to garnish.

3 cups chicken or turkey stock (homemade, if possible), plus more as needed

2 lb boneless, skinless chicken thighs

Toasted sesame seeds, for garnish

➣ **TIP**

You can prepare and serve a mole the same day, but the flavors really improve if you let the sauce rest overnight (or even for a couple of days) in the refrigerator.

DOUBLE CHOCOLATE COOKIES

A killer cookie for chocolate lovers. Be careful to not overbake—these cookies should be crispy on the outside and a little chewy inside. **MAKES ABOUT 24 COOKIES.**

In the bowl of an electric mixer, beat together the butter, sugar, salt, and vanilla until fluffy.

Add the cocoa to the butter mixture, beating to incorporate. Add the eggs, one at a time, beating at medium speed.

In a bowl, combine the flour and baking powder and fold into the batter until smooth. Fold in the chopped chocolate.

Pile the cookie dough onto a piece of plastic wrap or parchment paper and roll into a log, twisting the ends of the plastic or parchment to enclose. Chill until firm.

Preheat the oven to 350°F. Line a baking sheet with parchment paper. Cut the chilled dough log into ¼-inch to ½-inch slices and place the slices 2 inches apart on the baking sheet. Sprinkle lightly with more sugar. Bake until firm, about 10 to 12 minutes. Transfer the cookies to a wire rack to cool.

Store in an airtight container for up to 2 weeks.

¾ cup unsalted butter

¾ cup granulated sugar, plus more for sprinkling

Pinch salt

1 tsp vanilla extract

½ cup Dutch-process cocoa powder

2 eggs

1¼ cups all-purpose flour

1 tsp baking powder

4 oz 70% cacao chocolate, chopped

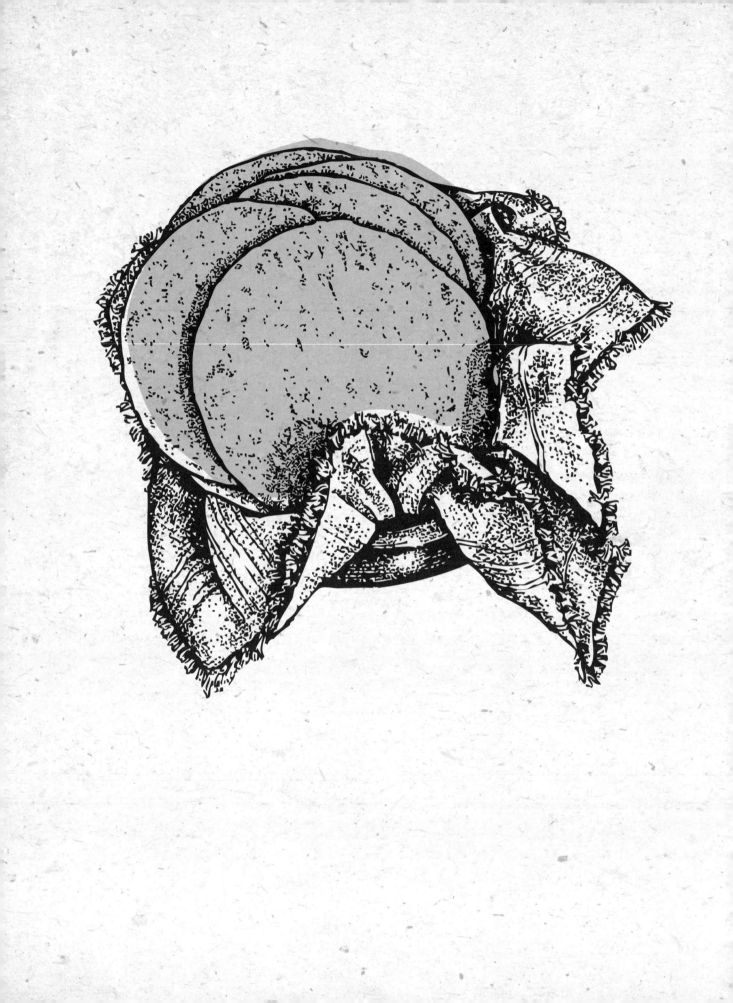

CORN TORTILLAS

Buy

Look for a local maker and buy good-quality corn tortillas fresh or frozen.

Store

Keep them wrapped in waxed paper in a plastic bag in the refrigerator for 1 week, or freeze for longer storage.

Serve

Fresh, handmade corn tortillas are a rare treat (unless you live in Mexico), but essential when you want to serve authentic Baja fish tacos or need a tender and tasty vehicle for pulled pork.

Don't Waste It!

- Spread corn tortillas with salsa, top with pulled pork, chopped cilantro, and cheese, sandwich with a second tortilla, and grill or panfry for fast quesadillas. (Or make BBQ duck quesadillas with shredded duck from your local Asian BBQ joint, mozzarella cheese, hoisin sauce, and cilantro.)
- Wrap corn tortillas in a clean damp cloth and warm in the microwave for 30 seconds to serve as wrappers for crispy fish tacos or fajitas.
- Sauté chopped tortillas in butter to crisp, then scramble with eggs for breakfast.
- Fry yesterday's corn tortillas until crisp and top with salsa and eggs for huevos rancheros.
- Make fast tostadas: top a fried corn tortilla with refried beans and/or chopped chicken, and shredded lettuce, fresh tomato salsa, avocado, and cheese.
- Cut corn tortillas into strips and fry until crispy to top soups and salads.
- Cut corn tortillas into wedges and fry or bake for chips to scoop up salsa and guacamole.
- To make edible salad bowls, warm corn tortillas in a microwave, brush lightly with oil, then drape over the back side of a muffin tin, pressing lightly into the spaces to form bowls, and bake at 375°F for 15 minutes until firm and crisp.
- Overlap corn tortillas in a pie plate and fill with a Mexican-style quiche mixture (eggs with tomatoes, cilantro, chives, chiles, and corn), then bake until set.
- Warm corn tortillas until pliable, fill with cooked chicken, roasted chiles, grated cheese, and cumin, roll tightly and secure with toothpicks, then fry in hot canola oil until crisp, about 5 minutes.
- Fill warm corn tortillas with chili and cheese for fast sloppy joes.
- Use corn tortillas for gluten-free individual pizza shells.

FISH TACOS

Use a food processor to whirl up this easy coating for your favorite fish fillets and you'll be dining in no time. These fillets can also be served with steamed rice—just arrange the crispy fish on a platter and spoon some salsa overtop. **SERVES 4**.

Whirl the chips in a food processor until ground to fine crumbs. Add the flour, cumin, and chili powder, and pulse to combine. Place the coating on a plate.

Roll the fish in the corn chip crumbs. Set aside on a plate.

In a nonstick sauté pan over high, heat the oil and when the oil is very hot, add the fish. Cook quickly, 2 minutes per side, until the fish is crisp. Use tongs to turn the fish to keep the coating intact. Set the cooked fish on a paper-towel-lined plate and place in a warm oven.

Rinse out the food processor and dry with a paper towel. Place the garlic and jalapeno in the processor and pulse until finely chopped. Add the cilantro, and pulse to combine. Add the tomatoes, onion, and lime juice, and whirl for 1 or 2 seconds to combine. Place the salsa in a bowl and set aside to allow flavors to meld (you can make this in advance and refrigerate it).

To serve, break the fried fish into chunks and wrap up in warm corn tortillas with the salsa and shredded lettuce.

1 cup organic yellow or blue corn chips

2 Tbsp all-purpose flour

¼ tsp ground cumin

¼ tsp chipotle chili powder or smoked paprika

1 lb boneless, skinless white fish fillets (halibut, pickerel, sole)

¼ cup canola oil, for frying

Salsa:

1 clove garlic

1 fresh jalapeno chile, seeded and quartered

2 Tbsp chopped fresh cilantro

2 ripe Roma tomatoes, seeded and chopped

¼ cup chopped white or red onion

1 Tbsp fresh lime juice

Warm corn tortillas

Shredded romaine lettuce or cabbage coleslaw mix

CHICKEN and CORN TORTILLA CASSEROLE

This is sort of a south-of-the-border lasagna made with chicken and day-old corn tortillas. You can even use leftover roast chicken and recycle two items at once. Just be sure you start with good-quality corn tortillas. Look for them at authentic Mexican markets. For a vegetarian version, substitute a big can of black beans, drained and rinsed, for the chicken. **SERVES 4–6**.

To make the salsa, combine the tomatoes, jalapenos, garlic, onion, salt, cumin, oregano, and chili powder in a blender or food processor and whirl into a chunky purée. Taste the salsa. If it's not spicy enough for you, add some hot sauce. Set aside.

In a sauté pan over medium, heat the oil, add the bell pepper, onions, and chicken, and sauté for 10 minutes, until the chicken is browned. Stir in the salsa and simmer for 10 minutes. Remove from heat and add the olives and cilantro.

Preheat the oven to 350°F. Grease a 13- × 9-inch casserole dish with olive oil and arrange 4 of the tortillas in the dish in a single layer, cutting 1 or 2 in half if necessary to fill the space.

Top with one-third of the sauce and one-third of the cheese. Repeat the layers twice, ending with cheese.

Cover the casserole with foil. Bake for 30 minutes. Remove the foil and bake for an additional 10 minutes, until the cheese is browned and bubbly. Let the casserole stand for 10 minutes before cutting. If desired, garnish with sour cream, shredded lettuce, and chopped tomatoes.

Speedy salsa:

1 (14 oz) can plum tomatoes

1 (4 oz) can jalapeno chiles, drained

1 tsp minced garlic (or puréed through a press)

½ medium onion, chopped

1 tsp salt

1 tsp ground cumin

1 tsp dried oregano

1 tsp chili powder

Hot sauce or Asian chili paste, to taste (optional)

Tortilla casserole:

1 Tbsp canola oil

1 red bell pepper, seeded and chopped

2 cups chopped onions

1½ lb boneless, skinless chicken thighs, cubed (or substitute leftover roast chicken)

½ cup pitted black olives, chopped

1 to 2 Tbsp chopped fresh cilantro

12 fresh corn tortillas

2 cups grated mozzarella, Monterey Jack, or medium cheddar cheese

Optional garnishes:

Sour cream

Shredded lettuce

Chopped tomatoes

TEX-MEX BREAKFAST

These ranch-style eggs are easy to make for a crowd if you precook the eggs. Just poach until barely set (about 3 minutes), then lift with a slotted spoon into a bowl of ice water to quickly chill. You can refrigerate the eggs in water overnight and reheat by dipping them into boiling water for 30 to 60 seconds, just before assembling the dishes. **SERVES 4**.

In a sauté pan over medium-high, heat the oil and sauté the onion and garlic for 5 minutes until tender. Add the tomato sauce, oregano, cumin, and jalapeno. Bring to a boil, then reduce heat to medium-low, cover, and simmer for 10 minutes.

Preheat the broiler.

Divide half of the sauce between 4 individual baking dishes. Heat the refried beans in a saucepan until warmed through (or microwave for 2 minutes) and spread a thick layer of beans over each tortilla. Set a tortilla into each baking dish (cut in half if necessary to fit) and top each with an egg. Season with salt and pepper. Spoon the remaining sauce evenly over the eggs and top each with ¼ cup of the grated cheese.

Set the dishes on a baking pan and slide under the broiler. Broil just until the cheese is melted, about 1 minute. Serve immediately, garnished with chopped cilantro.

1 Tbsp olive oil

1 cup chopped onion

2 cloves garlic, minced

1 (14 oz) can tomato sauce

1 tsp dried oregano

¼ tsp ground cumin

1 fresh jalapeno chile, chopped (or hot sauce, to taste)

1 (14 oz) can low-fat refried beans

4 fresh corn tortillas

4 eggs, soft poached or lightly fried, sunny side up

Salt and freshly ground black pepper, to taste

1 cup grated jalapeno jack cheese, divided

Chopped fresh cilantro, for garnish

EGGS

Buy

Get the freshest, tastiest eggs straight from farms or backyards where chickens are allowed to dig around and forage. Otherwise, buy local and organic for eggs with orange yolks and the most flavor. Most recipes call for large eggs.

Store

How fresh are your eggs? The air space inside the shell grows as the eggs age, so very fresh eggs sink in water while older eggs float. Make sure to cook the latter well. Eggs actually keep for several weeks in the refrigerator if raw. But once hard-cooked, you'll need to consume your eggs quite quickly—within 5 to 7 days. Once peeled, hard-cooked eggs can be stored in the refrigerator in a bowl of cold water for 3 days. Extra egg whites freeze well for later use in angel food cake, meringues, frothy cocktails, etc.

Serve

Eggs are not only for breakfast. After you've had them fried, poached, coddled, and scrambled on toast, try perching a soft-cooked egg atop a green salad, on a pile of sautéed asparagus, or even on a burger. For hard-cooked eggs that peel perfectly, steam eggs in a pressure cooker for 9 minutes, then plunge into ice water.

Don't Waste It!

- For deviled eggs, peel hard-cooked eggs, cut in half lengthwise, remove the yolks, and mash them with mayo and Dijon, and stuff them back into the egg-white halves. For fancier versions, add chopped chives, Italian parsley, or wasabi paste, and top with smoked salmon, baby shrimp, caviar, sundried tomatoes, or chopped olives.

- Omelet for one: Whisk 2 eggs with 1 tablespoon of milk and salt and pepper to taste. Heat a little butter in a 7-inch nonstick pan over medium heat, pour in the egg, reduce heat, and push back the edges to let the egg run over and underneath. Scramble up the middle a bit too. When golden on the bottom and just a little wet on top, fill the center with cooked mushrooms, onions, cheese, etc., and slide away from you onto a plate, flipping the handle up to fold the omelet over as it leaves the pan.

- Make hollandaise by blending 3 egg yolks in a blender with 2 tablespoons of lemon juice, a dash of cayenne, and salt to taste. With the motor running, slowly add ½ cup of melted butter to emulsify and thicken. Serve over eggs Benedict on English muffins or with steamed asparagus.

- For easy egg drop soup, boil some chicken broth with a dash of soy sauce and sesame oil, a slice of ginger, and some green onion, then beat an egg and whisk it into the hot broth.

- To make mayonnaise, place 1 egg yolk, 2 teaspoons of mustard, 2 tablespoons of vinegar or lemon juice, and some salt in a food processor. With the machine running, slowly add ¾ cup of olive oil until thickened and emulsified.

- For fast spaghetti carbonara, toss hot cooked pasta with beaten eggs, grated Parmesan, chopped Italian parsley, and chopped ham or crispy bacon. Season with pepper. Serve immediately.

- Make holiday eggnog by heating beaten eggs with sugar, milk, cream, nutmeg, vanilla, and bourbon or brandy.

- Fill a pie shell with sautéed mushrooms, onion, and garlic, then top with beaten eggs, and bake into a savory quiche. Or use cooked salmon, dill, and goat cheese for salmon quiche.

- Whisk egg yolks, sugar, and Marsala wine in a double boiler until thick to make zabaglione, an Italian custard to serve over strawberries.

EASY EGG FOO YUNG

Egg foo yung is one Asian dish anyone can make, even without a wok. Serve it atop a bowl of rice for a simple supper, or slap a few pancakes between slices of brown toast and you've got an Asian twist on a classic Western (AKA Denver) sandwich. When you have eggs in the fridge and leftover ham or roast chicken, get some bean sprouts for this easy and delicious dish. SERVES 4.

In a large bowl, combine the garlic, ginger, bean sprouts, green onions, and carrot. Stir in the eggs, soy sauce, and salt; combine well. Fold in the ham, chicken, or shrimp.

In a large nonstick frying pan over medium-high, heat a little canola oil. When the oil is hot, ladle some of the egg mixture into the pan, making 3-inch "pancakes." If you want one omelet per sandwich, make each as big as your bread (that may mean making them one at a time). If the egg runs out beyond the vegetables, push them back into the omelet with a spatula to keep the edges even.

Cook until brown on one side, 3 to 4 minutes, then flip over to brown the other side. Keep warm on an ovenproof plate in a warm oven until all of the omelets are finished.

In the same pan, make the sauce. Combine the stock, soy sauce, sugar, and cornstarch in a bowl and pour into the hot pan. Cook and stir the sauce until bubbling, clear and thick, about 30 seconds to 1 minute.

Divide the omelets into 4 servings and drizzle with the sauce. Sandwich the omelets between slices of toast.

1 clove garlic, minced

1-inch knob ginger, minced

3 cups fresh bean sprouts

3 green onions, minced

1 carrot, peeled and grated

6 eggs, lightly beaten

1 tsp soy sauce

½ tsp salt

1 cup finely chopped ham or cooked chicken, or 1 can small shrimp, rinsed and drained

Canola oil, for frying

Sauce:

½ cup chicken stock

1 Tbsp soy sauce

½ tsp granulated sugar

2 tsp cornstarch

8 slices grainy bread, toasted and buttered

POTATO and SPICY SAUSAGE FRITTATA

A frittata is an all-purpose egg dish, a "mother" recipe and technique you can modify to suit what's in the fridge, whenever there are leftover potatoes around. Always bake or boil an extra potato or two on the weekend, and you'll have the basis for a fast frittata during the week (or substitute 1 cup frozen hash browns). Use any kind of cheese you have, and add leftover sautéed mushrooms, steamed broccoli or asparagus, and different meats, like ham or prosciutto. Make a frittata for breakfast or enjoy it for a fast supper with a salad on the side. **SERVES 4.**

2 Tbsp olive oil

1 large potato, cooked, chilled, and thinly sliced or chopped

½ cup chopped onion

1 red bell pepper, seeded and slivered

1 yellow bell pepper, seeded and slivered

2 cloves garlic, minced

½ lb fresh spicy Italian or chorizo sausage, meat removed from the casings and crumbled

8 eggs

4 oz aged Fontina cheese, grated

1 oz Parmigiano-Reggiano, grated

In a large nonstick, ovenproof pan over medium-high, heat the oil. Add the potato and sauté for 5 minutes, until beginning to brown. Add the onion and cook for 3 to 4 minutes, until it starts to color. Add the red and yellow peppers, garlic, and sausage, cooking until the meat is no longer pink.

Beat the eggs in a bowl and pour over the ingredients in the pan. Reduce the heat to medium. Stir the mixture until the eggs begin to set, then reduce the heat to low and let the eggs cook on the bottom, shaking the pan to keep the mixture loosened.

Meanwhile, preheat the broiler. When the frittata is nicely browned on the bottom, remove the pan from the heat. Top with the cheeses and place the pan under the broiler. Broil for 1 to 2 minutes, just until the top of the frittata is set and the cheese is melted and beginning to brown.

Let the frittata stand for a couple of minutes to cool, then cut into 4 wedges.

LYONNAISE SALAD

This simple salad is a classic bistro dish. Make it when you have bacon, eggs, and greens (romaine lettuce, spinach, arugula, or kale) to use up for a healthy, satisfying supper. SERVES 4.

In a skillet over medium heat, fry the side pork or bacon until crisp. Remove to a plate lined with paper towel, reserving the fat in the pan.

In the same pan (with the bacon fat) over medium heat, sauté the shallot for 3 minutes, then remove from heat and whisk in 1 tablespoon of the white wine vinegar, the olive oil, and the mustard. Set aside on low heat to keep warm.

Combine the greens in a bowl.

Fill a straight-sided 10-inch sauté pan with 2 inches of water. Add the remaining white vinegar and bring the liquid to a bare simmer (not a rolling boil). Gently crack the eggs into small dishes or teacups and slip them into the water, taking care not to break the yolks. Cover the pan and let the eggs cook until the whites have set and the yolk is done to the desired consistency, 3 to 5 minutes. Use a slotted spoon to remove the eggs from the water one at a time.

Toss the greens with the warm vinaigrette, then divide among 4 shallow bowls.

Place 1 egg on each portion of greens. Sprinkle the pork evenly over each salad and season with salt and pepper.

2 slices side pork or thick smoky bacon, cut into ¼-inch strips or cubes

1 small shallot, minced

2 Tbsp white wine vinegar, divided

2 to 3 Tbsp olive oil (depends on how much fat renders from your bacon)

2 tsp Dijon mustard

4 eggs

1 head frisée (curly endive), or a mix of greens (kale, spinach, dandelion, arugula, radicchio, etc.), torn into bite-sized pieces (about 4 to 6 cups)

Sea salt and freshly ground black pepper, to taste

LEMONY STRAWBERRY PAVLOVA

Lemony custard tempers sweet meringue in this version of classic pavlova. You can fill this with any seasonal fruits or berries, from blueberries to fresh peaches, but ripe strawberries are especially delicious and dramatic. **SERVES 8.**

4 eggs, separated

1 tsp vanilla extract

¼ tsp cream of tartar

¼ tsp salt

1⅓ cups granulated sugar, divided

⅓ cup fresh lemon juice

2 Tbsp finely grated lemon zest

1 cup heavy cream

4 cups ripe strawberries, sliced

Preheat the oven to 250°F. Line a baking sheet with parchment paper and on it draw a 9-inch circle, or eight 4-inch circles for individual pavlovas.

Using an electric mixer at high speed, beat the egg whites, vanilla, cream of tartar, and salt until soft peaks form. Add 1 cup of the sugar gradually, a tablespoon at a time, with the mixer running, and continue to beat until the whites are glossy and stiff.

Using the parchment as a guide, spoon the meringue onto the baking sheet. Mound it higher around the edges, forming a bowl in the middle for the custard.

Bake the meringue for 1½ hours, until crisp. Turn off the heat, leave the oven door ajar, and allow to cool in the oven.

In a saucepan over low heat, whisk the egg yolks with the remaining ⅓ cup of sugar and the lemon juice. Cook, stirring constantly, until the mixture is thick and smooth, about 5 minutes. Stir in the lemon zest and set custard aside to cool.

In another bowl, use an electric mixer to whip the cream until stiff. Fold the whipped cream into the cooled lemon custard, just to lighten it.

Just before serving, fill the meringue with the lemon cream mixture and top with the strawberries.

> **TIP**
> Extra egg yolks will keep in a container of cold water for 2 days in the refrigerator. Or use up extra egg yolks in a yellow cake, homemade ice cream, eggnog cocktails, or hollandaise to serve over poached salmon or asparagus (or more eggs).

NUTS

Buy

The best buys for the freshest nuts are often in bulk food stores, especially ethnic markets with a high turnover. You can buy raw nuts for baking or roasted and salted nuts for snacking. Nuts are harvested in the late fall, so that's when they are freshest.

Store

Unshelled nuts will keep for a couple of months at room temperature, though all nuts are best stored in a cool, dark place. Refrigerate nuts and seeds, or freeze, for longer storage. Nuts are high in oils and can go rancid. Discard rancid nuts.

Serve

You can toast and flavor nuts with herbs and spices to serve as snacks, add them to home-made granola or salads, even chop them to use in nutty coatings for fried fish or chicken.

Don't Waste It!

- Use your food processor to make healthy nut butters. Just whirl unsalted roasted almonds, peanuts, or cashews until they release their oils and become smooth pastes, no salt or sugar needed.

- Mix ground almonds or hazelnuts with bread crumbs and herbs, coat fish fillets or chicken breasts, and bake.

- Toss mixed nuts with popcorn, drizzle with melted butter, cinnamon, paprika, cayenne, sea salt, ginger, and maple syrup, then bake at 300°F for 30 minutes, tossing, until crisp.

- For fresh almond milk, soak whole raw almonds in water (1 part almonds to 2 parts water) for 24 hours, drain, and blend with fresh water in a Vitamix blender or food processor (2 to 4 minutes), then strain through cheesecloth. Refrigerate the milk; use the almond meal in baking.

- Brown sliced almonds in butter and pour over steamed green beans or broccoli.

- Use ground nuts, especially almonds and cashews, to thicken sauces, like mole and pesto, and Indian butter chicken.

- Roast nuts to refresh and bring out their flavors—10 minutes on a baking sheet at 325°F, or a few minutes, watched carefully, in a dry pan over medium-high heat.

- Add roasted cashews to stir-fries or top Thai salads with chopped roasted peanuts. Toasted nuts—like almonds, walnuts, or pine nuts—add flavor and crunch to salads.

- Make a vegan pâté to spread on crackers: sauté chopped mushrooms, onion, and garlic in butter, purée with walnuts, season with salt and pepper and fresh thyme, and chill.

- Top cakes and crumbles with chopped or slivered nuts, softened butter, and brown sugar.

ROSEMARY PECANS

These sweet and spicy nuts, flavored with fresh rosemary and zippy cayenne, are simple to make and addictive, too. **MAKES 3 CUPS**.

3 cups raw pecans

2 Tbsp olive oil

2 Tbsp brown sugar

1 tsp salt

¼ tsp cayenne

2 Tbsp minced fresh rosemary

Preheat the oven to 400°F. Place the pecans on a rimmed baking sheet in a single layer and toast for 5 to 10 minutes. The nuts should just be hot and fragrant—watch carefully as they can burn quickly.

Meanwhile, in a large bowl, combine the olive oil, brown sugar, salt, and cayenne, mixing well to form a slurry. Stir in the rosemary.

Pour the hot, toasted pecans into the bowl and toss with the seasoning mix for several minutes, until all of the nuts are coated and cooled.

⸎ FOOD FOR THOUGHT

The resources wasted to produce wasted food are vast. It takes 260 US gallons (1,000 liters) of water to produce a quart (liter) of milk, or 4,200 gallons (16,000 liters) to make enough ground beef for a hamburger.

CRUNCHY ALMOND BARK

Here's a home-style version of an expensive almond and pecan candy. Pack it into pretty holiday tins for gourmet gifts. **MAKES ABOUT 8 CUPS.**

In a heavy sauté pan over medium heat, melt the butter and sugar together. When the mixture begins to bubble, add the almonds and increase the heat to medium-high.

Stirring constantly, cook for 5 to 7 minutes, until the mixture turns a nice caramel color and the nuts are lightly toasted. Be careful—you can easily overdo it and burn the nuts.

Line a baking sheet with parchment paper (or use a Silpat silicone sheet) and pour the caramelized sugar mixture onto the pan. Use a metal spoon to quickly spread it evenly and, while it's hot, grate the milk chocolate overtop, then evenly sprinkle with the pecans. Use the spoon to press the pecans down evenly over the entire surface of the hot candy. Cool.

When the candy is cold and stiff, break into chunks and store in sealed containers.

1 cup butter

1 cup granulated sugar

1 cup blanched almonds, coarsely chopped

6 oz good-quality milk chocolate

¾ cup pecans, finely ground

VEGETARIAN NUT ROAST

I developed this recipe based on a vegetarian haggis I enjoyed in Scotland. It makes a perfect "roast" for vegetarians to enjoy during family holiday feasts. Leftovers can be stuffed into a small, hollowed-out winter squash (sweet dumpling, delicata, kabocha) and baked. Serve with mashed potatoes and turnips. **SERVES 6.**

In a large sauté pan over medium-high heat, melt 1 tablespoon of the butter. Add both kinds of oats and the nuts and toast for 5 to 10 minutes, stirring often, until starting to brown. Dump into a bowl and set aside

In the same sauté pan over medium, heat the remaining butter and the oil. Sauté the onion until softened and starting to color. Add the carrots, garlic, and mushrooms and sauté for an additional 5 minutes. Stir in the lentils and 1 cup of the stock. Bring to a boil.

Mix another cup of the stock with the beans and soy sauce, and add to the pan. Cover and simmer for 10 minutes.

Stir in the toasted oats and nuts as well as the thyme, savory, celery salt, cayenne, and black pepper, bring to a boil, then return the lid to the pan and simmer on low for 15 minutes.

Add the remaining ½ cup to ¾ cup of stock as necessary. This mixture should be moist, but not soupy.

Stir in the lemon juice. Taste and adjust the seasoning. It may need salt, depending on what kind of stock you've used.

Preheat the oven to 375°F and butter a loaf pan. Turn the mixture into the pan and bake for 30 minutes.

3 Tbsp butter, divided

⅔ cup steel-cut oats

⅔ cup rolled oats

⅔ cup chopped nuts (mix of almonds, cashews, hazelnuts, etc.)

1 Tbsp olive oil

1 large onion, minced

2 medium carrots, shredded

2 to 3 cloves garlic, minced

8 mushrooms, chopped

⅓ cup red lentils, rinsed

2½ to 2¾ cups vegetable or chicken stock (or water), divided

½ cup kidney or romano beans (canned/cooked), mashed

1 Tbsp soy sauce

½ tsp dried thyme

½ tsp dried savory

¼ tsp celery salt

¼ tsp cayenne

½ tsp black pepper

1 Tbsp fresh lemon juice

NUTTY APRICOT FRUITCAKE SOAKED in WHISKY

Even if you think you are in the fruitcake-loathing camp, you should try this nutty version. Studded with dried apricots and lots of nuts, it's then soaked with whisky (or Scotch) for added appeal. If you can't find good-quality candied peel, substitute another dried fruit, like currants or cranberries. **MAKES 2 CAKES**.

2 cups sultana (golden) raisins

2½ cups chopped dried apricots

1 cup mixed candied lemon and orange peel

2 cups rye or Scotch whisky, plus more for aging fruitcake

1 lb butter, at room temperature

2 cups granulated sugar

2 cups packed brown sugar

8 large eggs, separated

3 cups chopped pecans

5 cups all-purpose flour, divided

2 tsp ground nutmeg

1 tsp baking powder

1 tsp salt

½ tsp ground cloves

Cover the raisins, apricots, and peel with the whisky and soak overnight at room temperature. Drain and reserve the whisky.

Preheat the oven to 300°F. Butter and flour two 8-inch tube pans or springform pans.

In a large bowl, cream the butter with the granulated sugar and brown sugar using an electric mixer, then beat in the egg yolks one at a time. Toss the pecans with ½ cup of the flour; set aside. Combine the remaining flour, nutmeg, baking powder, salt, and cloves. Alternate adding the flour mixture and the reserved whisky (a little at a time) to the egg mixture, beating between additions, to make a smooth batter. Carefully fold in the marinated fruit and the pecans. In another bowl, beat the egg whites until stiff and fold them into the batter to lighten it.

Pour the batter into the prepared pans. Pans should be no more than three-quarters full.

Place a shallow pan of water in the oven on the lowest rack to keep the cakes moist during baking. Bake the fruitcakes for 2 to 2½ hours, until the cakes are set and browned and a skewer inserted comes out clean. Brush the top of the cakes with 2 tablespoons of whisky as soon as they're out of the oven.

Allow the cakes to cool and remove them from the pans. Wrap them in several layers of cheesecloth that has been soaked in whisky, then wrap well in foil. Let the cakes ripen for 2 to 3 weeks, then again soak the cheesecloth in whisky and rewrap. Fruitcakes need this kind of aging to develop and meld the flavors—you must age this cake for at least a month, dousing it regularly with more whisky. Like all good fruitcake, it will keep indefinitely if tightly wrapped.

> **TIP**
>
> You can also use a deep square pan; line it with waxed paper or buttered parchment to prevent overbrowning. To make smaller cakes (6 mini loaf pans), reduce the baking time to 1½ to 2 hours.

OLIVES

Buy

There are a lot of different kinds of olives to buy, from big, brined kalamata olives to inky air-dried olives, big Queen Spanish green olives, and olives stuffed with things like anchovies or garlic. Find a market with a good turnover, whether you get your olives from a deli olive bar or in a jar. The longer they're cured, the more intense the flavor.

Store

Olives should be submerged in brine and refrigerated after opening. Air-dried olives are stored dry in the jar and can get a white "bloom" of salt on the outside but are still perfectly safe to eat. Always use a clean utensil (i.e., not your fingers) to fish them out of the jar.

Serve

Serve olives whenever you serve cheese and charcuterie. Consider warming them in a little olive oil before serving for extra flavor. To pit olives, press them under the flat side of your chef's knife and the pits will pop out.

Don't Waste It!

- Whirl pitted black olives with garlic, anchovies, lemon juice, and olive oil into a paste in the food processor for tapenade to spread on toasts.

- Top cheese and tomato pizzas with artichokes and chopped black olives.

- Add black olives to a lamb stew made with red wine and rosemary, for a real south-of-France feel.

- Add chopped black olives and hot chili flakes to a basic tomato sauce for pasta puttanesca.

- Make spiced olives by tossing a mixture of green and black olives from the deli with olive oil, chili flakes, puréed garlic, lemon zest, and herbs.

- Marinate olives with cubes of feta cheese, garlic, olive oil, chili flakes, rosemary, and lemon zest to pile onto crostini for easy appetizers.

- Use frozen bread dough to make olive bread: roll into a rectangle, sprinkle with chopped olives, olive oil, and shredded cheese, then roll into a loaf (like a jellyroll), let rise, and bake.

- Skewer olives on toothpicks with sundried tomatoes and chunks of Asiago cheese for easy appetizers.

- Toss any leftover marinated olives into your favorite pasta dish for a blast of flavor.

- Wrap pitted or stuffed olives in a pastry made with butter, flour, grated cheddar, and cayenne, then bake at 400°F for 15 minutes, until golden, for warm appetizers.

SEARED HALIBUT with TOMATO and OLIVE RELISH

You can make the relish in advance and sear the halibut steaks at the last minute. Roasted potatoes with lemon and rosemary or sautéed spinach with garlic finishes the plate nicely. **SERVES 4.**

Combine the relish ingredients in a small bowl and set aside at room temperature.

Season the fish with salt and pepper. In a nonstick sauté pan over medium-high, heat the oil and sear the fish, flesh side down, for 5 minutes.

Turn the fish over, skin side down, reduce heat to medium, and cook for 5 minutes, until fish is just cooked through.

Set the fish on warm individual serving plates, and top each portion with a little of the tomato and olive relish.

Relish:

½ cup sundried tomatoes, minced (see Tip)

½ cup pitted kalamata olives, minced

1 clove garlic, minced

1 Tbsp extra-virgin olive oil

½ tsp chili paste

2 Tbsp chopped fresh Italian parsley

1 Tbsp basil pesto

Black pepper, to taste

2 lb boneless halibut fillet, cut into 4 portions

Salt and freshly ground black pepper

3 Tbsp extra-virgin olive oil

> **TIP**
> There are two kinds of sundried tomatoes—dried and dried and then packed in oil. For this recipe, use the kind that has been packed in oil; drain before measuring.

EASY PASTA with CHICKPEAS, OLIVES, and FETA

This simple and healthy vegetarian supper is redolent of the rustic flavors of Greece. **SERVES 4**.

In a saucepan over medium-high, heat the olive oil and sauté the onion and garlic until tender, about 5 minutes. Add the spinach or chard and cook for 5 minutes or until just wilted and bright green.

Meanwhile, cook the fusilli according to package directions until al dente. Drain but don't rinse.

Scrub the lemon. Use a lemon reamer and zester to remove the juice and zest from the lemon. Stir the lemon juice, lemon zest, oregano or basil, chickpeas, and olives into the pan with the spinach and heat through.

Add the drained pasta and toss well. Season with salt and pepper, and pile into bowls. Divide the feta cheese overtop.

⅓ cup olive oil

1 onion, thinly sliced

3 cloves garlic, minced

1 bunch fresh spinach or chard leaves, washed well and chopped

1 lb fusilli pasta (corkscrew or other short pasta)

1 large lemon

2 Tbsp chopped fresh oregano or basil

1½ cups cooked chickpeas (or canned chickpeas, rinsed and drained)

½ cup sliced kalamata or other black olives

Salt and freshly ground black pepper, to taste

½ cup crumbled feta cheese

TIP

Buy prewashed spinach and all you need to do is rinse it lightly. To easily chop leaves into a chiffonade (strips), stack them up, roll them like a fat cigar, and slice against the grain. Voila!

FASTA PASTA

This is a fast feast from the pantry that uses olives, sundried tomatoes in oil, artichoke hearts, and basil pesto, along with some deli ham or turkey, and a little goat cheese or feta. **SERVES 4.**

In a large sauté pan over medium-high, heat the oil and cook the ham and garlic together, just until the garlic sizzles. Add the olives, sundried tomatoes, artichokes, and chiles, and heat through. Keep warm on low heat.

Meanwhile, bring a very large pot of salted water to a boil, and cook the pasta until al dente, about 8 to 12 minutes for most short pasta.

When the pasta is tender, drain, then return to the pot and add the contents of the sauté pan. Toss. Stir in the pesto. Add in the cheese and toss until it just begins to melt. Season with salt and pepper. Serve immediately.

¼ cup extra-virgin olive oil

6 oz ham (or smoked turkey), slivered

3 cloves garlic, minced

¾ cup black, green, or mixed olives, pitted and chopped or sliced

¾ cup sundried tomatoes (in oil), chopped

1 can artichoke hearts, drained and chopped

1 to 2 dried red chiles, crumbled

1 lb short pasta (gemelli, rotini, penne, etc.)

2 Tbsp basil pesto (or 2 Tbsp chopped fresh basil)

½ lb goat cheese or feta cheese, crumbled

Salt and freshly ground black pepper, to taste

BRAISED LAMB with RED WINE and OLIVES

Here's a beautiful braise, inspired by the flavors of Provence. Serve the lamb alongside creamy polenta flavored with goat cheese or garlic mashed potatoes and fresh, skinny green beans that have been barely steamed. **SERVES 8.**

The day before you plan to serve the lamb, make the marinade. In a saucepan over medium, heat the oil and sauté the onion, celery, carrot, and garlic until soft and starting to brown, about 10 minutes. Stir in the bay leaves, rosemary, and thyme, then add the wine and bring to a boil. Simmer for 20 minutes. Remove from the heat and chill. When the marinade is cold, add the lamb pieces and marinate overnight in the refrigerator.

The next day, remove the lamb from the marinade. Strain the marinade, discarding the solid bits but reserving the liquid to add to the sauce later.

To peel the onions, bring a pot of water to a boil. Trim each onion at the base. Add the onions to the boiling water and blanch for 1 minute. Drain and cool in ice water, then slip off the papery skins. Set aside.

Preheat the oven to 325°F.

Combine the flour and salt and pepper in a plastic bag and toss in the lamb pieces, shaking to coat. In a large nonstick sauté pan over medium-high, heat the olive oil and brown the floured meat in batches.

As they're browned, remove the lamb pieces to a heavy covered ovenproof Dutch oven. Add the bacon to the sauté pan and cook until the fat is rendered and the bacon is nearly crisp. Remove the bacon with a slotted spoon and add to the Dutch oven.

In the bacon fat, sauté the peeled onions over medium-low heat for 15 minutes, until they begin to brown. Remove the onions with a slotted spoon and add to the lamb. Lightly sauté the celery, carrots, and garlic in same pan, until they begin to brown, then deglaze with the reserved marinade, boiling until the liquid in the pan is reduced by half.

Marinade:

2 Tbsp extra-virgin olive oil

1 onion, minced

1 stalk celery, finely chopped

1 carrot, peeled and finely chopped

8 cloves garlic, halved

2 bay leaves

1 Tbsp chopped fresh rosemary

1 sprig fresh thyme

1 bottle dry red wine

Pour this mixture over the meat and stir in the olives, beef stock, and 2 cups red wine. Cover the Dutch oven and bake for 2 to 3 hours, or until the meat is very tender and the sauce has thickened.

Before serving, skim any excess fat from the sauce and simmer, uncovered, on the stove to further thicken the gravy (a bit of flour mixed into some softened butter or a solution of cornstarch and water can help thicken the sauce). Garnish with a sprinkling of rosemary or parsley and serve immediately (or chill overnight and reheat, adding the herbs just before serving).

4 lb boneless lamb shoulder, trimmed of visible fat and separated into fairly large pieces

25 small boiling onions

⅓ cup all-purpose flour

Salt and freshly ground black pepper, to taste

2 Tbsp extra-virgin olive oil

2 thick slices double-smoked bacon, cut into matchstick pieces

1 stalk celery, chopped

2 medium carrots, peeled and cut into chunks

6 whole cloves garlic, peeled

1 cup Niçoise olives or other good-quality air-cured black olives

2 cups beef stock

2 cups red wine

Minced fresh rosemary or Italian parsley, for garnish

PEANUT BUTTER

Buy

Look for natural, organic peanut butter with one ingredient on the label: roasted peanuts. Many products are loaded with added fats and sugar. So read the label and avoid hydrogenated products.

Store

Natural peanut butter should be refrigerated, which is why this is the peanut butter you should be eating. The sugar and preservatives in processed peanut butter mean it can stay in the pantry, without refrigeration, for 3 months or more.

Serve

Mainly used to spread on sandwiches or toast, natural peanut butter (with no added fats or sugar) is a great ingredient to have on hand to include in cookies or Asian peanut sauce.

Don't Waste It!

- Make a fast satay peanut sauce—for dipping grilled chicken skewers or salad rolls—by combining natural peanut butter with a little chili paste, soy sauce, and coconut milk or water.
- Make "ants on a log": celery sticks filled with peanut butter and topped with raisins.
- Peanut butter and jelly, peanut butter and banana, even peanut butter and dill pickle or sliced onions are all classic sandwiches.
- Combine peanut butter with milk, sugar, corn syrup, and butter for fudge.
- For a peanut butter cheesecake, add smooth natural peanut butter to a cream cheese batter, and pour into a chocolate wafer crust.
- Purée plain yogurt with peanut butter and frozen bananas, then swirl in a chocolate hazelnut spread (like Nutella) and freeze for an easy dessert.
- Make a creamy peanut soup with onions and celery sautéed in butter, 4 cups of chicken broth, 1 cup of peanut butter, and 1 cup of heavy cream. Season with salt and pepper, and serve garnished with chopped peanuts.
- Marinate boneless chicken breast strips in a sauce of coconut milk, curry paste, peanut butter, and lime. Skewer, accordion style, and grill.
- Use peanut butter as the binding agent in savory vegetarian burgers, and in pâtés of puréed chickpeas or lentils flavored with onion, garlic, and oats or mashed potatoes.
- Combine ¼ cup of smooth peanut butter with a bit of miso paste, a bit of chili paste, some minced garlic, and lime juice, thin with a splash of hot water, and drizzle over grilled salmon or cod.

COLD NOODLE SALAD with SESAME PEANUT SAUCE

This sauce is great over noodles, but equally good for glazing satay chicken kabobs on the grill. SERVES 4-6.

Bring a large pot of salted water to a boil. Add the noodles and cook for 3 to 5 minutes, just until the noodles are until tender but firm. Do not overcook.

Drain well, rinse in cold water, and place in a large bowl. Toss with the canola oil.

For the dressing, combine the sesame oil, garlic, peanut butter, soy sauce, brown sugar, and sushi vinegar in a blender or food processor and purée until smooth. Add the chili paste and the chicken stock and pulse to combine.

Toss the noodles with the sauce to coat well. Add the bell pepper, carrot, bean sprouts, green onions, and cilantro and toss again.

Arrange the salad in a serving bowl and top with the sesame seeds or chopped peanuts.

1 lb fresh Chinese egg noodles

1 Tbsp canola oil

1 red bell pepper, seeded and thinly sliced

1 large carrot, grated

2 cups fresh bean sprouts

2 green onions, cut into 1-inch slivers

¼ cup minced fresh cilantro leaves

2 Tbsp toasted sesame seeds or finely chopped peanuts

Dressing:

1 Tbsp sesame oil

2 cloves garlic, minced (optional)

⅓ cup crunchy or smooth natural peanut butter (no sugar or fats added)

¼ cup soy sauce

2 tsp brown sugar

1 Tbsp seasoned sushi vinegar (or wine vinegar)

1 tsp Asian chili paste

¼ cup chicken stock or water

AFRICAN SWEET POTATO and PEANUT SOUP

Crunchy peanut butter adds a unique but subtle flavor to this comforting but exotic chicken soup. **SERVES 6-8.**

In a large saucepan over medium, heat the oil and add the onion, garlic, and pepper. Sauté for about 10 minutes, until tender, then add the chicken, ginger, and paprika. Sauté for an additional 5 minutes, then stir in the chili paste, stock, tomato juice, sweet potato, potato, corn, and salt.

Bring the soup to a boil over medium-high heat, then cover, reduce heat to low, and simmer for 30 minutes.

Stir in the peanut butter and heat through. Serve immediately, topped with green onions.

2 Tbsp olive oil

1 large onion, chopped

4 cloves garlic, minced

1 red or green bell pepper, seeded and chopped

1 lb boneless, skinless chicken breasts, chopped

1 Tbsp grated fresh ginger

2 tsp sweet paprika

1 tsp Asian chili paste (or ½ tsp cayenne)

4 cups chicken stock

1 cup tomato juice

1 medium orange-fleshed sweet potato, peeled and cubed

1 medium white baking potato, peeled and cubed

1 cup fresh, canned, or frozen corn kernels

1 tsp salt

⅓ cup crunchy natural peanut butter

2 green onions, minced, for garnish

PEANUT BUTTER GRANOLA BARS

These bars actually get better after a couple of days. Wrap them individually in plastic and take them on your next hike. **MAKES 24 BARS.**

Preheat the oven to 350°F. Butter a 13- × 9-inch rimmed baking sheet.

In a large bowl, combine the oats, flour, baking powder, cinnamon, ginger, and salt. Add the apricots, raisins, peanuts, coconut, and sunflower seeds.

In another large bowl, cream the butter, peanut butter, and brown sugar with an electric mixer until light and fluffy. Add the eggs, one at a time, beating well after each addition. Beat in the molasses and vanilla until blended.

Gradually add the dry ingredients, stirring with a wooden spoon, until thoroughly blended.

Evenly press the mixture into the prepared pan and bake for 35 to 40 minutes, or until the edges begin to pull away from the side of the pan. Cool on a wire rack before cutting into individual bars.

1½ cups large-flake rolled oats

1½ cups all-purpose flour

1 tsp baking powder

1 tsp ground cinnamon

1 tsp ground ginger

½ tsp salt

½ cup chopped dried apricots

½ cup raisins

½ cup chopped peanuts

½ cup unsweetened shredded coconut

¼ cup toasted sunflower seeds

¼ cup butter, softened

½ cup crunchy natural peanut butter

½ cup packed brown sugar

2 eggs

½ cup light molasses

2 tsp vanilla extract

SUNDRIED TOMATOES

Buy

You can buy sundried tomatoes in jars, packed in oil, or dried. (You can even dry your own Roma tomatoes in a dehydrator when you have a windfall—see page 139 under "Don't Waste It.")

Store

Jars should be kept in a cool, dark place (in the pantry) or in the refrigerator once opened. After opening, they will last indefinitely in the refrigerator, as long as the tomatoes are submerged in oil.

Serve

Sundried tomatoes may be a bit of a California cliché but they make fast and delicious additions to dips, pasta dishes, salads, pizza, and even soups. A great pantry staple whether packed in oil or oven-roasted. Drying simply intensifies the tomatoes' sweet tart flavor.

Don't Waste It!

- Skewer cubes of fresh mozzarella, pieces of sundried tomato (in oil), and basil leaves on toothpicks for fast snacks. Drizzle the cheese with the oil from the tomatoes before skewering to add extra flavor.

- Purée sundried tomatoes with their oil and some toasted nuts, Parmesan, and fresh basil for an instant pesto for pasta.

- Make homemade tomato soup with onions, garlic, chicken stock, sundried tomatoes, fresh thyme, and a little cream. Simmer together, then purée with an immersion blender.

- For a tasty dip, finely chop sundried tomatoes from a jar and add to cream cheese that has been lightened with a little sour cream.

- Mince or purée straight out of the jar and add to any recipe that requires tomato paste (easier than opening a tin and throwing half of it away!).

- Sliver sundried tomatoes and serve atop crackers and cheese.

- Add puréed sundried tomatoes to cream sauces to serve over pasta.

- Chop sundried tomatoes and add to scrambled eggs, frittata, or quiche.

- Add chopped sundried tomatoes to the mix when you're baking savory breads and scones.

- Layer sundried tomatoes with olive tapenade, provolone, grilled eggplant, bell peppers, and zucchini inside a crusty loaf for a picnic muffuletta sandwich.

- Sauté kale or other winter greens in olive oil with chopped garlic and sundried tomatoes, then season with a little wine vinegar.

- Mince sundried tomatoes in oil and add to lean ground beef when making burgers or meat loaf.

- Make an intense tomato ketchup by combining in a blender 20 sundried tomatoes in oil with 3 fresh tomatoes, 5 pitted dates, a bit of fresh garlic, and cayenne, and whirring until smooth.

- Mix chopped sundried tomatoes in oil with minced garlic, toss with day-old bread cubes and grated Parmesan, soak in a mixture of beaten eggs and milk, then bake in a casserole at 350°F for 35 minutes until golden, for a savory breakfast bake.

PASTA SHELLS with SPICY TOMATO PESTO and GREENS

Healthy and fast, especially if you make the tomato pesto in advance to keep on hand in the fridge. Whole-wheat pasta needs assertive sauce like this spicy tomato pesto. The wilted greens add a healthy jolt of color. Arugula and mustard greens add the most flavor, but you can also use prewashed baby spinach to save time. SERVES 4.

Soak the sundried tomatoes in 1 cup of boiling water for 10 minutes to soften. Drain and reserve the soaking liquid. In a food processor, combine the softened sundried tomatoes, garlic, basil, almonds, cheese, salt, and chile. Process until smooth, scraping down the sides of the bowl as necessary. With the machine running, slowly add the oil. Add 2 to 4 tablespoons of the reserved tomato soaking liquid, a tablespoon at a time, until you have a smooth pesto. Set aside or refrigerate for up to 1 week.

Bring a large pot of salted water to a boil and cook the pasta until al dente, about 10 to 12 minutes. Drain.

Meanwhile, roll the leafy greens and slice into strips. Chop any stems fine or discard if too woody.

In a wide sauté pan over medium-high, heat the oil. Add the onion and cook, stirring, until it begins to brown, about 5 minutes, then reduce heat to low and continue to cook until the onion is nicely caramelized, about 20 minutes.

Add the greens to the pan and stir-fry until the leaves turn bright green. Add the stock or water, cover, and steam for 2 minutes.

Toss the pasta with the tomato pesto and steamed greens. Season with salt and pepper. Pass additional Parmigiano-Reggiano at the table.

Sundried tomato pesto:

½ cup sundried tomatoes (not packed in oil)

2 cloves garlic, minced

¼ cup chopped fresh basil

¼ cup sliced almonds

¼ cup grated Parmigiano-Reggiano

½ tsp salt

1 small dried red chile (or ¼ tsp crushed red chili flakes)

2 to 3 Tbsp extra-virgin olive oil

¾ lb whole-wheat pasta (small shells, orecchiette, or other short pasta)

3 cups fresh greens (chard, arugula, mustard, or baby spinach)

1 Tbsp olive oil

1 large onion, slivered

¼ cup stock or water

Salt and freshly ground black pepper, to taste

Grated Parmigiano-Reggiano, for garnish

CHICKEN with SUNDRIED TOMATO and CHIPOTLE CREAM SAUCE

Spice things up with this saucy combo to serve over chunky pasta, polenta, or egg noodles. **SERVES 4.**

For the sauce, heat the oil in a saucepan over medium and add the onion and garlic. Cover the pan and let the onion sweat (think of a sauna—it's like frying or sautéing with the lid on) until just translucent, not brown, about 5 minutes.

Add the wine and cook over high heat until it is almost boiled away. Stir in the sundried tomatoes, and add the chipotle chile along with the cream and milk. Simmer the sauce over medium-low heat until reduced by about one-third. This should take about 15 minutes. The sauce should just simmer, not boil. Cool the sauce and purée in a blender, or using a hand blender, until smooth. Adjust the flavor with a little salt and pepper and/or sugar. You should have about 2 cups of sauce. The sauce may be made ahead to this point and refrigerated.

To cook the chicken, season the flour with salt and pepper and dredge the chicken breasts to coat on both sides, shaking off any excess flour.

In a nonstick sauté pan over medium, heat the olive oil and cook the breasts, for 6 to 8 minutes on each side, until nicely browned.

Add the prepared sauce to the pan, spooning around the chicken, then simmer together for 5 minutes, until the chicken is cooked through and the sauce is nicely thickened.

Serve the chicken and sauce over bowls of hot cooked pasta.

Sauce:

2 Tbsp olive oil

½ cup chopped onion or shallots

1 large clove garlic, minced

¼ cup white wine

¼ cup chopped sundried tomatoes (drained if in oil or softened in hot water and drained if dry)

1 canned chipotle chile in adobo sauce, minced

2 cups heavy cream

1 cup milk

Salt and freshly ground black pepper, to taste

Granulated sugar, to taste

3 Tbsp all-purpose flour

Salt and freshly ground black pepper, to taste

4 boneless, skinless chicken breasts

2 Tbsp olive oil

2 to 3 cups hot cooked pasta

the
WEEKLY FEAST

SALMON

Buy

Look for fresh wild salmon—spring, chinook, coho, sockeye. Avoid farmed Atlantic salmon, whether it's from Chile or Canada. If you buy frozen salmon, look for FAS (Frozen at Sea) fish, which can actually be higher quality than fresh. Canned salmon is nearly always wild, and a cheap alternative. Check the Seafood Watch or OceanWise programs for tips.

Store

Fresh fish is extremely perishable—transport freshly caught fish on crushed ice. Eat fresh fish within a day of purchasing. To freeze, seal fillets using a vacuum-sealing system. Or dip fish in water, freeze, and redip (several times) to coat in ice before freezing. Eat frozen fish within 6 months.

Serve

Serve a cold side of salmon for summer buffets, garnished with chopped tomatoes and Niçoise olives, or slathered in a mayonnaise sauce and decorated with radish "scales." You can also "cook" a side of fresh salmon gravlax-style (marinated in fresh dill, salt, and sugar for a few days in the refrigerator and sliced like cold-smoked salmon).

Don't Waste It!

- Combine flaked grilled salmon with cream cheese, sour cream, chopped green onions, and dill for a dip for crackers and vegetables.
- Roll up grilled salmon with arugula and spiced mayo in flour tortillas for a fast lunch.
- Add flaked salmon to creamy pasta sauces.
- Make salmon salad sandwiches with mayonnaise, minced green onion, and dill.
- Add leftover flaked salmon to an egg frittata or omelet.
- Serve cold grilled salmon atop a mixed green or Caesar salad.
- Make a breakfast hash of sautéed onions and fried potatoes, then add chunks of grilled salmon, heavy cream, and chopped parsley to finish.
- Serve pieces of grilled salmon on a toasted burger bun with tomato, lettuce, avocado, and dill mayo.
- Make a creamy potato and onion chowder and add chunks of boneless salmon.
- Mix flaked salmon with mashed potatoes, chopped green onion, parsley, and a beaten egg for salmon cakes to fry for lunch (or make them small for appetizers topped with lemony mayo).

SLOW-ROASTED SALMON

It can be tricky to poach a side of salmon—most people don't have the special vessel for such things. But anyone can slow-roast a side of salmon in the oven, and the results are similar—a clean, simple, unembellished piece of fish that takes well to whatever sauce or accompaniment you choose. It's idiot-proof, too. Just preheat the oven, rub the fish with oil and salt, and it's done in 30 minutes flat. Try this technique with other fish, too. It works well with snapper, cod, and even tuna. **SERVES 4–6.**

1 side of salmon, skin on, about 2 inches thick (2 to 3 lb)

2 tsp olive oil

Salt

Preheat the oven to 275°F and line a baking sheet or baking pan with parchment paper. Rub the salmon all over with olive oil and season with salt. Place it on the baking sheet and bake for 30 to 40 minutes. The fish should flake easily and should be 120°F internally. Serve warm from the oven, garnished with a simple sauce or glaze; or cool the fish to room temperature, lift it onto a serving platter, then cover and refrigerate it for several hours, to serve cold, drizzled with aioli or herb oil.

> **TIP**
>
> You can also "poach" a side of salmon in the oven. Wrap the entire fillet in a heavy foil (season it with salt and pepper and throw in a splash of white wine), seal it up, slide it onto a baking pan, and bake it at 250°F for about 45 to 60 minutes. Let it cool in the foil, pour off any juice, and refrigerate until you're ready to serve it.

SALMON POT PIE

Start with fresh or leftover salmon for these classic fish pies, or substitute a mixture of cod, halibut, scallops, and shrimp. MAKES 4 INDIVIDUAL PIES, OR 1 LARGE POT PIE TO SERVE 4.

In a sauté pan over medium heat, sauté the mushrooms and garlic in 2 tablespoons of the butter for 10 minutes, until they are tender and almost dry. Cool. Spread the mushroom mixture over the bottom of 4 individual 2-cup ovenproof ramekins or one 8-cup soufflé dish.

In the mushroom pan over medium heat, sauté the onion in the remaining butter until tender and golden. Stir in the flour and cook for 1 minute. Slowly whisk in the wine, stock, and cream. Simmer, stirring, until you have a thick, smooth sauce. Mix in the parsley, thyme, and lemon juice. Season with salt and pepper.

Meanwhile, boil the potatoes in lots of salted water until tender, about 20 to 30 minutes, then drain and mash with the butter, cream, and black pepper. If you wish to pipe the potatoes over the pot pies, they should be very smooth. Otherwise, leave them a little chunky for texture.

Preheat the oven to 350°F.

Arrange the salmon chunks over the mushroom mixture in the baking dishes. Pour the sauce overtop. Cover each pie decoratively with mashed potatoes. Bake for 30 to 40 minutes, or until pies are bubbly and the tops are golden.

4 Tbsp butter, divided

1 cup finely chopped fresh mushrooms

2 cloves garlic, minced

1 medium onion, minced

1 Tbsp all-purpose flour

½ cup white wine

1 cup fish stock or water

½ cup heavy cream or milk

¼ cup chopped fresh parsley

1 Tbsp chopped fresh thyme or dill

1 Tbsp fresh lemon juice

Salt and freshly ground black pepper, to taste

1½ lb salmon fillet, skin and bones removed, cut into large cubes (or leftover salmon, cubed or flaked)

Topping:

2 lb Yukon Gold or other yellow-fleshed potatoes, boiled and mashed

3 Tbsp butter

¼ cup milk or heavy cream

Freshly ground black pepper, to taste

FARFALLE with SALMON and SOYBEANS

Here's an easy dish for a spring fling when you just want to get something fresh and green back into your life. SERVES 2.

Wash the spinach well to remove any grit and spin to dry. Stack the leaves and roll like cigars, then cut across into thin "chiffonade" strips. Set aside.

Bring a big pot of salted water to a boil and add the pasta and soybeans. Cook for 8 to 10 minutes, until the pasta is tender but still al dente. Drain well and dump into a large serving bowl. Add the spinach strips to the hot pasta and toss until the spinach is wilted. Stir in the dill, lemon zest, lemon juice, olive oil, and salt and pepper. Break the salmon into chunks and toss with the pasta. Serve immediately.

2 cups fresh spinach

1½ cups farfalle (butterfly) pasta

1 cup shelled soybeans (edamame), from the frozen food section of the Asian grocery

1 Tbsp chopped fresh dill

1 tsp finely grated lemon zest (use a Microplane grater)

1 Tbsp fresh lemon juice

2 to 3 Tbsp fruity extra-virgin olive oil

Salt and freshly ground black pepper, to taste

6 oz cooked salmon fillet

CHICKEN

Buy

Try to find a good organic, free-range chicken for roasting. You'll be amazed at the difference in flavor. Smaller chickens are meant for frying—a chicken that's older, 5 to 6 pounds, will be much tastier than a 3-pound fryer.

Store

A fresh chicken will keep for 2 to 3 days in the fridge (1 year in the freezer). Once cooked, roast chicken should be consumed within 3 to 4 days (it will keep for 2 to 6 months in the freezer). Refer to sell-by or freeze-by dates on fresh poultry.

Serve

A whole roast chicken is welcome at a family dinner or a dinner party. While chicken is a staple ingredient in everything from appetizers to main dishes, roast chicken can be easily recycled into soups, hot chicken or chicken salad sandwiches, salads, pasta and grain dishes, even pizza.

Don't Waste It!

- Make chicken salad sandwiches with leftover white meat and chopped green onion, celery, and mayo (add halved red grapes if you want to serve the chicken salad over greens).
- Add chopped chicken to a creamy tomato sauce to serve with pasta.
- Make chicken soup with the leftover carcass (see Turkey Stock on page 240 for instructions).
- Make a Spanish rice dish with Arborio, tomatoes, paprika, chorizo, and chunks of leftover chicken.
- Combine leftover chicken with a wild rice pilaf and grated cheese to stuff small winter squash for a tasty fall supper.
- Make tacos with cabbage salad, cilantro, salsa, and shredded chicken.
- Add slivered roast chicken to a Caesar salad for a main meal.
- Toss chicken with hoisin sauce and sesame oil and wrap in a small flour tortilla with shredded lettuce, carrots, cucumbers, and bean sprouts.
- Use leftover roast chicken with salsa, sliced avocados, cilantro, and grated cheese in crispy, smoky grilled quesadillas.
- Toss chopped roast chicken with cold rice, oil, and soy sauce in a hot wok, then add green onion, green peas, and peppers for speedy fried rice.
- A toasted panini sandwich, with sliced chicken and Swiss cheese, plus a slather of tomato pesto (or red pepper and eggplant spread), makes a fast hot lunch.

ROAST CHICKEN

The wonderful flavor of this simple chicken dish is achieved by stuffing herbs and garlic under the skin before roasting. SERVES 6.

Clean the chicken and pat dry. Preheat the oven to 450°F.

Using your fingers and starting around the neck cavity, slowly and carefully pull the skin away from the breast, working your hands down to pull skin away from the thighs and legs.

In a small bowl, combine the garlic, rosemary, and 1 tablespoon of the oil. Reserve 1 tablespoon of the mixture for the inside of the bird and, using your hands, evenly spread the rest of the mixture over the breast and leg meat but under the skin.

Season the inside of the bird with salt and pepper and the reserved garlic and rosemary mixture. Place a couple of pieces of lemon inside the bird and tie the legs together. Fold the wings under the chicken to hold the breast skin tight. Rub the breast with the remaining oil and set on a rack in a roasting pan, just large enough to hold the bird. Squeeze fresh lemon juice from the remaining lemon pieces overtop.

Place the chicken in the oven and roast for 30 minutes. Reduce heat to 400°F and continue roasting for about 50 minutes, basting occasionally. The chicken is done when the juices run clear and the leg moves easily in its socket. Remove the chicken to a platter to rest.

To make the gravy, pour the pan juices into a glass measuring cup and set aside for 5 minutes. The fat will rise to the top. Return 3 to 4 tablespoons of the fat to the roasting pan and set over medium heat. Stir in the flour to make a thick paste, adding more if necessary. Skim away any remaining fat from the pan juices, and slowly add the pan juices to the flour mixture in the pan, whisking as you go.

Let the gravy come up to a boil and stir in 1 cup of the stock or water; continue adding more stock, a little at a time, just until you have a gravy of the proper consistency. Season with salt and pepper.

Serve chicken and gravy with potatoes.

1 roasting chicken, preferably organic, about 5 to 6 lb

8 cloves garlic, minced

2 Tbsp minced fresh rosemary (do not substitute dried)

2 Tbsp canola oil, divided

Salt and freshly ground black pepper

1 whole lemon, cut into quarters

Gravy:

2 Tbsp all-purpose flour, plus more if needed

3 to 4 cups chicken stock or water

Salt and freshly ground black pepper, to taste

PANANG CHICKEN CURRY

With leftover roast chicken, some eggplant, red pepper, and exotic spices, in 10 minutes you'll be dining on this amazing Thai curry. Serve it over jasmine or basmati rice and that's it—dinner's done. Try this dish with leftover turkey, too. **SERVES 2-4.**

Bring a pot of water to a boil and blanch the eggplant for 2 minutes to soften.

Drain and set aside. Remove the chicken from the bones and chop into chunks.

In a large wok over high, heat the oil until it begins to smoke. Add the garlic and fry for 10 seconds, then stir in the red pepper and curry paste. When the curry paste sizzles, add the stock, lemongrass, peanut butter, sugar, coconut milk, fish sauce, and wine, and bring to a rolling boil.

Stir in the blanched eggplant and the chicken, and toss to coat well with the sauce. Bring back to a boil, stir in the cornstarch solution, and simmer until the sauce is thickened and the eggplant is cooked, about 3 to 4 minutes. Serve immediately, sprinkled with chopped peanuts and cilantro.

TIPS

It's easy to cook authentic-tasting Thai food with a bit of red or green curry paste. Both come in resealable tubs and keep in the fridge for months. Find curry pastes at Asian groceries along with the lemongrass, fish sauce, and fat-reduced canned coconut milk you'll need for this fast dish.

Lemongrass looks like tall, pale green onion, but it's tough as nails. Use the bottom 10 inches of the stalk only, and mince it finely or pulverize it in a blender or food processor. Freeze the tougher tops to add whole to curries or soups to add subtle lemony flavor, then remove before serving.

---

1 medium eggplant, peeled and cut into ½-inch cubes

Half of a leftover roast chicken (about 1 lb boneless meat)

1 tsp vegetable oil

1 clove garlic, minced

1 red bell pepper, seeded and cut into chunks

2 to 3 tsp Thai red curry paste

1 cup chicken stock

1 (2- to 3-inch) piece lemongrass, minced or pulverized in a blender (or 2 tsp finely grated lemon zest)

1 tsp natural peanut butter

2 tsp granulated sugar

1 cup regular or low-fat coconut milk

1 tsp Asian fish sauce

1 tsp Chinese cooking wine

1 Tbsp cornstarch mixed with 1 Tbsp cold water

1 tsp chopped roasted peanuts

1 tsp chopped fresh cilantro

TORTILLA SOUP

With a ripe avocado, a few corn tortillas, and a little leftover chicken, this simple soup comes together in minutes. Serve with grilled or panfried quesadillas, filled with salsa, cheese, and refried beans, for a fast weekday dinner. **SERVES 4.**

In a sauté pan over high, heat the canola oil until nearly smoking. Reduce heat to medium-high and add the tortilla strips, cooking until crisp and lightly browned. Set aside on a plate lined with paper towel to absorb excess oil.

In a large saucepan over medium-high heat, combine the stock, tomatoes, and lime juice, and bring to a boil. Reduce the heat to medium, and stir in the hot sauce and leftover chicken. Simmer for 1 to 2 minutes, just until the chicken is heated through. Taste and adjust seasoning with more hot sauce or a touch of salt or pepper, if necessary.

Arrange the crispy tortilla strips in the bottoms of 4 shallow soup bowls, and top each with a quarter of the cheese. Add the avocado to the bowls and ladle the hot soup overtop, making sure to divide the chicken equally among the bowls. Garnish with the green onions and cilantro (if using) and serve immediately.

¼ cup canola oil

2 fresh corn tortillas, cut into thin strips

4 cups chicken or turkey stock (canned or homemade)

2 ripe Roma tomatoes, seeded and finely chopped

Juice of 1 lime (about 2 Tbsp)

6 drops hot sauce (or more to taste)

½ lb leftover roast chicken, cut into strips

Salt and freshly ground black pepper, to taste

½ cup grated Monterey Jack or mozzarella cheese

1 firm but ripe avocado, chopped

2 green onions, chopped, for garnish

Chopped fresh cilantro, for garnish (optional)

SPEEDY THAI CHICKEN SALAD

With leftover roast chicken, steamed Asian noodles, and romaine lettuce, this spicy chicken salad makes a super summer meal for dining on the deck. SERVES 4.

Whirl the dressing ingredients together in a food processor or blender until smooth. Dressing may be made a day in advance and refrigerated.

Bring a very large pot of water to a boil and add the noodles. Cook them just for a couple of minutes, then drain well in a colander in the sink and rinse under cold water to chill.

In a large salad bowl, combine the lettuce, half the mint, half the cilantro, and the carrot. Add just enough dressing to lightly coat the vegetables and toss well. In a separate bowl, toss the cold noodles with some of the remaining dressing (leftover dressing keeps well in the refrigerator for several days).

Divide the salad mixture among 4 large bowls. Top each salad artfully with a pile of noodles, some cucumber and chicken, the remaining mint and cilantro, and the onion. Sprinkle with the chopped peanuts to garnish.

Dressing:

1 Tbsp minced garlic

1 Tbsp Asian garlic chili paste (sambal oelek)

½ cup sweet Indonesian soy sauce (ketjap manis) (see Tips)

6 to 8 Tbsp fresh lime juice (juice of 3 to 4 limes)

1 Tbsp sesame oil

Salad:

½ lb thin Asian steamed noodles (bagged in the produce department)

6 cups chopped romaine lettuce or mixed baby greens

½ cup fresh mint leaves, shredded if large

¼ cup chopped fresh cilantro

1 large carrot, peeled and shredded

½ English cucumber, seeded and cut into matchstick pieces

Leftover roast chicken

½ cup finely diced red onion

½ cup dry-roasted peanuts, chopped (see Tips)

TIPS

Ketjap manis, a thick, sweet soy sauce from Indonesia with the consistency of molasses, is the key ingredient in this easy dressing. If you can't find it, combine 1 cup soy sauce with 1 cup dark brown sugar, 1 cup water, ½ cup dark molasses, and 1 crushed garlic clove, and simmer for 5 minutes. Cool, strain, and store in the refrigerator.

To "chop" the dry-roasted peanuts, simply dump them on the cutting board, place the flat side of your big chef's knife over them, and press down. The nuts will crumble into nice small bits, and you won't have them flying around the kitchen.

TURKEY

Buy

Look for a local, free-range bird for the best flavor and avoid anything labeled "butter basted" (read: injected with saturated or hydrogenated fat). Big free-range, organic birds often tip the scales at nearly 20 pounds, so invite an army or plan for lots of leftovers.

Store

Fresh turkey should be cooked within 2 to 3 days of purchase. Turkey labeled "previously frozen" must be cooked within 48 hours of purchase. A frozen whole turkey will keep for a year in the freezer. Do not leave turkey (cooked or raw) at room temperature for longer than 2 hours. Cooked turkey may be refrigerated for up to 4 days or frozen for up to 4 months.

Serve

If the turkey is frozen, it will take about 4 hours per pound (10 hours per kg) to thaw the bird in the fridge (that's 2 to 3 days for a small bird). Don't thaw it at room temperature or cook a partially frozen bird, or you risk salmonella poisoning. To save time, place the turkey, still in its plastic wrap, in a sink and cover completely with cold water. Allow 1 hour per pound (2 hours per kg) to thaw, and keep the water cold. You can roast a turkey stuffed or unstuffed, grill or smoke a whole bird, or even deep-fry a turkey in a giant fryer (with a pitchfork to submerge it in the hot oil).

Don't Waste It!

- Of course, you will save the turkey carcass to make homemade turkey stock (if you don't have time now, just freeze the bones and make stock later).
- Make turkey/mashed potato/gravy/stuffing/peas TV dinners— just freeze in a shallow plastic or metal container to pull out on busy nights.
- Use roast turkey breast meat in a classic clubhouse (AKA Dagwood) sandwich: stack it with toast, bacon, ham, cheddar, tomato, and mustard mayo.
- Reheat the small bits of leftover turkey in the leftover gravy and pour over toasted bread for hot turkey sandwiches.
- Add leftover turkey to stir-fries, curries, and pasta dishes (any place you might use chicken).
- Shred leftover turkey and mix with mole sauce to wrap up in corn tortillas.
- Combine shredded turkey with leftover rice and fry in a wok with oil, soy sauce, bean sprouts, ginger, green onions, and peas for fried rice.
- Toss turkey with spicy tomato salsa and roll up in flour tortillas with grated cheese, lettuce, cilantro, and refried beans.

ROAST TURKEY

It always amazes me that so many people have never cooked a whole turkey, and forget about things like thawing the frozen bird or using the giblets. So here's a primer, to pull out for every holiday (and on other occasions when a big bird is an appropriate centerpiece to the feast). SERVES 12, WITH LEFTOVERS.

Preheat the oven to 325°F.

Remove the plastic from the turkey, take the neck and giblets out of the cavity (they should be in a bag), rinse inside and out with cold water, and pat dry with paper towels. Put the neck and giblets in a pot of water with the onion, carrot, peppercorns, and parsley, and simmer to make a broth for your gravy.

Place the turkey on a rack in a large roasting pan, breast side up. Brush with the oil or melted butter and season inside and out with a little salt and pepper.

If stuffing the bird, wait until just before roasting. Do not pack the stuffing; the bird should be loosely filled. (See Tip for a bread stuffing recipe.)

Cover the bird loosely with foil. Roast until the internal temperature reads 180°F for a stuffed turkey, or 170°F for an unstuffed bird. Use an instant-read meat thermometer, inserted in the thickest part of the thigh to test the internal temperature (don't leave it in while the bird is roasting; just use it for testing). Make sure you take the temperature of the stuffing, too. It should be at least 165°F in the center of the stuffing. It doesn't take as long as you think to roast a turkey to perfection—about 3 to 4 hours for a stuffed bird, about 15 minutes per pound. Start checking the temperature early.

When the turkey is done, remove the pan from the oven and let the bird rest on a cutting board, covered loosely with a piece of foil, for 20 to 30 minutes. This will allow the juices to set and give you time to make the gravy.

12 to 16 lb turkey, thawed (see "Serve" on p. 237)

½ onion

1 carrot

10 whole black peppercorns

Handful fresh parsley

2 Tbsp oil or melted butter

Salt and freshly ground black pepper

3 to 4 Tbsp all-purpose flour

Pour the juices from the roasting pan into a heatproof glass measuring cup and set aside. (If there is just a small amount of fat/juice in the pan, drain off all but 3 tablespoons.) Place the roasting pan on the stove over medium heat and sprinkle the flour over the fat and browned bits in the roasting pan. Stir with a wooden spoon to moisten the flour and loosen the browned bits. Add the reserved juices and a little water and stir in well, creating a thick paste. When the mixture is hot and bubbling, strain the broth you have been simmering on the stove, and add it to the pan, a little at a time, stirring as you go to avoid lumps. Let the gravy come back to a boil each time, and add a little more liquid if it's still too thick. Season to taste with salt and pepper. Keep warm in a gravy boat or small pitcher.

Using a large spoon, remove all of the stuffing from the cavity of the bird and place it in a covered dish in the oven to stay warm.

Carve the turkey. Remove the leg and thigh pieces first and slice the meat from the bone, arranging the dark meat at one end of the platter. Slice the breast meat. Start at the base of the breast (where you've removed the legs) and slice vertically, parallel to the breastbone, into thin, even slices. Arrange on a platter, and pass the stuffing and the gravy.

✎ TIP

For dressing to stuff a turkey, dice 1 loaf of day-old bread (you can use a combination of white and grainy breads), combine with 2 to 3 cups of minced onion and celery that's been sautéed in ½ cup of butter until tender, and season with 1 teaspoon each of dried thyme, dried sage, and celery salt (or to taste). To serve alone, as a side dish, add some stock and bake in a covered casserole dish. You can also use this dressing to stuff squash or layer with fish fillets before baking.

TURKEY STOCK

Always save all of the bones, wings, and trimmings from your holiday turkey (or roast chicken) to make stock. Just add egg noodles for a comforting soup or freeze this healthy broth—it is the perfect base for other soups or to cure a cold in flu season. Really is like money in the bank. MAKES ABOUT 12 CUPS.

Place the turkey carcass and any leftover bones in a large stockpot. Add the remaining ingredients to the pot and cover with cold water (the carcass should be submerged; break it into pieces if necessary).

Bring to a boil over high heat, reduce heat to low, cover partially, and simmer for several hours, topping up with more water as it boils away. You can also do this in a pressure cooker in about 30 minutes.

Let the mixture cool somewhat before straining through a sieve or cheesecloth. Discard the bones and vegetables. Skim excess fat.

1 roast turkey carcass (meat removed) and scraps

1 large parsnip, peeled and cut into chunks

2 carrots, peeled and cut into chunks

2 stalks celery, with leaves, cut into chunks

1 onion, quartered

2 tsp salt

4 to 5 black peppercorns

3 sprigs fresh parsley

TURKEY POT PIE with WHITE CHEDDAR CRUST

You'll never know you're eating leftovers. Cooked chicken or even pork roast could stand in for the turkey in this comforting dish. SERVES 6.

Boil the squash cubes in salted water until just tender, about 8 minutes. Remove with a slotted spoon to a casserole dish, reserving 1 cup of the cooking liquid.

Preheat the oven to 400°F.

In a saucepan, melt the butter and sauté the onion for 5 minutes, until soft. Stir in the flour and cook for 1 minute. Slowly add the stock and reserved squash-cooking liquid. Bring to a boil. Stir in the sage and pepper and simmer until thick, about 10 minutes.

Stir in the beans, turkey, and parsley. Pour over the squash in the dish. Check seasoning and adjust if necessary.

For the biscuit topping, combine the flour, baking powder, and salt in a bowl. Blend in the butter using your hands or a pastry cutter until crumbly. Stir in the cheese and enough milk to form a sticky dough. Drop by the tablespoonful over the turkey mixture in the baking dish.

Bake the pot pie for 25 to 30 minutes, until topping is golden. Dust with cayenne or paprika before serving.

2½ cups water

1 tsp salt

1 lb peeled butternut squash, cubed

2 Tbsp butter

1 medium onion, slivered

2 Tbsp all-purpose flour

1 cup turkey or chicken stock

2 Tbsp minced fresh sage

½ tsp freshly ground black pepper

1 cup cooked white beans (or canned white beans, rinsed and drained)

3 cups cubed leftover roast turkey

1 Tbsp chopped fresh parsley

Cheddar biscuits:

1 cup all-purpose flour

1 tsp baking powder

½ tsp salt

2 Tbsp cold butter

1½ cups grated aged cheddar cheese

⅔ cup skim milk

Cayenne or paprika, for dusting

TURKEY and CORN CHOWDER

You'll never recognize the holiday bird in this spicy soup. This is a meal in a bowl garnished with crushed tortilla chips or curly strips of corn tortillas that have been fried until crisp. SERVES 4–6.

In a large soup pot over medium, heat the oil and sauté the onion and garlic for 5 minutes. Add the celery, pepper, and carrots, and cook for 5 minutes.

Stir in the oregano, cumin, and chili paste, and heat for 1 minute, then add the stock, tomato sauce, and jalapeno. Bring the soup to a boil over high heat, then reduce heat to low and simmer for 10 minutes.

Stir in the corn and chopped turkey and continue to simmer for 15 to 20 minutes, until all of the vegetables are tender. Stir in the lime juice and season the soup with salt and pepper and extra chili paste to taste, if desired.

Serve in shallow bowls, with a few corn tortilla chips crushed on top.

1 Tbsp canola oil

1 onion, minced

2 cloves garlic, minced

3 stalks celery, finely chopped

1 red bell pepper, seeded and finely diced

2 carrots, finely diced

2 tsp dried oregano

1 tsp ground cumin

1 tsp chili paste

4 cups chicken stock

1 (7½ oz) can tomato sauce

1 fresh jalapeno chile, seeded and minced

2 cups fresh, canned, or frozen corn kernels

2 cups chopped leftover roast turkey (or chicken)

2 Tbsp fresh lime juice

Salt and freshly ground black pepper, to taste

Crushed tortilla chips (or fried corn tortilla strips), for garnish

HURRY CURRY

Add your leftover roast turkey to this quick curry sauce and you'll have a dish reminiscent of your favorite butter chicken from the local curry house. Find garam masala and fenugreek leaves at Indian groceries. This curry is even better reheated the next day, after the flavors have had lots of time to marry. **SERVES 4–6.**

In a saucepan over medium, heat the butter, and sauté the onion, ginger, and garlic together for about 10 minutes, until starting to brown. Stir in the garam masala, turmeric, and dried fenugreek, and cook for 1 minute to release the aromas.

Add the chicken stock and tomatoes. Stir in the chili paste. Bring to a boil and simmer for about 1 hour, until the mixture is thickened. Add a little honey or salt to adjust the balance, and more chili paste if needed.

Stir in the cream and return to a simmer.

Add the leftover turkey and heat through. Add two-thirds of the cilantro, and heat the mixture for an additional 10 minutes. Serve with the hot basmati rice, sprinkled with the remaining cilantro (or chill to reheat and serve a day later).

¼ cup butter

1 medium onion, minced

1-inch knob ginger, minced

3 cloves garlic, minced

2 Tbsp garam masala

1 rounded tsp ground turmeric

1 tsp dried fenugreek leaves (kasoori methi), crushed

1½ cups chicken stock

1 (24 oz) jar plain Italian strained tomatoes

1 tsp Asian chili paste

Honey, to taste

Salt, to taste

½ cup heavy cream

2 to 3 cups leftover roast turkey, cut into large cubes

2 Tbsp chopped fresh cilantro, divided

Hot cooked basmati rice, for serving

> ✐ **TIP**
> To save time, use a food processor to mince the onion, ginger, and garlic.

PORK

Buy

Pork roasts range from inexpensive shoulder (or butt) cuts (best for braising) to the lean leg (boneless for fast oven roasts), tenderloin (to grill), and cured hams. Look for pork belly with crispy crackling intact to roll and stuff. Heirloom breeds and ethically raised, grass-fed, or pastured pork is some of the most delicious pork around. Meat should be firm and rosy pink. Keep in mind that wild boar is extra lean and should be treated like game meats.

Store

Cook fresh pork within 2 to 3 days or wrap well and freeze for up to 6 months. A cooked ham doesn't freeze well, but leftovers can be frozen and used in soups or casseroles.

Serve

Roast pork for about 25 minutes per pound (start with a room temperature roast), to an internal temperature of 145°F to 160°F (140°F for cured ham). It's perfect when cooked to a juicy medium, not well done. Remove at 150°F and let rest for 10 minutes.

Pork butt is perfect for smoking (AKA pulled pork), as it's naturally larded with just enough fat to keep it moist and juicy for hours on the grill, even if the heat rises above the magic 225°F mark.

Whether you roast a whole, bone-in ham or a leg, or make pulled pork, it's always good to have leftover pork on hand.

Don't Waste It!

- Add some heavy cream or sour cream and sweet Hungarian paprika to your leftover gravy, stir in slivers of cooked pork, add some sautéed mushrooms, onions, and bell peppers, and serve over egg noodles, for an almost instant goulash.

- Chop leftover roast vegetables and pork, add some chicken stock and canned white beans, and simmer, for a hearty soup.

- Try a Cuban sandwich: layer roast pork with ham, Swiss cheese, mustard, and a garlicky cilantro pesto, and toast in your panini press until hot and gooey.

- Make a Mexican-style posole with canned hominy, cubed pork, chicken stock, oregano, cumin, onions, and roasted tomatillos.

- Make mu shu: shred leftover roast pork and toss with hoisin sauce, then stir-fry with shredded cabbage and minced ginger, garlic, and shiitake mushrooms, and fold into small flour tortillas.

- Chop cooked ham in the food processor and combine with mayonnaise, mustard, and chopped capers for a sandwich spread or picnic pâté.

- Combine cubes of cold baked ham with cooked short pasta, chopped red onions, yellow peppers, green beans, and a mustard-mayonnaise dressing for a colorful pasta salad.

- Make individual ham and pineapple pizzas with tomato sauce and mozzarella cheese on pita breads.

- Add ham to creamy sauces for pasta along with Parmesan and sautéed mushrooms or green peas.

- Line muffin tins with slices of ham, top each with an egg and some cheese, and bake for brunch.

- Stuff ham and cheese inside a boneless chicken breast, then bread the chicken, and bake or fry for speedy chicken Cordon Bleu.

- Ham and slivered peaches with salsa and mozzarella make great grilled quesadillas.

ROAST LEG of PORK with ROASTED ROOTS

Take a boneless pork leg roast, season it with garlic, herbs, and chiles, and surround it with caramelized root vegetables. Could Sunday dinner be any easier? This method of partially braising the roast keeps it moist and tender. SERVES 6.

Mince the rosemary, garlic, and salt together until fine. Combine with the pepper, sage, chile pepper, and 1 teaspoon of the olive oil to form a paste. Using a long, thin-bladed knife, cut 12 slits into the roast and press some of the seasoning mixture into each slit. Rub any excess over the roast and let stand at room temperature for 30 minutes.

Preheat the oven to 325°F.

Heat the remaining oil in a heavy roasting pan over medium-high. When the oil is very hot, brown the roast on all sides.

Set the meat in the pan, fat side up, and pour in the wine.

Cover the pan and roast for 1 hour. Remove the lid and place the onions, potatoes, beets, carrots, and rutabaga around the roast. Stir to coat them in pan drippings. Return the roast to the oven, uncovered, and roast for an additional hour, until the meat reaches an internal temperature of 160°F. Add more wine or water if necessary during roasting if the pan gets dry.

Remove the roast and vegetables from the pan. Place the roast on a platter, tent with foil, and let rest for 15 minutes before carving.

Slice the roast and serve surrounded by roasted vegetables.

2 Tbsp minced fresh rosemary

3 cloves garlic, minced

2 tsp salt

¼ tsp freshly ground black pepper

½ tsp dried sage

1 dried red chile pepper, crumbled

3 Tbsp olive oil, divided

4 lb pork leg roast, deboned and rolled

1 cup white wine

12 small boiling onions, peeled, or 1 large white onion, cut into wedges

12 baby potatoes, scrubbed but not peeled

3 medium beets, peeled and quartered

4 carrots, peeled and cut into chunks

1 small rutabaga, peeled and cubed

↵ TIP

Scatter a couple of tablespoons of flour over the drippings in the pan and slowly whisk in a little white wine and water, stirring up the brown bits to make a light gravy.

PORK and BEANS

Make this easy campfire classic from scratch and you'll never go back to the canned version. Use any leftover pork, whether you have pork chops, pork tenderloin, or roast pork shoulder (even pulled pork). Serve these beans on their own, with barbecued meats, or alongside eggs for breakfast. SERVES 4.

In a heavy saucepan or Dutch oven over medium, heat the oil and sauté the onion and garlic for 5 minutes, until soft. Stir in the cold coffee, stock, or water, stirring up any browned bits from the bottom of the pan, then add the tomato juice, maple syrup, molasses, dry mustard, and chile. Bring to a boil.

Rinse the beans in a strainer, under running water, to remove all of the thick canning liquid. Drain well. Stir the beans into the pot along with the pork. Season with salt and pepper.

Bring the beans to a boil, reduce heat to low, cover the pot, and simmer for 1 hour, or transfer the beans to a covered casserole dish or bean pot and bake them in the oven for 1 hour at 250°F.

1 Tbsp olive oil

1 medium onion, or
4 fat shallots, minced

1 clove garlic, minced

½ cup cold coffee,
chicken stock, or water

1 cup V8 or plain
tomato juice

¼ cup maple syrup

2 Tbsp molasses

2 tsp dry mustard

1 canned chipotle
chile, minced (or 1 tsp
Asian chili paste)

2 (15 oz) cans white beans

1 lb leftover lean
roast pork, cubed

Salt and freshly ground
black pepper, to taste

BARBECUE PORK BUTT
(FOR PULLED PORK SANDWICHES)

Use this technique for creating tender meat out of pork butt (AKA shoulder). This is the perfect cut to smoke as it has just enough fat to keep it moist and juicy for hours on the grill, even if you accidentally let the heat rise above the magic 225°F mark. If you don't have a grill, you can cook the pork butt on a rack in a roasting pan in a low (200°F) oven for 8 hours, until the pork is so tender that it tears when you try to lift it with a fork. It won't be the same, but you can add some smoked Spanish paprika to the rub or add some smoky barbecue sauce at the end for extra BBQ flavor. **SERVES 6.**

Rub the pork with the mustard to coat on all sides. Combine the dry rub ingredients and massage generously into the pork. Leave the pork at room temperature for 10 minutes, for the rub to get tacky. The salt will draw some of the moisture out of the meat, forming a crust as it cooks that will seal in the juices.

Preheat the smoker or barbecue. If you're using coals, place the pork on a rack above the coals; toss some presoaked apple or mesquite wood chips on the coals to generate some smoke. If you're using a gas grill, turn one burner off and place the roast on the unlit side of the grill. (Put the wet wood chips into a metal smoking box or a pouch of heavy foil, punched with holes, and set it right on top of the fire bricks or gas flame.)

Keep the heat constant and low (about 200°F to 225°F) and cook the pork until the internal temperature reaches 180°F. The pork should be tender and falling apart, easy to "pull" into shreds with a fork. This will take 6 to 8 hours.

Combine the sauce ingredients in a saucepan over medium heat and whisk until warm and well combined.

Shred the cooked pork and pile it on the crusty rolls, then drizzle with the mustard sauce. Serve the sandwiches with coleslaw on the side or piled on the sandwich.

> **TIP**
> Pork is safe to eat at an internal temperature of 165°F. At this point the pork will be cooked and sliceable. But for pulled pork you must cook the meat to the "falling apart" stage (around 185°F to 190°F).

1 pork butt or shoulder, bone-in, about 3 lb (leg is too lean for this process)

¼ cup regular ballpark mustard such as French's (don't use fancy Dijon, as it doesn't contain enough sugar)

Dry rub:

¼ cup Hungarian paprika (or other good-quality, sweet paprika)

¼ cup granulated sugar

2 Tbsp brown sugar

2 Tbsp ground cumin

2 Tbsp ground ginger

2 Tbsp chili powder

2 Tbsp black pepper

2 Tbsp garlic powder

1 Tbsp dry mustard

1 Tbsp salt

Mustard sauce:

¼ cup mustard

2 Tbsp honey

1 Tbsp mayonnaise

1 Tbsp ketchup

1 Tbsp apple cider vinegar

1 tsp Tabasco sauce

1 clove garlic, puréed through a press

6 to 8 crusty rolls

PULLED PORK TOSTADAS

An easy and classic recipe—BBQ pork piled high on crispy tostadas with cabbage slaw, fresh salsa, and avocados. SERVES 4.

In a sauté pan over medium-high, heat about ½ inch of vegetable oil and fry the tortillas, one at a time, until crisp and lightly browned. When the oil is hot enough, this will take about 1 minute.

Set the fried tortillas on a baking sheet that's lined with paper towels to drain, and fry remaining tortillas.

In a bowl, combine the cabbage, radishes, lime juice, and salt and pepper. Set aside to allow to wilt.

Set the slaw, pulled pork, salsa, crème fraîche, and avocado out in small bowls along with the tortillas, and let guests assemble their own tostadas.

Vegetable oil, for frying

8 fresh corn tortillas

2 cups shredded napa cabbage

3 radishes, thinly sliced

2 Tbsp fresh lime juice

Salt and freshly ground black pepper, to taste

2 cups shredded leftover pulled pork, warmed (see p. 248)

½ cup fresh tomato salsa

½ cup crème fraîche or sour cream

1 ripe avocado, sliced

SPINACH, PORK, and
POBLANO TORTILLA CASSEROLE

Make this creamy casserole when there's too much spinach in the garden and leftover pulled pork in the fridge. You can also use shredded barbecued or rotisserie chicken. SERVES 6–8.

In a large pot of boiling water, blanch the spinach for 1 minute. Drain and chill in a large bowl of ice water. Once cooled, squeeze the spinach dry, then chop and set aside.

Roast the chiles on the barbecue, over a direct gas flame, or under a broiler until blackened on all sides. Place them in a bowl, cover with plastic wrap, and set aside to steam. When the peppers are cool, scrape off the blackened skin and discard the stems and seeds. Chop the roasted chiles. Set aside two-thirds for the filling, and one-third for the sauce.

In a large saucepan over medium heat, melt the butter, stir in the olive oil, and sauté the onion until tender. Stir in the chili powder, cayenne, and flour to form a smooth roux. Slowly whisk in the milk and cream to make a thick sauce. Stir in the spinach, two-thirds of the roasted poblanos, the pork, and the corn. Cook together until very thick. Remove from heat. Stir in the mozzarella and allow to cool.

When cool, stir in three-quarters of the jalapeno jack cheese.

Place the tortillas into a covered container and microwave for 1 minute to soften (or soften each tortilla for about 10 seconds per side in a hot pan).

Preheat the oven to 350°F. Lightly oil a large shallow baking pan.

Place a warm tortilla on your work surface, spoon about ⅓ cup of filling down the center, roll into a cigar, and set, seam side down, into the baking pan. Continue until you have filled all of the tortillas.

For the sauce, melt the butter in a saucepan over medium-high, stir in the flour, then gradually whisk in the stock. Bring to a boil, then add the cream, tomato, and remaining chopped poblano.

Pour the sauce evenly over the filled tortillas. Scatter the remaining jalapeno jack and a little extra mozzarella overtop.

Bake for 30 to 45 minutes, until bubbly and browned. Let rest for 10 minutes before serving.

8 cups fresh spinach

3 large fresh poblano chiles

2 Tbsp butter

1 Tbsp olive oil

1 onion, minced

1½ to 2 tsp chili powder

½ tsp cayenne

¼ cup all-purpose flour

1 cup milk

1 cup heavy cream

2 to 3 cups leftover pulled pork, chopped (see p. 248)

1 cup fresh, canned, or frozen corn kernels

½ cup grated mozzarella cheese, plus extra for the top of the casserole

½ lb jalapeno jack cheese, chopped (divided)

24 fresh corn tortillas

Sauce:

3 Tbsp butter

3 Tbsp all-purpose flour

2 cups chicken stock

¼ cup heavy cream

1 large tomato, seeded and chopped

BAKED HAM

Buy a fresh ham, glaze, and bake for special occasions—then use the leftovers for sandwiches, breakfasts, fried rice, and soups (if there's a bone, save it for flavoring pots of beans or pea soup). A whole ham weighs 10 to 20 pounds, so they're usually sold in sections or halves. SERVES 8.

Preheat the oven to 325°F.

Remove all but ¼ inch of fat from the ham and score the fat in a diamond pattern.

Place the ham on a rack in a large roasting pan with a lid and add a little water, juice, wine, or beer to the bottom of the pan. Bake, covered, basting every 30 minutes. Since most hams are already fully cooked, you just need to heat it through—it should take about 10 to 15 minutes per pound. Use an instant-read thermometer and pull the ham out of the oven when the internal temperature reaches 155°F.

Meanwhile, simmer your preferred glaze ingredients together for a few minutes.

Increase the oven temperature to 425°F, then spoon or brush the ham with the glaze, and bake for an additional 20 to 30 minutes, basting with the glaze every 10 minutes to glaze the outside nicely.

Set the ham on a cutting board, tent with foil, and allow to rest for 20 minutes before slicing. Pour the pan juices into a measuring cup and skim off excess fat. Return the pan juices to the roasting pan and simmer over high heat to reduce and thicken slightly.

Carve the ham, saving the bones and trimming for soup. Pass the sauce to drizzle over the sliced ham.

Bone-in half or quarter ham, 5 lb

Water, juice, wine, or beer, for basting

Glazes:

½ cup apricot jam

¼ cup Dijon mustard

3 Tbsp orange juice or lime juice

OR

½ cup marmalade

¼ cup Dijon mustard

3 Tbsp orange juice or lime juice

OR

½ cup dark beer or stout

¼ cup honey

¼ cup packed brown sugar

1 Tbsp fresh lemon juice

SPECIAL FRIED RICE

When you prepare rice, do a big batch and then make fried rice with the leftovers. You can add almost anything to your fried rice, from ham and chicken to barbecue pork or prawns and bell peppers or frozen peas. This version has ham, baby bok choy, and mushrooms, but get creative and use what you have in the fridge. Just remember the garlic, egg, and soy sauce, then make it special with your own leftovers. SERVES 4.

2 cups baby bok choy

1 cup fresh shiitake or other brown mushrooms

3 Tbsp canola oil

1 Tbsp minced garlic

3 to 4 cups leftover cooked rice, cold

½ lb ham (or roast chicken), cut into small cubes

2 eggs, lightly beaten with 1 tsp sesame oil

2 Tbsp light soy sauce

1 Tbsp oyster sauce or hoisin sauce

2 green onions, chopped

Separate the leaves of the bok choy and rinse well (it can be gritty), then stack and slice into shreds. Rinse the mushrooms quickly to remove any debris, trim the stems, and cut into slivers.

Place a large wok over high heat for 30 seconds, then add the oil, drizzling it around the top of the wok so it falls down the sides. Immediately add the garlic and stir-fry for 1 minute. Turn the heat down slightly to medium-high, then add the cold rice, spreading it evenly over the surface of the pan. Stir-fry the rice for 1 to 2 minutes, then add the bok choy and mushrooms, stirring and cooking for 3 to 5 minutes, until both begin to wilt and give up some liquid. Add the ham and stir to combine.

Push the rice to one side and add the beaten eggs to the pan, stirring to scramble softly. When the eggs are set, mix them into the rice and continue to stir-fry.

Whisk together the soy sauce and oyster sauce. Add to the rice, tossing to combine. Add the green onions and serve immediately.

HAM and WHITE BEAN, SPLIT PEA, or LENTIL SOUP

This is a versatile soup recipe that uses the leftover ham bone. Feel free to add more vegetables—a cup of frozen green peas or shredded cabbage is a nice addition at the end—or use some fresh chopped herbs like parsley. I like to add some leftover cooked rice or barley to this soup for added texture, too. **SERVES 6–8.**

In a deep stockpot over medium, heat the olive oil and sauté the onions, garlic, celery, and carrot until tender and starting to color.

Add the potato, chicken stock, wine, water, and ham bone. Stir in the thyme, bay leaf, cayenne, and beans.

Bring to a boil, cover, reduce heat to low, and simmer for 1 hour. Remove the ham bone. Remove any cooked ham from the bone, chop, and stir back into the soup along with the tomato. Adjust the seasoning if necessary and add the peas, cooked rice, cabbage, or parsley, if desired. You can crush some of the potato against the side of the pot, to help thicken the mixture, or partially purée the soup with a hand blender to make it smoother, if desired.

2 Tbsp olive oil

2 cups chopped onions

2 Tbsp chopped garlic

½ cup chopped celery

½ cup chopped carrot

1 medium potato, peeled and chopped or shredded

4 cups chicken stock

1 cup white wine

2 cups water

1 meaty ham bone or chunk of ham

½ tsp dried thyme

1 bay leaf

Pinch cayenne

2 cups small white beans, soaked overnight (or use 2 cups rinsed split peas or brown lentils, no soaking necessary)

1 tomato, seeded and chopped

Salt and freshly ground black pepper, to taste

1 cup frozen green peas, thawed (optional)

½ cup cooked rice or barley (optional)

½ cup slivered cabbage (optional)

1 Tbsp chopped fresh Italian parsley (optional)

LAMB

Buy

Lamb is associated with spring or Easter, but today you can buy fresh young lamb year round. Imported lamb from New Zealand is 100 percent grass fed and leaner than domestic lamb, which is usually grain finished like beef. North American animals—and roasts—are therefore much larger. A "sirloin end" leg roast is meatier than a "shank end" roast. Meat should be pink to red in color with slight marbling.

Store

Store fresh lamb roasts for 3 to 5 days in the refrigerator or vacuum-seal to freeze for up to 4 months. Refer to sell-by or freeze-by dates on fresh meat.

Serve

A boneless leg is easiest to roast. Buy a bone-in roast and ask the butcher to debone and tie the roast, then take the bones home for soup. Or get a boneless lamb shoulder roast to braise. Leftovers are perfect for Indian curries and shepherd's pie.

Don't Waste It!

- Add leftover roast lamb to white bean cassoulet with carrots, celery, onions, garlic, tomato, and chicken sausage, topped with buttered bread crumbs.
- Use leftover roast lamb in an Indian rice biryani with lots of fried onions, garlic, and curry powder, and a bit of mango chutney.
- Make couscous and top with a tagine of leftover lamb simmered with tomatoes, roasted peppers, carrots, chickpeas, cumin, paprika, and mint.
- Make a meat pie with leftover lamb, leeks, and potatoes in a short crust.
- Mix minced lamb with tomato sauce and Greek spices like oregano and cinnamon for a filling for phyllo pastries.
- Chop roast lamb and combine with caramelized onions, feta cheese, and mint for a stuffing for calzones (you can adapt the recipe on page 267).
- Make a spicy lamb curry with tomatoes, onions, garlic, garam masala, and cilantro and seasoned with chiles and turmeric.

ROAST LEG of LAMB

A leg of lamb is easy and fast to cook, and will leave you with some premium leftovers. Just rub it with lots of fresh rosemary and garlic and cook to medium-rare for a spectacular party centerpiece or a family dinner. Or try stuffing a boneless roast with a tapenade made of minced black olives, parsley, and olive oil before roasting. SERVES 6.

1 leg lamb (bone-in or boneless), about 5 lb

2 cloves garlic, slivered

1 tsp minced fresh rosemary

1 Tbsp olive oil

Salt and freshly ground black pepper

Preheat the oven to 450°F.

Trim any excess fat and sinew from the exterior of the roast.

Using a sharp paring knife, cut slits into the roast on all sides and insert the slivers of garlic. Combine the rosemary and olive oil and rub over the outside of the roast (if the roast is deboned and tied, press some of the rosemary and garlic into the interior, too). Season on all sides with salt and pepper.

Set the roast on a rack in a roasting pan. Add a cup of water to the pan. Place the roast into the oven and roast for 20 minutes. Reduce the heat to 325°F and continue to roast until the internal temperature reaches 130°F, about 1 hour for boneless roasts, and slightly longer for bone-in legs. Start checking the temperature after 1 hour.

Remove the roast from the oven and let it rest for about 15 to 20 minutes. This allows the juices to settle in the meat, and the internal temperature to rise to about 135°F to 140°F, for perfectly medium-rare results.

To make a jus, add a little water or wine to the drippings in the pan, stirring up the browned bits, and simmer for 1 to 2 minutes.

Slice the roast and serve drizzled with the jus. Save any bones in the freezer for soup.

GREEK LAMB PITAS

This is the sandwich to serve the day after you've roasted a leg of lamb. You can either sauté the vegetables in olive oil, or skewer them and grill over medium heat until tender. Make sure to get fresh pita breads that you can cut open to form pockets. **SERVES 4.**

To make the sauce, combine the cucumber with the yogurt, olive oil, garlic, mint, and salt and pepper. Stir well and chill.

Cut the onion into segments (to skewer) or slivers (to sauté). Cut the peppers into chunks (to skewer) or slivers (to sauté).

Thread the onion and pepper chunks on metal skewers, brush with the olive oil, and grill for 10 minutes, until lightly charred and tender. Alternatively, in a sauté pan over medium-high, heat the oil and sauté the slivered vegetables until tender.

To make the sandwiches, cut the pita breads in half to form pockets. Divide the onion and peppers, roast lamb, and cherry tomatoes between the pita pockets and top each sandwich with a generous dollop of cucumber sauce.

Sauce:

½ English cucumber, finely chopped or shredded and drained

2 cups plain Greek yogurt

1 tsp olive oil

3 cloves garlic, minced

1 Tbsp chopped fresh mint

Salt and freshly ground black pepper, to taste

1 medium red onion, peeled

1 red bell pepper, stem and seeds removed

1 yellow bell pepper, stem and seeds removed

2 Tbsp olive oil

4 thick Greek-style pita breads

1 lb leftover roast lamb, cut into thin slices

16 cherry tomatoes, halved

SCOTCH BROTH

A great way to use the last bits of roast lamb and squeeze more flavor from the bones. MAKES 8 MAIN DISH SERVINGS (AND KEEPS WELL IN THE REFRIGERATOR FOR SEVERAL DAYS).

In a large stockpot over medium-high, heat the olive oil and sauté the onion and celery until beginning to brown.

Add the lamb bones to the pot and brown the bones for 10 minutes before adding the stock, water, rutabaga, and carrots. Bring to a boil, cover the pot, reduce heat to low, and simmer for 30 minutes.

Add the barley, garlic, pepper, and thyme and continue to simmer for 45 minutes, until the barley is tender and the soup is thickened.

Remove the lamb bones and discard.

Stir in the leftover roast lamb and heat through. If the soup is too thick, thin with a little more water or stock. Season to taste with salt and serve each bowl topped with a little chopped parsley.

1 tsp olive oil

1 medium onion, chopped

3 stalks celery, chopped

Leftover roast lamb bones

4 cups chicken stock

4 cups water

2 cups diced peeled rutabaga

1 cup diced carrots

1 cup pearl barley

1 Tbsp minced garlic

1 tsp freshly ground black pepper

1 tsp chopped fresh thyme (or ½ tsp dried thyme)

½ lb leftover roast lamb, cut into small cubes

Salt, to taste

1 Tbsp chopped fresh Italian parsley, for garnish

CASEROLE of LAMB, ROSEMARY, and WHITE BEANS

This flavorful oven braise with added roast lamb is a great meal to come home to. Serve with a pile of creamy polenta and a rustic French Syrah. SERVES 4–6.

Start by precooking the beans. Drain the soaked beans and place them in a large pot with the onion, celery, carrot, and herb bundle. Cover with 7 cups of cold water, bring to a boil, and simmer for 20 to 30 minutes. Drain the beans, discarding the vegetables and herbs. If you have a pressure cooker, you can do this in about 10 minutes. Set the beans aside.

In a nonstick sauté pan over medium-low, heat the oil and sauté the sweet onions until golden brown, about 20 minutes. Add the garlic and white wine, and simmer until the wine is evaporated and the onions are very tender.

Preheat the oven to 350°F.

In a wide, oval baking dish (or a heavy casserole with a lid), spread half of the onions. Top with the beans and rosemary. Layer the lamb over the beans, and spread the remaining onions overtop.

Whisk the chicken stock and tomato paste together, and pour over the casserole. Cover tightly with foil or a lid, and bake for 1 hour. Remove the cover and bake for an additional 30 to 40 minutes.

Remove the baking dish from the oven and let stand for 10 minutes. Tilt the pan and skim off the accumulated fat.

Meanwhile, make the polenta. Bring the water to a rolling boil and add the salt and butter.

Slowly add the polenta in a steady stream, whisking as you go to prevent lumps from forming. Stir for 5 minutes, then reduce heat to low and continue to cook for 10 to 15 minutes, stirring to make sure the polenta does not stick to the pot.

Remove from heat and stir in the sour cream, Parmigiano-Reggiano, and rosemary or basil. Keep warm until serving.

To serve, bring the casserole dish to the table and serve family-style in deep soup plates with the creamy polenta (or some French bread).

Beans:

1 cup dried flageolet or small white beans, soaked for at least 4 hours

1 small onion, peeled and stuck with 3 whole cloves

1 stalk celery, quartered

1 carrot, quartered

Sprigs fresh thyme, rosemary, and parsley, tied in a bundle

Casserole:

2 Tbsp olive oil

8 cups thinly sliced Vidalia or other sweet onions

1 Tbsp chopped garlic

½ cup white wine

2 Tbsp minced fresh rosemary

2 lb leftover roast lamb, cut into large cubes

2 cups chicken stock

2 Tbsp tomato paste

Polenta:

5 cups water or stock

1 tsp salt

1 Tbsp butter

1 cup coarse ground polenta

3 Tbsp sour cream

2 oz Parmigiano-Reggiano, grated

1 Tbsp chopped fresh rosemary or basil

BEEF

Buy

The Sunday dinner roast beef can be a quick round roast, a homey pot roast, or fancy prime rib. Choose a cut labeled "premium oven roast" for dry roasting. (If it's labeled "pot roast" or "braising roast," you will need to cook the beef slowly, for a much longer time, in a covered roasting pan, with vegetables and wine, broth, or tomato sauce.) Higher grades mean more marbling (intramuscular fat, which equals tenderness), so you'll find everything from AA, Select or Choice, and Prime to highly marbled Japanese Wagyu. Aging also affects tenderness and flavor—dry-aged beef is premium. One hundred percent grass-fed beef often grades lower (less fat) but is flavorful, and it means that animals were not fattened in feedlots on GMO grains or corn. Buy about 2 pounds of boneless beef for 6 servings.

Store

Beef will keep refrigerated for 5 days; otherwise vacuum-seal and freeze. Refer to sell-by or freeze-by dates on fresh meats. Cooked leftover roast can also be frozen but will lose some juices when thawed.

Serve

As a general rule, brown roast in a very hot oven to start, then cook for about 15 minutes per pound for medium-rare. Don't overcook or your meat will be tough.

Don't Waste It!

- Use any leftover bones with chopped onion, carrot, and celery to make beef stock or start a pot of beef and barley soup.
- For shepherd's pie, mix cubed leftover roast beef with gravy and leftover vegetables (peas, carrots, etc.) in a baking dish, top with leftover mashed potatoes, and bake.
- Make a curry or Moroccan stew with canned tomatoes, onions, garlic, and spices, then add cubed leftover roast beef at the end, once the vegetables have already cooked down and married.
- Cook up some quinoa and add chopped cooked mushrooms, caramelized onions, chopped parsley, and your leftover roast beef. Some chopped cherry tomatoes are tasty in the mix, too.
- Make a Thai beef salad with slivered cold cooked beef, cucumbers, carrots, tomatoes, peppers, mint, and peanuts, with a sweetened sesame/soy/lime dressing.
- For beef stroganoff, sauté mushrooms and onions in butter, add a little flour and then stock and sour cream, and cook until thickened. Stir in slivers of roast beef and some paprika, and toss with cooked egg noodles.
- Try sliced leftover roast beef in wraps with fresh spinach, mango salsa, black beans, onions, and bell peppers.
- Make fresh rice paper rolls with slivers of cold rare steak, bean sprouts, sliced radishes, and Thai basil, with a spicy sesame soy dip.
- Make steak and potato soup with beef stock, red wine, sautéed onions, and bell peppers, adding cubed leftover baked potatoes and slivers of rare steak near the end. Spice it up with black pepper and hot sauce.
- Top mixed romaine and vegetable salads with thick slices of cold rare steak and dress with Asian soy and garlic dressing or classic garlicky Caesar dressing.
- Roll up thin slices of grilled steak in flour tortillas with chopped lettuce, tomatoes, onions, and sour cream.
- Serve sliced roast beef on toasted crusty buns or baguette with horseradish mayonnaise, caramelized onions, and blue cheese, plus leftover gravy or jus from the roast for dipping.

MINI ROAST BEEF

For roast beef sandwiches all week long, nothing beats this simple and inexpensive little boneless roast that's done in 45 minutes flat. Start with an eye of the round or boneless top sirloin roast (often labeled "quick roasts"), rub it with spices, and roast. SERVES 6.

1 Tbsp extra-virgin olive oil

1 Tbsp Dijon mustard

1 tsp Worcestershire sauce

1 boneless eye of round roast (about 2 lb), or substitute a small top round roast

½ tsp crushed black peppercorns

¼ tsp garlic powder

¼ tsp paprika

¼ tsp salt

Bring the roast out of the refrigerator for at least 30 minutes before cooking to bring the meat to room temperature. Preheat the oven to 500°F.

Combine the olive oil, Dijon, and Worcestershire and rub all over the outside of the roast. Sprinkle all sides with the black pepper, garlic powder, paprika, and salt, pressing to adhere the spices to the roast.

Place on a rack in a shallow roasting pan. When the oven is hot, place the roast in the oven and sear for 10 minutes. Reduce the heat to 300°F and continue to roast for 35 to 45 minutes. Remove the roast from the oven and let rest for at least 15 minutes before cutting across the grain into thin slices. The roast will be rare (which is great for cold roast beef sandwiches), but if you want to test it with an instant-read thermometer before you slice it, cook to an internal temperature of 125°F to 130°F—no more or it will be tough. Slice it very thinly and serve warm, or chill and slice for sandwiches.

ROAST PRIME CUT

Make sure to choose a premium cut for this kind of roasting. Feel free to vary the flavor—try an Italian rub with oregano, basil, and garlic, or an Asian rub with soy sauce instead of Worcestershire, ground ginger, chiles, and five-spice powder. SERVES 8–12.

Bring the roast out of the refrigerator for at least 30 minutes before cooking to bring the meat to room temperature. Preheat the oven to 500°F. In a small bowl, combine the peppercorns, brown sugar, salt, garlic, thyme or rosemary (if using), mustard, and Worcestershire. Rub this mixture over the meat and let stand for at least 10 minutes.

Place the meat on a rack in a shallow roasting pan, fat side up, and roast for 15 minutes. Reduce heat to 325°F and continue to roast until the internal temperature is 135°F to 150°F for rare to medium-rare, or 160°F for well done. Use an instant-read thermometer. At 138°F to 140°F you will have a perfect, juicy, medium-rare roast.

Remove the roast from the oven and let it rest on a platter, tented with foil, for 15 minutes. This is an important step. If you carve the roast too soon, the juices will run out and the meat won't be juicy. Once it rests, and the juices settle into the meat, the roast will appear less rare and it will be firmer and easier to carve.

To make gravy, set the roasting pan over medium-high heat and whisk 2 tablespoons of the flour into the drippings, stirring to form a smooth paste. Add more flour if necessary. Slowly whisk in the beef stock and red wine (or some of the water from cooking side potatoes or vegetables). Bring to a boil, stirring until it is smooth and thickened to your liking. Thin with additional stock, wine, or water and season to taste. Strain for a completely smooth sauce.

To carve a prime rib, lay it on its side on a cutting board and slice along the ribs to separate the meat from the bone. Then slice the meat toward the bone—the slices will come away from the bone as you carve. To carve a boneless roast, like a rib eye or strip loin, simply slice across the grain. Pass the gravy separately.

> **TIP**
> Make sure to use a shallow roasting pan with a rack, large enough to allow the dry heat to circulate around the roast. If it's too small or deep, the roast won't properly sear and brown.

4 to 6 lb premium oven roast (prime rib, top sirloin, rib eye, strip loin, tenderloin)

Rub:

1 Tbsp crushed black peppercorns

1 tsp brown sugar

½ tsp salt

1 Tbsp minced garlic

3 Tbsp chopped fresh thyme or rosemary (optional)

1 Tbsp Dijon mustard

1 tsp Worcestershire sauce

Gravy:

2 to 4 Tbsp all-purpose flour

1 cup beef stock

1 cup red wine

PORTABLE BEEF PIES

Use frozen bread dough to make portable hand pies (AKA calzones) for speedy lunches. Any leftovers can go inside (think sausage, caramelized onions, and mozzarella; or meatballs in tomato sauce; even vegetarian combos of chopped olives, roasted peppers, artichokes, basil, and ricotta). Here's a beefy filling for your calzones reminiscent of the stuffing found in pastries in eastern European cuisine. For a vegetarian version, substitute 3 cups of finely chopped eggplant for the beef. The dill is an authentic touch—don't leave it out. **MAKES 12 CALZONES**.

In a sauté pan over medium, heat the butter and olive oil and sauté the onions and garlic until the onions begin to brown. This will take about 10 minutes. Stir occasionally so that the onions don't burn.

Add the mushrooms to the pan and cook until they release their liquid and begin to brown. Add the beef to the pan, and sauté.

Remove the pan from the heat, stir in the cheese and dill, and season with salt and pepper. Cool.

Preheat the oven to 400°F. Coat a baking sheet with cooking spray and sprinkle with cornmeal.

Cut each loaf of bread dough into 6 equal pieces. On a floured surface, roll each piece into a 5-inch circle. Wet the edges. Fill each with 3 tablespoons of the beef filling, fold the dough overtop, and press the edges well to seal. Brush the calzones with milk and poke them with a fork to allow steam to escape during baking.

Set the calzones on the prepared baking sheet. Bake for 20 minutes, until brown. Cool on a rack. These freeze well.

2 Tbsp butter

1 Tbsp olive oil

2 cups minced onions

3 cloves garlic, minced

1 cup finely chopped mushrooms

1 lb finely chopped leftover roast beef

1 cup grated cheddar cheese

2 Tbsp chopped fresh dill

Salt and freshly ground black pepper, to taste

2 loaves frozen bread dough, thawed (whole-wheat)

Milk, for brushing

TIP

Calzones or hand pies make great lunches—bake a bunch, freeze, then grab and go. They'll be thawed by noon and you can eat them cold or reheat them in the microwave. They make great portable lunches for hiking or cycling because they don't get squished in your pack.

GRILLED STEAKS

Strip loin steaks are so big these days, you can easily split one between two people. But if they come two in a package, you can also plan for tasty leftovers to serve over salads, in toasted paninis stacked with caramelized onions and blue cheese, or tossed into an Asian noodle dish. SERVES 4 OR 2 WITH LEFTOVERS.

To make the chimichurri, roast the tomatillos and garlic in a hot dry pan for 5 to 10 minutes, until starting to brown. Cool slightly, then combine with the parsley, cilantro, oregano, chile, salt and pepper, oil, lime juice, and water in a food processor or blender and blend until smooth. Cover and chill. (Makes 2 cups.)

Combine the olive oil and garlic and brush over the steaks. Drizzle on both sides with Worcestershire sauce and grind a generous amount of black pepper overtop.

Heat the barbecue grill to medium-high and grill the steaks to rare or medium-rare, about 4 to 5 minutes per side.

Let the steaks rest for 5 minutes before serving with the chimichurri sauce.

Chimichurri sauce:

1½ cups tomatillos

4 whole cloves garlic

¼ cup minced fresh Italian parsley

¼ cup minced fresh cilantro

¼ cup minced fresh oregano

1 fresh jalapeno or serrano chile, seeded and minced

Salt and freshly ground black pepper, to taste

¼ cup extra-virgin olive oil

2 Tbsp fresh lime juice

1 Tbsp cold water

Steaks:

1 Tbsp olive oil

1 tsp minced garlic

2 sirloin steaks, each about 10 oz and 1 inch thick

2 tsp Worcestershire sauce

Freshly ground black pepper

SATAY BEEF SUBS

These Vietnamese sandwiches (AKA bánh mì) combine slivers of leftover grilled steak (or try chicken breast or pork tenderloin) with a lightly pickled carrot salad, cucumber, and cilantro in big crusty rolls. The result is something fresh, exotic, and yet so simple. Even faster if you use a store-bought satay sauce in place of this sauce. MAKES 2 SUB SANDWICHES.

Combine the sauce ingredients in a jar or bottle and shake.

Place the meat in a bowl and add 1 tablespoon of the sauce (the rest can be refrigerated). Toss to coat.

Place the carrots in a colander or strainer, sprinkle with the salt, and let them drain for 1 hour to remove moisture. Rinse under cold running water and pat dry. Place the carrots in a bowl or other container and add the sugar, vinegar, and 1 cup water. Cover and refrigerate for at least an hour (or up to 3 days) to lightly pickle.

Preheat the broiler. To assemble the subs, split the baguettes lengthwise and slather each side with mayonnaise. Top with the meat and cheese and arrange on a baking sheet. Slide under the broiler and broil for 1 to 2 minutes, just to toast the bread and melt the cheese.

Top each sandwich with half of the shredded carrot salad, strips of cucumber, onion, chopped chiles, and a handful of cilantro leaves. Drizzle each with a few tablespoons of the sauce. Press the baguette halves together to enclose and wrap the sandwiches in waxed paper to keep everything inside while you eat.

Sauce:

¼ cup fresh lime juice

¼ cup Asian fish sauce

2 Tbsp rice or wine vinegar

1 Tbsp granulated sugar

¼ cup water

1 tsp Asian garlic chili paste (or cayenne and garlic powder)

6 oz grilled steak, sliced into thin strips

1 cup matchstick or shredded carrots

1 Tbsp salt

2 Tbsp granulated sugar

¼ cup rice vinegar

2 (6-inch) lengths fresh baguette (or 2 crusty sub buns)

Mayonnaise

Thin slices mozzarella cheese

½ English cucumber, sliced in thin lengthwise strips (use a vegetable peeler)

½ cup finely sliced white onion

2 to 3 chopped fresh chiles (serrano are good)

Large handful fresh cilantro leaves

OYSTER SAUCE BEEF NOODLES

Start with a bag of fresh Chinese steamed noodles from the supermarket produce department and some sliced veggies (whatever you have, from carrots to green beans), toss in your leftover steak, and you'll be in noodle nirvana. Add a 1-quart box of chicken stock if you prefer your Asian noodles in soup. **SERVES 2.**

In a small bowl, combine the sauce ingredients. Stir to combine and dissolve the cornstarch. Set aside.

Heat a large pot of water to a rolling boil and add the noodles, breaking them apart as they cook. Cook for 1 minute, then drain in a colander in the sink. Return them to the pot and toss with the sesame oil.

In a wok over medium-high, heat 2 tablespoons of canola oil and sauté the ginger and garlic for 30 seconds. Add the onion and cook for 2 minutes, until starting to brown, then add the red pepper, mushrooms, and snow peas. Stir-fry together for 2 to 3 minutes, until tender.

Add another tablespoon of oil to the wok, then add the noodles, stirring and tossing to combine. Allow the noodles to sit in the hot pan for a couple of minutes to brown on the bottom before tossing again.

Push the noodles to one side and add the sauce to the wok.

When the mixture boils and thickens, combine with the noodles and vegetables in the wok, tossing to coat everything with the sauce.

Add the steak and heat through. (For soup, just add chicken stock to the wok and heat.)

Sauce:

½ cup chicken stock or water

¼ cup oyster sauce

1 Tbsp soy sauce

1 tsp Asian chili paste

½ tsp brown sugar

1 to 2 tsp cornstarch

½ lb steamed Chinese egg noodles (fresh)

1 tsp sesame oil

Canola oil, for stir-frying

2 tsp minced fresh ginger

2 cloves garlic, minced

1 small onion, slivered

1 small red bell pepper, seeded and slivered

1 cup sliced mushrooms

2 cups fresh snow peas

½ lb leftover grilled steak, thinly sliced across the grain

> ⮜ **TIP**
> Always keep fresh ginger on hand in the fridge or freezer. To peel the thin skin from the root, use the edge of a teaspoon, then cut the root into ½-inch chunks and smash under the flat blade of your chef's knife (like garlic) to make mincing quicker. Freeze peeled ginger in chunks. Use a Microplane grater to grate it while it's still frozen for instant fresh ginger flavor.

METRIC CONVERSION CHARTS

Volume	
⅛ tsp	0.5 mL
¼ tsp	1 mL
½ tsp	2 mL
¾ tsp	4 mL
1 tsp	5 mL
3 tsp = 1 Tbsp	15 mL
1½ Tbsp	22.5 mL
2 Tbsp	25 mL
4 Tbsp = ¼ cup	60 mL
1/3 cup	75 mL
½ cup	125 mL
⅔ cup	150 mL
¾ cup	175 mL
1 cup	250 mL
2 cups	500 mL
3 cups	750 mL
4 cups = 1 quart	1 L
5 cups	1.25 L
6 cups	1.5 L
8 cups	2 L
10 cups	2.5 L
12 cups	3 L

Cans and Jars	
2 oz	57 mL
3½ oz	104 mL
4 oz	114 mL
5 oz	142 mL
5½ oz	156 mL
6 oz	170 mL
7½ oz	213 mL
13 oz	385 mL
14 oz	398 mL
15 oz	426 mL
19 oz	540 mL
24 oz	684 mL
28 oz	796 mL

Weight	
1 oz	30 g
2 oz	60 g
3 oz	90 g
4 oz = ¼ lb	115 g
5 oz	140 g
6 oz	170 g
8 oz = ½ lb	225 g
10 oz	285 g
12 oz = ¾ lb	350 g
1 lb	450 g
2 lb	900 g
3 lb	1.3 kg
4 lb	1.8 kg
5 lb	2.3 kg
6 lb	2.7 kg
12 lb	5.4 kg
16 lb	7.3 kg

Length/Thickness/Diameter	
⅛ inch	3 mm
¼ inch	6 mm
½ inch	1 cm
1 inch	2.5 cm
2 inches	5 cm
3 inches	8 cm
4 inches	10 cm
5 inches	13 cm
6 inches	15 cm
7 inches	18 cm
8 inches	20 cm
9 inches	23 cm
10 inches	25 cm

Temperatures	
120°F	48°C
125°F	52°C
130°F	54°C
135°F	57°C
138°F	59°C
140°F	60°C
145°F	63°C
150°F	66°C
155°F	68°C
160°F	71°C
165°F	74°C
170°F	77°C
175°F	80°C
180°F	82°C
185°F	85°C
190°F	88°C
195°F	90°C
200°F	95°C
225°F	105°C
250°F	120°C
275°F	135°C
300°F	150°C
325°F	165°C
350°F	175°C
375°F	190°C
400°F	200°C
425°F	220°C
450°F	230°C
475°F	240°C
500°F	260°C

Pans	
8-inch square baking pan	20 × 20 cm
8- × 4-inch loaf pan	20 × 10 cm
9-inch springform pan	23 cm
10-inch tart pan	25 cm
13- × 9-inch baking sheet	33 × 23 cm

ACKNOWLEDGMENTS

Somewhere at the intersection of inspiration and perspiration is where great ideas and great books happen.

This book required a lot of the latter from the team at TouchWood Editions—a small but mighty group who literally rolled up their sleeves and made this special book come together in record time, whether it meant helping to cook and style food for photos, pouring over hundreds of pages of copy, or digging out illustrations.

Thank you, Pat Touchie, for collecting such a devoted and talented staff, especially smart and savvy associate publisher Taryn Boyd, who heard my idea and understood immediately why it was a message that the world needed, and quickly. It is truly a joy to work with a woman who is clearly so passionate about books and everything they bring to us.

Thanks, too, to editor Cailey Cavallin, who so carefully combed through my copy to give it continuity and clarity. And thanks for her team spirit—like designer Pete Kohut, who helped behind the scenes on our crazy photo shoot, she did double duty as our lithe and mysterious model in the beautiful images created by photographer DL Acken. Thank you to Cory Pelan from The Whole Beast, who was kind enough to let us shoot photos in his beautiful shop.

I'd also like to thank Dana Gunders, a staff scientist at the Natural Resources Defense Council and food waste warrior, who introduced me to the global problem of wasted food. And to all of the other inspiring people I discovered while researching this timely topic: farmers, writers, scientists, chefs, municipal governments, even the United Nations, all working to end food waste.

I am not a scientist, but as a journalist and longtime food writer, I have always hoped to inspire my readers to support local producers and sustainable food systems when they choose their food. The broad social and environmental impact of food waste is just another reason why we should buy our food locally, from organic farms and sustainable fishers, factoring the land, water, air, and oceans into the cost of the food we eat. Only then can we truly know the impact of our daily decisions.

Thank you for being part of this important shift, and for making a few changes in your home to eat better, save money, and, ultimately, protect the planet we share.

INDEX

Copyright © 2015 Cinda Chavich

TouchWood Editions
touchwoodeditions.com

LIBRARY AND ARCHIVES CANADA CATALOGUING IN PUBLICATION
Chavich, Cinda, author
The waste not, want not cookbook: save food, save money,
and save the planet / Cinda Chavich.

Includes index.
Issued in print and electronic formats.
ISBN 978-1-77151-111-7

1. Low budget cooking. 2. Cooking (Leftovers). 3. Cooking
(Natural foods). 4. Cookbooks. I. Title.

TX652.C43 2015   641.5'52   C2014-908219-3

Editor: Cailey Cavallin
Proofreader: Grace Yaginuma
Design: Pete Kohut
All illustrations are from public domain sources.
Cover photo: *Vegetables and spices vintage border background*, by udra, istockphoto.com
Food photography: DL Acken

Canadian   Patrimoine
Heritage   canadien

We gratefully acknowledge the financial support for our publishing activities from
the Canada Book Fund and the British Columbia Book Publishing Tax Credit.

This book was produced using FSC®-certified, acid-free papers,
processed chlorine free, and printed with vegetable-based inks.

The information in this book is true and complete to the best of the author's knowledge.
All recommendations are made without guarantee on the part of the author.
The author disclaims any liability in connection with the use of this information.

1 2 3 4 5 19 18 17 16 15

PRINTED IN CANADA